EGYPTIAN TEMPLES

EGYPTIAN TEMPLES

BY

MARGARET A. MURRAY,

F.S.A. (*Scot.*), F.R.A.I.

Fellow of University College, London, Assistant Professor of Egyptology at University College, London

"When a man of sense beholds these ruins he finds himself able to excuse in the vulgar their belief with regard to the ancients that their lives were longer than ours and their bodies stronger, or that they possessed a magic rod with which when they struck the stones they leapt towards them. For the modern mind feels itself unable to estimate how much was required in these works of knowledge of geometry, and concentration of thought, and ardour of study, and patience in labour, and power over tools, and application to work."—*Abd el Latif*.

LONDON

SAMPSON LOW, MARSTON & CO., LTD.

MADE AND PRINTED IN GREAT BRITAIN BY PURNELL AND SONS
PAULTON (SOMERSET) AND LONDON

PREFACE

There is no book which gives a short *résumé* of the temples of Egypt, for there is nothing between a guide book and the enormous volumes of specialists. I have, therefore, tried in this small book to collect together the chief points of interest of many of the temples now remaining. This does not pretend to be an exhaustive account of any one temple, or even to give a complete list of all the temples; it merely gives a rapid survey of the architecture, some of the history, and a few details not usually found in books such as those I have mentioned above.

The study of Egyptian architecture is at present in its infancy. The broad distinctions between the capitals of Pharaonic and Ptolemaic types are well marked and can be distinguished at a glance, but the details of building of various periods, the forms of the pillars—shafts as well as capitals—the small differences which occur from period to period, are still awaiting investigation. A brick building can be dated to a dynasty, almost to a reign, as the sizes of the bricks are known for each period; but the stone temples require the same investigation and methodical classification as the buildings of mediæval Europe.

My thanks are due to Mr. Hector Corfiato, Reader in Architecture in the University of London, for much kind help and valuable suggestions; to Miss Eleanor Vaughan, Lecturer in Classics at University College, London, for her translations of the Greek and Latin inscriptions; to Mr. Percival Hart for many of the photographs; and, last but not least, to Dr. Edith Guest, Hon. Assistant in Egyptology at University College, London, for her continued and ungrudging help.

CONTENTS

ILLUSTRATIONS

EGYPTIAN TEMPLES

INTRODUCTION

ALL Egyptian temples are remarkable as being entirely rectangular, both in plan and elevation; at no period was a curved structure used. This is perhaps due to the fact that the landscape of Egypt is a landscape of lines, vertical, horizontal or diagonal; and, as the artist knew nothing else, his buildings conformed to their surroundings. This was the reason of the vertical columns, horizontal roofs and sloping pylons of Egyptian architecture. The round arch was known as a constructional feature from the IIIrd dynasty, but it was used only where it could not be seen, merely as an economical means of support. Occasionally, the false vault is found, as in the temple of Sethy at Abydos and the temple of Hatshepsut at Dêr el Bahri, where it covers stairways or small rooms, but even in these cases it is inside the building and not visible from without. In every instance, whether of the true or false arch, it is always the round, not the pointed, arch.

The rainless skies and continuous sunshine of Egypt are points to be considered in the architecture. It is a country of violent contrasts; the flat plain and vertical cliffs, the fertile fields and the dreary waste of desert, the brilliant sunshine and the dark shadows, the river which harboured edible fish and murderous crocodile; all these naturally had their effect on the mind of the Egyptian architect and showed themselves in the architecture. As Petrie notes

"The strongly marked horizontal and vertical lines of the scenery condition the style of the buildings which can be placed before such a background." The form of the temple repeats the form of the barren cliff before which it stands (pl. XXVII), but the interior decoration shows the wealth of detail and the vivid colouring of the fertile fields; brilliant sunshine poured into the open courts, and the dark sanctuaries were made darker by the contrast; the Giver of Life, who dwelt in the sanctuary, was propitiated by the death of human beings and animals.

The plan of a temple is simple in the extreme when once the essential facts are recognised. It consists of four parts—an outer court, an inner court, a vestibule and a shrine; the holy place, enclosed by mat hangings or wooden doors, being in the axis of the building opposite the main entrance. The earliest record of a temple is a representation of a hut-shrine engraved on an ebony tablet of the Ist dynasty (pl. II, 3). The outer court is shown enclosed by a lattice-work fence; at the gate are two masts with flags, and in the court is the emblem of the deity, in this case a goddess. The inner court and vestibule were possibly in one at this period, and were enclosed with the sanctuary in the hut, as is done at the present day in some parts of Africa.

From the beginning of the historical period there were two kinds of temples, those dedicated to the worship of the god and those dedicated to the worship of the dead King. Of temples dedicated to a god none are in existence from the early periods, although the foundations of several are known; e.g. at Abydos there was a temple of Osiris in the Ist dynasty, at Hierakonpolis the temple of the sacred falcon was probably as early, at Bubastis the temple of the cat-goddess is not later than the IVth dynasty, and the shrine of the crocodile-god in the Fayum had very primitive characters; and though the early temples of Neith of the Delta and Seth of Upper Egypt have been utterly destroyed representations of their hut-shrines still remain (pl. I, 3, 4).

The origin and development of the royal temples can be demonstrated with some facility. As the primitive king or chief always had a better house than the common people, so the god who was superior to the king had a better house than the king; the original temple was then merely a finer hut than those used by human beings. These early huts and temples were of reed or palm lattice smeared with mud, they therefore do not survive except in representations; it was only when the Egyptians were able to work in stone that the buildings have remained in existence. The earliest stone temples are those attached to pyramids and other royal burial places, and were intended for the worship of the dead King. Such temples were derived from the custom of making offerings of food at the royal tomb. To quote from Professor Petrie: "At first the place of offerings was closely connected with the tomb, as shown by the large steles found at the tombs of the Ist dynasty; and such continue to be the case for the ordinary Egyptian in all times. But the place of offering to the kings was, at the end of the IIIrd dynasty, in a separate court attached to the side of the tomb (Snefru at Medum); in the IVth dynasty the court became a separate temple (Khufu, Khafra, and Menkaura): in the XIIth dynasty the tomb was farther back on the desert, and the chapel was at the desert edge (Senusert II, Illahun; Senusert III, Abydos); in the XVIIIth and XIXth dynasties the chapels or temples were ranged along the desert edge at Thebes and not in any uniform relation to the tombs hidden in the desert."

This suggestive paragraph is well substantiated by the evidence. In the plan of the tomb of Perabsen, of the IInd dynasty (pl. I, 1), it will be seen that the elaborate underground structure has offering chambers for the objects which the King was supposed to require in his future life;

at the same time steles bearing the royal name were set up above ground at one corner of the enclosure, where the daily offerings of food might be made to the King. The underground chambers then contained the permanent endowment, the offerings above ground were for the daily needs of the royal soul. At Medum, in the IIIrd dynasty (pl. I, 2), the steles were enclosed with a wall which adjoined the actual burial-place, i.e. the pyramid; and chambers were built for the storage of the vessels and other objects used in the rites of commemoration and worship. From this simple beginning there grew up the more stately and elaborate temples belonging to the pyramids of Gizeh of the IVth dynasty, and to the pyramids of Abusir of the Vth dynasty. The temple of the Step-pyramid of Saqqara is a structure which has no parallel; the plan shows that it was experimental throughout; it was built without system, and it had no effect on the regular development of the royal mortuary temples.

The pyramid field extends from Abu Rowash in the north to Lahun in the south, a distance of about fifty miles, and is on the west side of the Nile. Isolated pyramids are found occasionally, as the pyramid of Aahmes I of the XVIIIth dynasty, at Abydos, and the pyramid of the XIth dynasty, at Thebes; these two, however, are of a different type from those further down the river.

Among the pyramids of the more northerly part of Egypt the temple is always on the east, the side nearest to the Nile; and a landing-stage and causeway were probably built for every pyramid; the best preserved examples of these are at Abusir. As the temple was on the east side the priest would face towards the west when conducting the service, an essential position for the ritual of the dead.

The plan of a pyramid-temple varies from two or three simple chambers, as at Medum, to elaborate colonnades and hypæthral courts, as at Abusir. At Abusir a roofed stone building (pl. IV, 1) stood on the bank of the Nile and served as a landing-place; from this a long passage—built, roofed and paved with stone—led to the temple. The passage walls were richly decorated with painted reliefs, showing the King as a sphinx trampling his enemies. Khafra appears to have introduced the custom of placing statues of himself in front of, or between, the pillars of his temple.

As a rule the pyramid-temples are even more ruined than those standing alone. Thus at Abu Rowash both temple and pyramid have gone; at Giza the temple of the Great Pyramid has vanished except for the basalt pavement; while of the temples belonging to the pyramids of Khafra and Menkaura the lower courses only of the walls are still in existence; the same is true of the Vth dynasty pyramids at Abusir, of the VIth dynasty pyramids at Saqqara, and of the XIIth dynasty pyramids at Lisht, Hawara and Lahun.

It is not yet certain when pyramids ceased to be burial-places. In the XIth dynasty Mentuhotep II was buried in a rock-cut tomb, near but not in or under his pyramid; in the next dynasty Senusert III was also buried in a rock-cut tomb at Abydos, while his pyramid was at Dahshur; the pyramid of Aahmes I is at Abydos, and is merely a dummy, his burial being at Thebes. When the pyramid was no longer for burial, the temple was unnecessary and became an entirely separate structure.

The temple for a deity developed in a different manner from the temple in honour of a dead King; it was always an independent structure, and not attached to a tomb or any other building. Petrie again gives a good summary of the rise of the god-temple: "The simplest shelter that we know in Egypt is a reed hut with projecting roof to shade the entrance, and this is the simplest shrine. The next step was to make the hut wider, and put a row of reed columns to carry the front shade, the portico thus begins. After that the back is divided into three chambers, as in the earliest temple at Abydos and Hierakonpolis. The house models must always have a courtyard in front of the portico, and the temples always had a similar court. Within the court stood the emblems of the god on a pole; and on either side of the door of the court stood poles with flags; these grew into the row of flag-staffs in front of the pylon. Besides these fixed features there were many chambers for stores and priests arranged on various plans." Petrie then notes that there were two types of sanctuary: "the statue temple which had a central box-shrine, in which the statue or emblem or animal was kept (e.g. Edfu, Dendera); and the processional temple for depositing a sacred bark, this had a doorway at both ends of the shrine, front and back (e.g. Tehutmes III at Medinet Habu, and Khonsu at Karnak). In these shrines was a stand on which the sacred bark could be deposited from the shoulders of the priests."

One of the principal difficulties in building in the Nile Valley is the annual movement of the ground. When the inundation begins, the seepage from the river causes the ground to rise for several inches, sometimes as much as a foot, and always unevenly; when the inundation subsides the ground subsides also, again unevenly, till it returns to its original level. The ancient Egyptian architect never overcame this difficulty, except by building beyond the reach of the effects of the inundation. In the desert at the foot of the cliffs there was no water, either from the heavens above or from the earth beneath, to destroy his buildings, and stones set up on the rock would remain standing; for such temples his foundations were so perfunctory as to be almost nil, as at Hatshepsut's temple at Dêr el Bahri. But when building on the moving ground the problem taxed his capacities to the utmost, and he failed to evolve any adequate method of coping

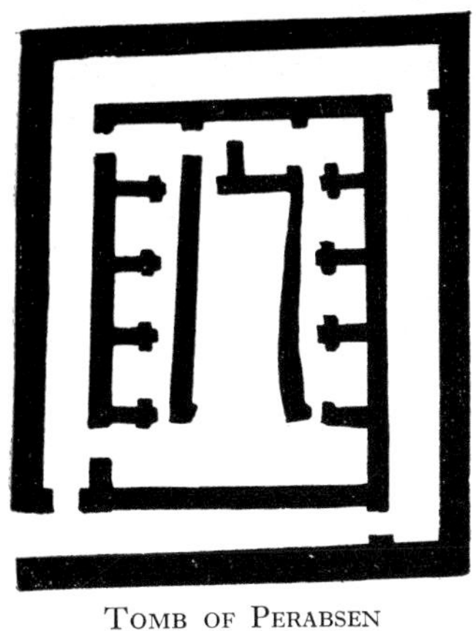

TOMB OF PERABSEN
(1)

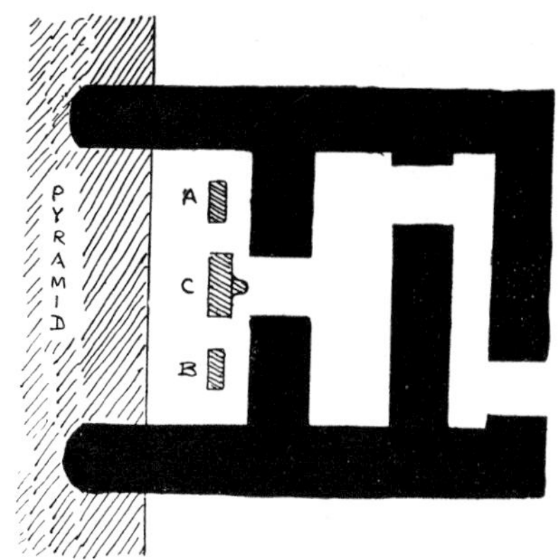

PYRAMID TEMPLE, MEDUM
(2)

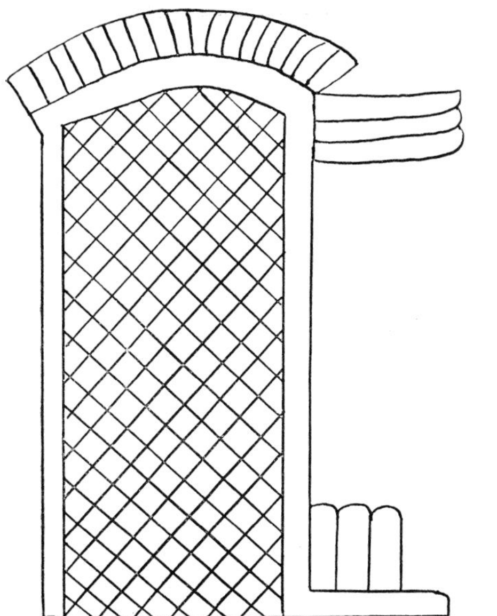

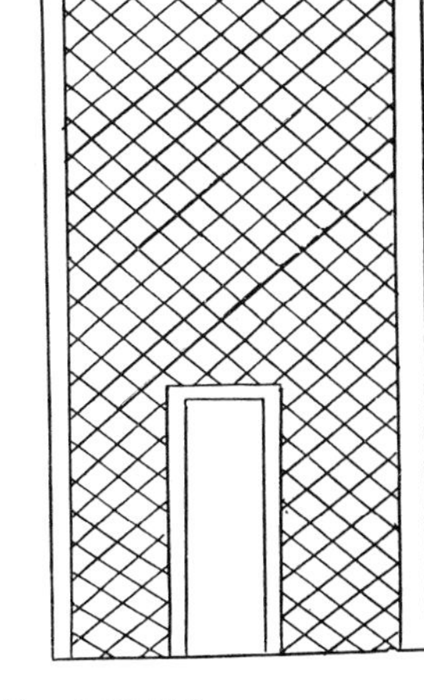

LATTICE-WORK SHRINES FROM THE HIEROGLYPHS
(3) (4)

[*Face page* 6

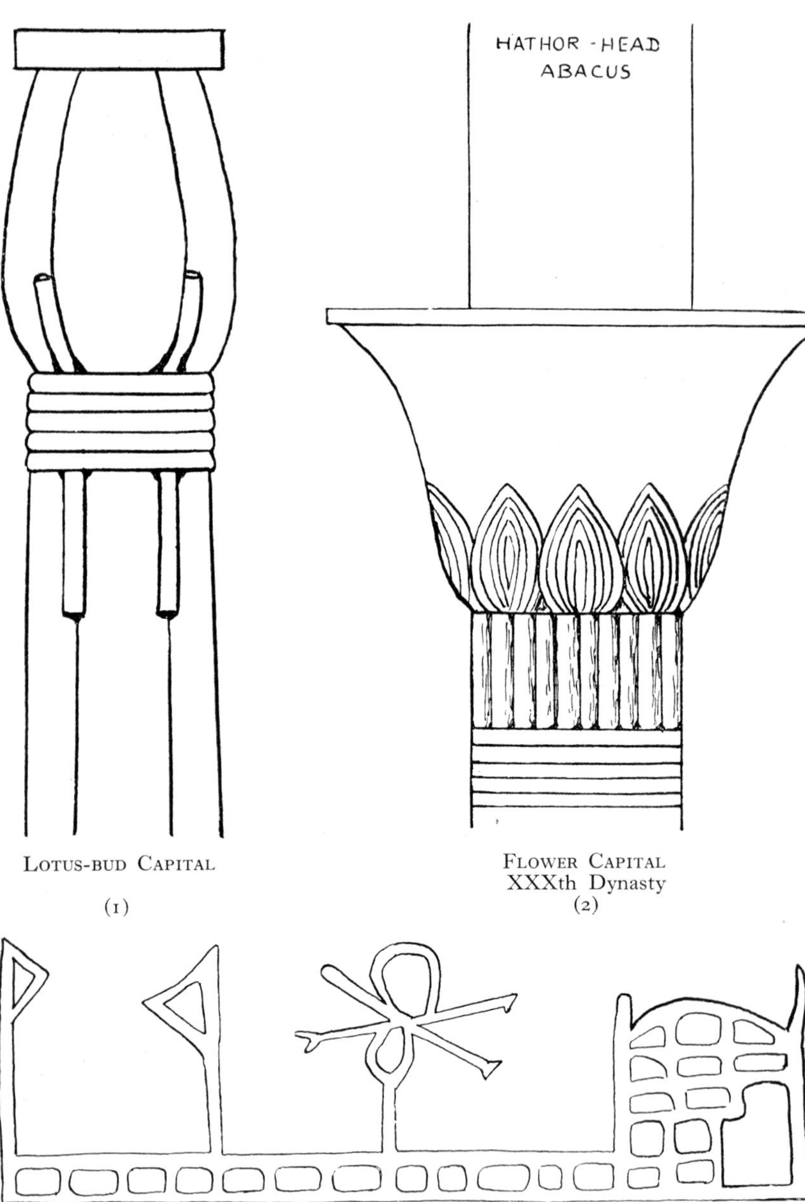

Lotus-bud Capital

(1)

Flower Capital
XXXth Dynasty
(2)

Lattice-work Shrine
Ist Dynasty
(3)

Face page 7]

with the difficulty. In the temples along the edge of the cultivation, where the ground is affected by the rising and falling flood, the foundations are pitifully weak and inadequate. They consist of a sandbed and small blocks of stones; but there is no attempt made to prevent the sand being washed away by the water, and the blocks of stone are too small to support the weight of the enormous buildings erected over them. It is surprising that the temples have lasted so long and have not collapsed long ago; the reason probably is that they were supported by the mass of debris accumulated round them in the course of centuries. Now that they have been cleared and that, owing to the silting of the river-bed, the level of the inundation has risen, the inadequate foundations are causing the destruction of some of the finest examples of Egyptian architecture. The Department of Antiquities is repairing with cement and reinforced concrete; it remains to be seen how these modern methods will resist the force of the uneven movements of the ground.

The rock-hewn temples were cut out like an Egyptian quarry in the side of a cliff so as to make an artificial cave. The cliff was pierced at the highest point required, and the temple was hollowed out by cutting downwards. The pillars were merely the props necessary to uphold the superincumbent mass of the hill in which the quarry or shrine was cut, and were part of the rock left *in situ*. The decoration, architectural or otherwise, was begun at the top; if architraves were to be represented they were cut in the overhanging roof, so also was the cavetto cornice along the tops of the walls. The abacus and capital of a pillar were finished first, then the shaft, and finally the base. The sculptured and painted decoration proceeded in the same way both on the walls and the pillars, beginning at the top and ending at the bottom. This method is best seen in the pillared and sculptured tombs at Tel el Amarna. Rock temples probably began in the

Middle Kingdom when rock-cut tomb-chapels became common.

One of the main features of an Egyptian temple is the colonnade, used chiefly as an interior decoration. The forms of the chief types of pillar show the development in stone of an original in reed and clay, these being the earliest building materials in the Nile Valley. Even at the present day reed-huts are still built for use in the heat of summer when the inhabitants require nothing more than shelter from the heat of the sun. The primitive pillar was made of bundles of papyrus-reeds lashed tightly together at the base, and also at the top under the flowering head. To keep the lashings taut a short stalk of papyrus was pushed down between the bundles. The inflorescence of the papyrus is in large corymbs, the flower-stems falling down on every side, like a loose untidy mop; the mass of flowering stems was tied together at the top, and a light plank placed on it; the weight of the plank made the corymbs curve outwards just above the junction with the stem. The reed-pillar was set up in a circular base of clay, and was freely smeared with clay. A row of such pillars was sufficiently strong to support a long light plank as an architrave, which, in its turn, held up a matwork roof. When this form of pillar was reproduced in stone the artist found it impossible to represent the minute detail of the flowering papyrus-head which formed the capital of his stone pillar; but, as the curved shape suggested the swelling bud of a lotus, he carved the capital as a lotus-bud with the calyx just parting to show the petals within (pls. II, 1, III, 1). This is the most common type of Egyptian pillar, and the form continues from the Old Kingdom till the XXIInd dynasty, though degenerating steadily. In the XVIIIth dynasty the shaft and capital are still lobed, and the shaft draws in at the base, the lashing is sometimes represented, and the short stalks which held the lashing taut are shown merely as vertical lines (see pl. XXV, 2). Later the shaft and capital are plain (see pl. XX, 1), or covered with sculpture but even in its most degenerate state the form is recognisable by the narrowing of the shaft at the base and by the slight overhang of the capital. This last feature is found in Ptolemaic capitals.

Another form of pillar is derived from the palm-stem. In this the stem is not represented with the same care as the bundles of papyrus in the papyrus pillar, for the shaft is perfectly cylindrical with no narrowing to the base. The lashing under the fronds of the palm is shown with as much care as in the other type, and the fronds themselves curve in a natural manner. This is not a very common form of capital, but it occurs from the Old Kingdom to the Ptolemaic period (pl. III, 2).

The reeded and fluted pillars in the temple of the Step-pyramid are the first example in stone-work of these types, but the form is known in small ornamental work as early as the Ist dynasty, and is found not uncommonly in the XVIIIth dynasty.

The bud-capital must naturally have led to the open-flower capital of the type seen in the colonnade of Harem-heb at Luxor, in the nave of the Great Temple at Karnak, and in the nave of the Ramesseum. The calyx of the flower is often represented at the base of the capital, but the petals are not reproduced, and the capital has a plain surface. The lashing is retained on the shaft of the pillar as with the bud-capital, but the shaft is always circular and not lobed. The capitals of Nectanebo's Porch at Philæ (pl. II, 2) are transitional; the form is like the capitals of the New Kingdom, and the calyx is also found; but the shafts of the pillars to which they are joined are of the Ptolemaic form, with reed-stems immediately below the capital, then comes the lashing, and below that again is a plain circular shaft. The Ptolemaic foliage-capital (pl. V, 1) is a development in a more richly decorated form from the Pharaonic flower-capital.

Two other forms characteristic of Egyptian architecture are also derived from the primitive building-materials of the early periods; these are the cavetto cornice and the torus roll. In ancient times, as at the present day, walls were made of interwoven palm-sticks thickly covered with mud, the tops of the palm fronds being left free to bend over; this gives a curved effect which, when translated into stone, produces the cavetto cornice (e.g. pl. XIX). The corners of lattice-and-mud walls need strengthening at the corners, which was done by lashing into place bundles of reeds or palm-sticks; the copy of this feature in stone is seen in the torus roll (e.g. pl. XIX).

The chief materials used in buildings were sun-dried bricks, limestone, granite, sandstone, and some alabaster, quartzite and basalt; the Imperial porphyry of the Romans, though actually found in the Eastern desert, was never used by the Egyptians.

The girdle-wall, which surrounded the sacred precincts, was usually of sun-dried bricks; it was always a high wall, with the intention of keeping the holy places apart from the common people; on account of the height it was extremely thick, and was built with a batter. The gateways in the wall were often of granite or more rarely of quartzite, and the flanking towers of limestone. The main walls of each temple were of limestone, or sandstone; the harder stones being used for the structural parts, such as pillars and door-frames; alabaster was used for the lining of small chambers, such as a sanctuary or a passage. As a general rule, basalt is found in the early temples, and quartzite in the Middle Kingdom, though both occur at other periods. Wood was very little used except for the actual doors and some of the internal fittings.

The method of building a thick stone wall was to erect two thin walls parallel to one another and at the desired distance apart; the space between was then filled with convenient-sized blocks thrown in without any arrangement and not in any way keyed to the outer "skin" (pl. III, 3). The stones of these outer walls were built up without any dressing of the faces, this was done later. The method is well seen in the construction of an internal angle; two blocks are placed at right-angles to and touching one another; in dressing the faces one block is cut further back than the other, so as to form the corner actually in the block; there are good examples of this in the temple of Sethy I at Abydos.

Temples appear to have been orientated by the river; the main direction of the stream is to the north, but it naturally varies somewhat and runs occasionally east or west of north, the temples, therefore, vary also in their orientation. The rule, however, is that the temples lie parallel or at right angles to the river, e.g. Luxor and Karnak. When there is any marked variation it is probably due to the conformation of the ground, as in the causeway of the Granite Temple, the side-chambers of the Sethy Temple at Abydos, and possibly the outer court of Luxor.

The lighting of the temple presented certain problems which differ materially from the problems of lighting in a cloudy country. In Egypt, where sunshine may be definitely an evil, only enough light was required to enable priests and worshippers to see their way; in other words, the temples were dark, and intentionally so. The exclusion of sunlight was a necessity, but there is, perhaps, another reason for the extreme darkness, and that was that the religion was a mystery-religion, for the practice of which darkness is an essential. The problem of lighting was solved by the Egyptians in their usual practical manner. Whether in tomb-chapels or in temples, openings in the form of long horizontal slits were made at the tops of the walls immediately under the ceiling. The light therefore was not direct sunlight, but was softened by the shadow from the ceiling and was diffused all over the chamber or hall. This was the earliest method; in later temples the light was often admitted by an opening in the roof; this was sometimes wide on the outside and narrowed downwards to a smaller aperture where the light entered the chamber (pl. XX, 2). The light so introduced gives a very delicate and pure illumination, and on those highly decorated walls the low relief sculptures, brilliantly painted as they are, glow like a rich mosaic. In many of the dark halls light was also reflected through open doors, and served to illuminate the lower part of the sculptured walls. In the temples of Thebes, which are almost entirely of the New Kingdom, the lighting of the hypostyle halls was by means of a clerestory. The nave of the hall was supported on pillars higher than those of the side aisles; the shorter columns supported not only the stone roof of the side aisle but also a wall which rose to the same height as the tall columns of the nave; this wall was pierced with windows; the nave then was lighted while the aisles were dark except for the indirect illumination from the clerestory. Cross-lighting of this kind is one of the most effective forms of illumination ever invented.

When Egypt was subjected to foreign influence there is a change in the architecture. Screen-walls were then introduced, slabs placed between the pillars of a colonnade to shut out the glare which strikes up from the ground, though sunlight was freely admitted above the slab. The change was probably due to the fact that Egyptian architects had become acquainted with the buildings of a more cloudy and rainy country than their own. Tehutmes III was the first to use screen-walls in his temple at Medinet Habu; as it is known that he went as far north as the Euphrates and that all the northern countries of the eastern Mediterranean sent their products to his court, it is clear that foreign influence was greatly felt in Egypt, and the architecture of the rainy lands of the north must have affected the architecture of rainless Egypt.

It is impossible to attempt to give an account of every temple in Egypt, for every town and village had a holy place, large or small, according to the number and wealth of the inhabitants. Of the five great cities of ancient Egypt—Memphis, Heliopolis, Sais, Thebes and Alexandria—Thebes alone has preserved its temples. Memphis, the earliest capital of the historic kings, once had a temple which roused Herodotus to enthusiasm; of ancient Heliopolis but one obelisk marks the spot where the greatest Pharaohs worshipped the royal god; Sais, the early capital of the Delta, had for its deity the personification of the Crown of Lower Egypt, and here the Pharaoh came to be made King of the North, to be crowned with the Red Crown, and to worship the goddess of the city; in Alexandria, only mounds or an occasional pillar show where the temples of the Ptolemies and the Cæsars once stood.

Throughout the Delta hardly a temple remains; Tanis lies in tumbled heaps of stone; Bubastis has yielded only a few sculptured blocks; at Behbit el Hagar a brick-built girdle-wall still guards the fallen grandeur of what was once a magnificent structure; at Letopolis few traces can be found of that sinister shrine where were celebrated the rites of "the Night of the Destruction of the Fiends."

In the valley of the Nile itself some few temples have escaped the almost universal ruin, a ruin which came upon them largely in the nineteenth century Less than a hundred years ago many temples were still complete, many more still showed colonnades, now vanished. The limestone buildings were a convenient quarry for building new houses or were burnt for lime; the granite pillars, cut into lengths, made good garden-rollers. Now nothing remains of many of these shrines but a few scattered blocks, and the sketches made by those adventurous European travellers who dared to visit Egypt.

Even in Nubia the lust of destruction prevailed in the nineteenth century. The temples, which had stood for thousands of years intact not only as to the stonework but as to the colouring also, were ruthlessly destroyed by the local inhabitants, and fragments of the sculptured blocks can be seen in the walls of the village houses. Here again the sketches of venturesome travellers reveal the number of temples then unruined.

At the present day the untrained digger completes the harm. It is perhaps pardonable when a peasant digs away the foundations of a standing temple in order to obtain the nitrogenous earth which he requires to fertilise his fields, and by removing that earth brings the whole structure crashing to the ground; he sins in ignorance. But what excuse can be made for a man who, without any training in archæology, ruins a whole site, destroying evidence which can never be recovered? Archæology is a subject which needs a long and strenuous training; it should not be regarded as a pleasant recreation for an elderly man who has retired from another profession, nor as a " soft job " for a young man who dislikes both office work and examinations. Egypt is a disastrous example of how much more harm can be effected by human means than by centuries of natural decay.

To understand the temples of Egypt it is necessary to understand a little of the religion. In Egypt, as in many other countries, the King was regarded as the Incarnate God, the Divine Spirit having taken up its abode in his body. Each district had its own local deity, and whatever temple the Pharaoh happened to visit he was there regarded as the incarnation of the local god. As the divine King he had the name of *Osiris*, "the Occupier of the Throne." Thus there were two strata of gods, the local deities and the King in whom the local gods

PAPYRUS PILLAR:
LOTUS-BUD CAPITAL

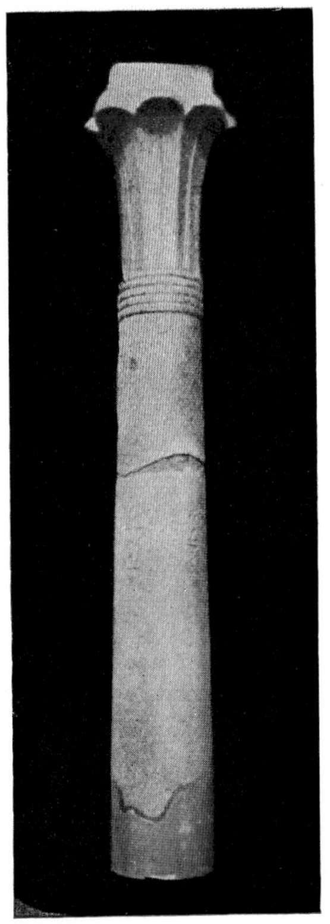

PALM-LEAF CAPITAL
(2)

METHOD OF BUILDING WITH TWO WALLS
(3)

[*Face page* 14

PLATE IV

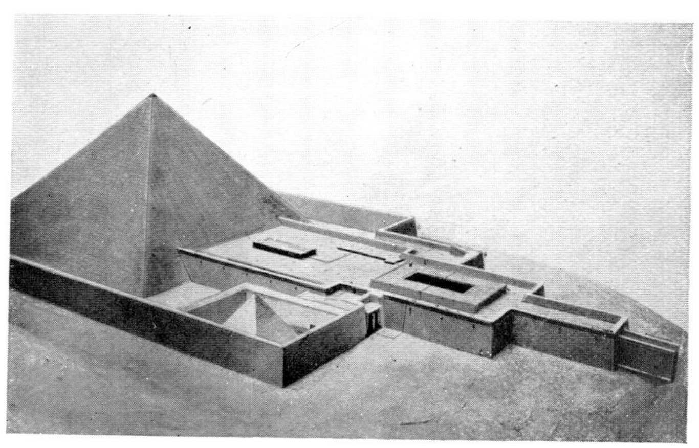

PYRAMID AND TEMPLE, ABUSIR
Vth Dynasty
(1)

STEP-PYRAMID
Ever Open Door
(2)

Face page 15]

were incarnate. There was still a third stratum, and this was the royal religion. The King heartily believed himself to be the Incarnate God, but not the incarnation of any small local deity; his own god was the sun, who was both his father and himself. As the temples owe their being chiefly to the piety of the Pharaohs it is natural that sun-worship should be found in them to a very marked degree; sun-worship has, therefore, assumed an importance in the eyes of modern writers which is not warranted by the facts.

The King being the incarnate deity during life, his body after death was holy as having once been the habitation of the spirit of God. Temples were erected to the dead King, where he was worshipped with divine honours. These temples were endowed and had their own priesthoods, and the dead King made his power felt by working miracles and giving oracles. The mortuary temples of the Kings are best seen at Thebes, where they reached their fullest development.

As every district had its own god, so every town of any size had a temple to the local deity; and the temple was large or small according to the wealth of the city in which it was built. When a district or town rose to importance the god rose also, and changes in the political condition can often be traced by the rise or fall of a deity. Within the precincts of a great temple there are often smaller shrines to the lesser gods.

A certain number of deities belong entirely to the religion of the people, and either never appear in the temples, or do so in a subordinate position. Among these are Ta-Urt, Bes, Renutet, Neheb-ka, and even the dreaded Anubis, the god of death; these were worshipped in the house or in the fields, and occasionally a chapel or shrine may be dedicated to them in or beside a large temple. The religion of the poor and the ignorant has naturally left fewer memorials than the religion of the wealthy, but it affected the higher religion as an underlying religion must always do. The animal deities belonged to the lowest stratum, yet they were of great importance to the very end, so much so that Strabo can say:

"All the Egyptians worship in common certain animals; three among the land animals, the ox, the dog and the cat; two among the birds, the hawk and the ibis; two among aquatic animals, the fishes lepidotus and oxyrhynchus. There are other animals which each people independently of others, worship; as the Saites and Thebans, a sheep; the Latopolites, a Nile-fish called *latus*; the people of Lycopolis, a wolf; the Hermopolites, a baboon; those of Babylon near Memphis, a cephus, which has the face of a satyr, and in other respects is between a dog and a bear, it is bred in Ethiopia. The people of Thebes worship an eagle; those of Leontopolis, a lion; those of Mendes, a male and female goat; and those of Athribis, a shrewmouse." While Clement of Alexandria declaims against the worship of "a beast rolling on a purple couch." Thus many of the primitive gods never lost their animal characteristics. Sekhmet and Bast were always feline, Sobk has a crocodile's head, Hathor has cow's ears even when in human form, Khnum has the head of a sheep.

As the chronology of Egypt is still a matter of dispute, it is easier to refer to the dates of the temples by dynasties rather than by years. The dynasties are numbered consecutively, the first being the earliest. For quick reference a method of grouping the dynasties together is used by all Egyptologists; this is given below, with the Pharaonic dates according to Manetho, the Ptolemaic historian. It need hardly be said that these are all before Christ.

	DYNASTIES	DATES
Proto-dynastic	I–III	5650–4777
Old Kingdom	IV–VI	4777–4077
First Intermediate	VII–X	4077–3760
Middle Kingdom	XI–XIII	3760–2976
Second Intermediate	XIV–XVII	2976–1587
New Kingdom	XVIII–XX	1587–1102
Late Period	XXI–XXVI	1102–525
Persian Period	XXVII–XXX	525–331
Ptolemaic Period	——	331–30

The periods in which the greater number of the temples are found are the Old Kingdom, the New Kingdom, and the Ptolemaic period.

I

THE GRANITE TEMPLE

FORMERLY this was known as the Temple of the Sphinx as it is in close proximity to that monument; the plan, however, shows that there is no reason to suppose that the Sphinx and the temple are necessarily connected in any way.

The temple was first excavated in 1853 by Mariette who, in his usual reckless manner, cleared every chamber without making records of anything except the statues. These interested the excavator; but the small objects and pottery, from which the modern archæologist learns so much, were entirely neglected. Consequently nothing is known of any finds within the precincts, with the exception of the Khafra statues, even the basalt figures of the apes of the god Thoth were left lying on the floor of the temple for many years.

The temple belongs to the Second Pyramid, and is part of the funerary buildings of the Pharaoh Khafra of the IVth dynasty. To the east of the Pyramid lies the Pyramid-temple, which is connected with the Granite Temple by a causeway, one of the most remarkable examples of Egyptian work (pl. V, 2). The road is skew to both temples, as it is cut in the ridge of rock which divides two shallow valleys across the desert. Though the ancient Egyptian engineer was probably not afraid of the labour involved in filling up one of these valleys with masonry, so as to make a flat surface for his road, and at the same time orientating it like the causeway of the Great Pyramid, he preferred the basis of natural rock rather than an artificial foundation. To hold the paving-blocks in place the rock itself was cut in squares, and now presents the appearance of ashlar masonry. On this foundation a layer of blocks of fine white limestone was fitted; a second layer of blocks was then laid over the first, making a smooth and even surface, fifteen feet wide and a quarter of a mile long. Time and human depredations have destroyed the greater part of the causeway, but enough remains to show the magnificence of the work.

The walls of the temple are built of rough-hewn blocks of limestone of great size, some weighing at least a hundred tons. Over these, on the outside of the wall, a fine ashlar masonry of white limestone was built, while on the inside of the wall the rough core was covered with great blocks of dark-red granite or veined alabaster.

The original entrance (pl. VI, 1) was by two great doors on the eastern side (A), opening into a long narrow hall (B), but the present entrance is in the south-west corner through a long corridor (C) lined with dark-red granite, which was actually the exit from the temple to the causeway. The corridor descends into a T-shaped hall with pillars (D), all of the same dark-red granite as the corridor. The hall has a single row of pillars along the whole length of the crossbar of the T, and down the stem of the T is a double row (pl. VI, 2). Each pillar is a monolith, square in section and standing eighteen feet high. On the pillars rest square beams of the same material and colour, which originally carried roofing-slabs across the whole extent of the hall. Against the walls stood formerly twenty-three statues, the emplacements of the pedestals being still visible on the pavement.

A doorway (E) on the east of the hall opens into the original entrance chamber, which is without decoration of any kind. It was in this chamber that Mariette found a well containing the famous diorite statues of Khafra, which had probably been hidden there to preserve them during one of the periodic political upheavals to which Egypt had always been subject. To every Memphite, whether priest or layman, all sculpture and especially statuary was peculiarly sacred, for the god of Memphis was Ptah, the god of stone-working in its most artistic form. Wanton destruction of artistic products was to the Memphite blasphemy against the god. It is a noticeable fact that statues found at Memphis often appear to have been deliberately lowered to the ground and there buried, presumably for safety, as only in a few cases are they ever battered and mutilated like the statues found further south.

From the south-west corner of the T-shaped hall a passage leads to three cupboard-like chambers (F), nineteen feet long and five feet wide, each divided into two floors by a granite shelf, twenty-eight inches thick; the lower floors are lined with red granite, the upper with alabaster. At one time these chambers were considered to be for burials, but the arguments against this supposition are very strong, the chief one being the impossibility of introducing a long object like a coffin into the side-chambers; they are now generally regarded as the storage rooms for the temple vessels and the less perishable offerings. The magnificence of the stonework is quite in keeping with the character of the Pharaoh, whose own statues are still the wonder and envy of all sculptors and stone-workers.

On the south of the present entrance-corridor a passage leads to a plain chamber lined with granite and alabaster (G); this was either the room of the temple-guardian, or where some of the priests rested while others performed the memorial ceremonies. Immediately opposite this chamber on the north side of the corridor there opens an inclined way (H) to the roof of the temple. The roof is flat, and at one time was surrounded with high walls, forming a kind of court open to the sky.

As the whole of the temple was roofed with stone the problem of lighting and ventilating the interior must have been carefully considered by the architect, for in all Egyptian temples light had to be excluded to as great an extent as possible. To obtain, therefore, a sufficiency of both light and air horizontal slit-windows were made at the top of the walls immediately below the ceiling. From each slit rose a square shaft of white limestone, which was taken high above the flat roof against the wall of the roof-courtyard, somewhat in the fashion of a chimney. The only light which entered the building was the reflection from the white walls of the shafts cast down through the slits; the light was also so arranged as to fall on the row of statues against the walls. The slits and shafts served at the same time as ventilators, and kept out the extreme heat in the "evil days of summer".

In all Egyptian temples a "dim religious light" was as essential to the cult of the god, and particularly to the cult of the dead, as the offerings themselves. The brilliant glare of the sunshine and the glowing sand outside made the contrast with the darkness within still more marked. In the dim twilight of the halls, where the dark-red walls and columns would absorb rather than reflect the light, the statues of polished stone would be clearly seen against the dark background, every detail softened by the subdued light which fell upon them from above. Barefooted priests and worshippers passing noiselessly among the huge columns would be lost to sight in the gloom. What more impressive building for the cult of the dead could be imagined?

Even in ruin the Granite Temple is the most stately of all Egyptian temples; for grandeur and simplicity of design and for beauty of workmanship no other can compare with it. Though it has no decoration of sculpture on the walls, no jewelling of colour, no inscriptions, it stands in its strength and dignity as one of the greatest

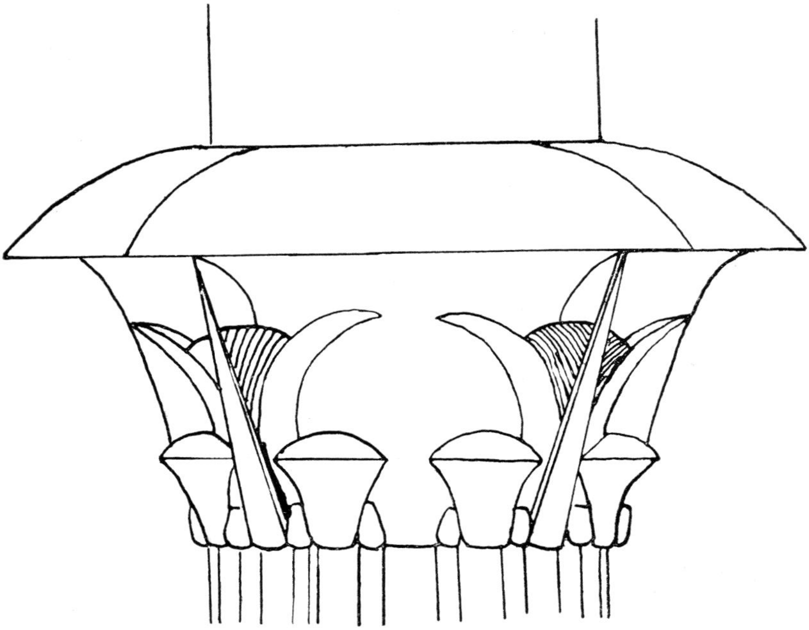

PTOLEMAIC FOLIAGE CAPITAL

(1)

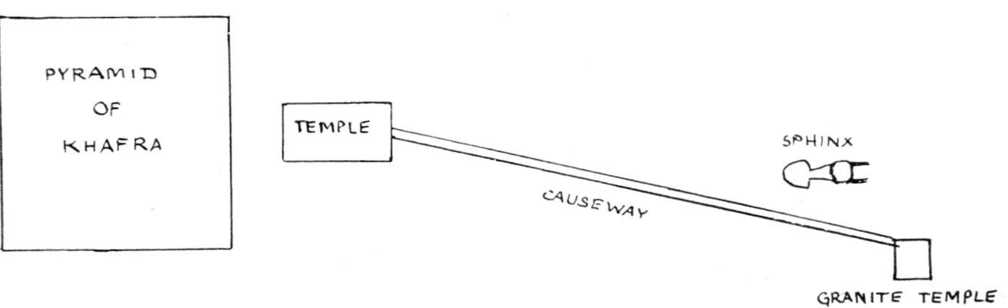

PLAN OF PYRAMID AND TEMPLES OF KHAFRA

(2)

[*Face page* 22

PLATE VI

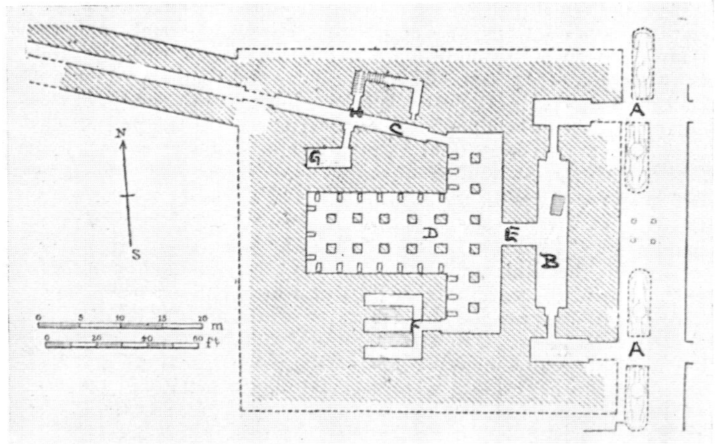

GRANITE TEMPLE (PLAN)
(1)

GRANITE TEMPLE (INTERIOR)
(2)

Face page 23]

religious monuments of past times. The squareness of pillar and architrave adds to the impression of strength and power, and the deep rich colour of its stones gives a magnificence which is lacking in the later more decorated temples. In the buildings of Zoser, beautiful as they are, over-decoration had already appeared; but the architect of Khafra, even with the example of the Zoser temples before him, resisted the temptation to hide bad work under pretty surfaces, and resolutely depended for his results on simplicity of design, solidity of building, and the splendour of an almost intractable material. He succeeded beyond his imaginings, for his work is known and appreciated by generations far removed from him in time, by peoples and nations who in his period were scattered tribes of barbarians.

II

THE SPHINX TEMPLE

BETWEEN the paws of the Sphinx is a small hypæthral chapel, too small to be called a temple. It was first discovered in 1817 by Caviglia, who was working for an English Society.

The breast and paws of the Sphinx form the walls of this tiny place of worship, which may date to the XVIIIth dynasty. Against the breast of the great lion is a smaller human figure, possibly representing a god, but more probably representing that King in whose likeness the Sphinx was sculptured; the figure is, however, so weather-worn as to be little more than a lump of rock. Below this figure is a stele recording the famous dream of Tehutmes IV; though the stele is of considerably later date than the event recorded, the tradition must belong to the time of the dream; the stele is probably a copy of an original record, for other steles of Tehutmes IV are found in the temple. Rameses II also left records of himself here. The whole area has been paved with great care, and just outside the paws is a platform, on which stands an altar of Ptolemaic date.

It is a remarkable fact that the classical authors never mention the Sphinx, though it must have been a more conspicuous object then than now, as it was complete. On the other hand, Arab authors evince great interest in it, and even state that there were two Sphinxes, one on either side of the Nile. If this statement were true the eastern Sphinx was destroyed long ago, for no trace of it remains.

III

TEMPLES OF THE STEP-PYRAMID

THE temples at the side of the Step-pyramid are the earliest known stone buildings in Egypt; they date to the IIIrd dynasty, and were erected by King Zoser the builder of the Step-pyramid. They are extremely important in the history of stone-building, and show the first efforts of Egyptian architects in that material. As early as the Ist dynasty granite and limestone had been used in the Royal Tombs at Abydos, though only for floors; actual stone building, i.e. the placing of stones one above the other to form a wall, does not appear to have been practised so early. Walls in the prehistoric and the earliest historic periods were of lattice smeared with mud, of wood, or of sun-dried brick, and it is not till the time of Zoser that stone building first appears. Manetho records that Tosorthros (now identified with Zoser) was the first to build a house of hewn stone. This might be a reference to the pyramid or to the temple or to its dependent mastaba-tombs; but the statement indicates that building in stone was so novel a method of construction as to be worthy of remark by those ancient recorders from whom Manetho drew his information.

The construction of both pyramid and temple bears out Manetho's statement, for it is evident that the builders were unaccustomed to their material and were experimenting, not always with success. The structures are built entirely of small blocks of stone, small enough to be lifted by a few men, quite unlike the great masses so common in the succeeding dynasty when stone had become the only material used for royal monuments. Zoser's architects and builders had no experience in handling and moving heavy blocks, and were obliged, perforce, to employ stones of a manageable size and weight.

The architecture, as well as the actual construction, shows that the builders were attempting to employ the technique of wood and brick in a different material, not understanding the capacity of stone in building. They had no knowledge of the stresses that stone would stand, and the resulting architecture is timid to a degree. But at least they had made a beginning, and although they themselves were not altogether successful they led the way to the magnificent architecture of later times.

A feature which occurs throughout the whole complex of buildings round the Step-pyramid is the door carved in stone, imitated from a wooden original. The doors are sometimes represented shut, and this is the prototype of the closed doors in the temple of Sethy I at Abydos. More often they are represented open (pl. X), the folding leaves are sculptured on either side of the doorway, and the detail of the pivot on which the door swung is carefully delineated; the ever-open door is found at almost every entrance; there is an occasional variation where the entrance is at an angle, then the door is shown half-open.

The Step-pyramid stands in the centre of a vast temenos, which is bounded by a thick wall recessed on the outside (pl. VII, 1). The entrance to the temenos is at the south-east angle (A), and the entrance corridor is one of the wonders of Egyptian architecture (pl. VII, 2). The forty pairs of piers, which are carried down its entire length, originally stood eighteen feet high; at each end of each pier is an engaged column carved to imitate a bundle of reeds. The piers are of white limestone, and the entrance was guarded at the outside by a pair of towers.

Opposite the second pair of piers is a passage, which turns twice at right-angles, and then runs due north for the greater part of its length; it finally turns to the west and opens into the south end of the temple of the Sed-festival (B); crossing the end of this temple it continues to an ever-open door which leads into another smaller temple (C). This building lies between the Sed-festival temple and the temenos (D); another entrance through a half-open door also gives access to the same temple. This building consists of a series of passages where were several little shrines, each approached by an ever-open door, while closed doors are found along the walls of the passages. There are two main sets of passages, one towards the west and the other towards the south.

The temple of the Sed-festival is the most complete example of the kind known; chapels for the celebration of the ceremony occur in later times, but none have been found so little destroyed. The exact significance of the Festival is not yet understood; it appears to have been of the utmost importance in the eyes of the Pharaohs, who throughout the historic period record its occurrence with great particularity. The idea that the festival was calendrical in the early periods cannot be proved though it may possibly have been celebrated at regular intervals in the Saite and later times. It was undoubtedly connected with fertility rites, and as the royal heiress played a prominent part it may represent the Sacred Marriage, such as was known among the ancient Greeks. The meaning of the words *Sed-heb* is "Tail festival," and it may therefore be connected with the custom of every Pharaoh to wear a bull's tail on great and ceremonial occasions. If, as is generally acknowledged, the dynastic Kings had a falcon as their totem some ceremony was necessary to admit them into membership with the Cattle-people who were the inhabitants of many parts of Egypt; the bull's tail would then represent the fact that the King was a bull as well as a falcon. The Sed-festival temple contains a series of chapels, each approached through an ever-open door, and each divided from the next by a stone wall carved to imitate a post-and-rail fence of the type seen in representations of early shrines (pl. X).

The temple of the pyramid (E) is set at the north side and adjoins the pyramid. The only entrance is through the temenos, and at all the narrow passages as well as at the actual entrances stands an ever-open door. The arrangement of the pyramid temple is not unlike a maze; the entrance is on the east into a corridor, which after several right-angled turns finally reaches the north-west corner, it then turns back on itself and runs eastward till it reaches the western hypæthral court, from which other passages lead into the eastern hypæthral court and into a labyrinth of chambers and passages. The two hypæthral courts, whose axes run north and south, are set side by side more or less in the middle of the building; engaged pillars form a façade to the south, from which access is obtained to a long gallery with openings into two chambers; from this gallery a corridor led to other chambers and corridors.

Every building within the temenos, with the exception of the pyramid, is asymmetrical. The innumerable chambers and passages appear to follow no known plan, and to have been altered and enlarged as the pyramid was altered and enlarged. The style of the buildings is unique; as far as is known it is not a development of any earlier form of temple, and it does not seem to have affected the later architecture, for the present therefore the whole complex remains *sui generis*.

IV

SPEOS ARTEMIDOS

About three miles to the south of the famous tombs of Beni Hasan is the Speos Artemidos, situated in a wady or ravine in the cliffs. It is hardly a temple in the ordinary sense of the word, as it is little more than a cave, which appears to have served as a wayside chapel for the men working in the quarries further up the wady.

The scenery of the ravine is extraordinarily fine; the gorge runs up into the heart of the cliffs, the floor is flat and is covered with hard white sand, while right and left the sides of the narrow valley tower upwards perpendicularly. The ravine is exactly suited to be a haunt of a beast of prey, and the cave was in all probability the lair of the wild-cat, one of the most savage of the cat tribe; hence, when it was used as a shrine, it was dedicated to Pakht, "the Tearer". The whole neighbourhood appears to have been full of wild animals; the nome, of which the ravine forms part, was called after the Hare, the adjoining nome to the south belonged to the Oryx-antelope, and beyond was the Jackal-nome. The names show that this was the land of wild game and of the animals which preyed on them.

The feline deities are a peculiar group, chiefly feminine. Sekhmet the lioness was the most feared, and therefore the most worshipped; her temple was at Memphis, where her High-priest made himself one with the deity by wearing a leopard-skin as a robe. Sekhmet was the fierce avenging goddess, the terror of evildoers; her name means "The

Powerful One ", often with the connotation of celestial or magical power. Bast was the cat; by the Greeks she was identified with Artemis, though the reason for the identification is obscure, for Artemis originated in a bear, not in a cat. The worship of Bast was orgiastic, and included frenzied dances; she was also a virgin-goddess without a male consort. Pakht must have been nearer to Bast than to Sekhmet for the Greeks called her shrine *Speos Artemidos*, "The Cave of Artemis." The reason for cat-worship is not far to seek in Egypt; even at the present day cats are more valued for their snake-killing powers than for ratting. The modern Egyptian cat kills a snake by jumping on the creature's back, and seizing it by the neck just behind the head, then with one shake and bite combined the snake's neck is dislocated or broken.

The Book of the Dead has many allusions to the cat. In the chapter of Repelling Snakes, the snake is said to have done everything that is most offensive to the sun-god, including eating a dead cat. But the most interesting, because the most tantalising in its allusions, is chapter 125; "I am pure of mouth, pure of hands. Those who see me say, 'Come, come in peace', because I have heard the great matter which the Ass said to the Cat in the House of Haped-re." This is evidently an allusion to a well-known story which is now utterly lost. The 17th chapter is perhaps the most ancient part of the whole compilation, it consists of a number of statements, with commentaries added at different periods; and it is in this chapter that there is one of the few references to a male cat-deity. "I am that cat who cleft the persea tree at his side in Heliopolis that night of exterminating the enemies of Neb-er-zer (Osiris). Who then is this? He, that male cat, is Ra himself." Another male feline deity is called "The Fierce-eyed," and is represented by a lion. In the New Kingdom the Pharaoh is likened to him; thus it is said of Amenhotep II "He was like a fierce-eyed lion,

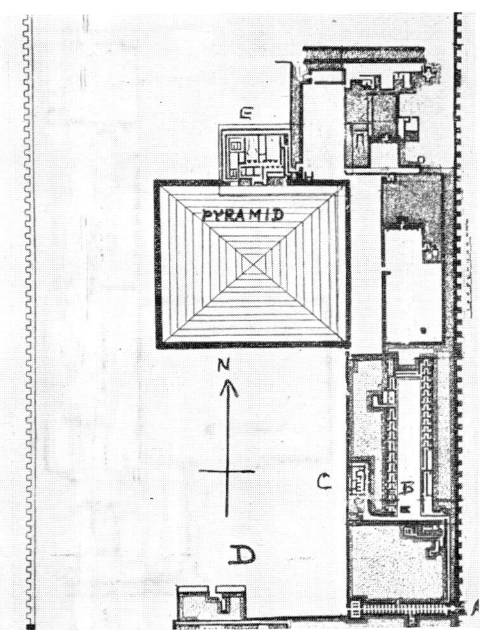

STEP-PYRAMID AND TEMPLES (PLAN)
(1)

STEP-PYRAMID (ENTRANCE CORRIDOR)
(2)

[*Face page* 30

PLATE VIII

SPEOS ARTEMIDOS

smiting the Lebanon," and of Sethy I, "His Majesty marched against them like a fierce-eyed lion, making them corpses in their valleys, overturned in their blood."

It is uncertain when the cave first became sacred; Hatshepsut of the XVIIIth dynasty claims to have restored it, and the names of Tehutmes III and Sethy I also occur. The entrance was fashioned like a temple façade, the pillars hewn out of the cliff itself, the overhanging rock smoothed and inscribed like an architrave (pl. VIII). The pillars were originally eight in number; three only remain, and on them are the names of Tehutmes III and Sethy I. The interior consists of a vestibule and a shrine, the two connected together by a short passage. The vestibule was decorated by Sethy with sculptured scenes, in which Pakht is the honoured deity. The shrine is undecorated, but in the rear wall is a niche where the statue of the goddess once stood.

The inscription above the entrance refers to the work of Hatshepsut in restoring the sacred places destroyed by the Hyksos. Manetho speaks of the way the Hyksos laid the whole country waste: "When they had our rulers in their hands, they burnt our cities and demolished the temples of the gods." It was this widespread and wanton destruction which the monarchs of the XVIIIth dynasty set themselves to repair. Hatshepsut's inscription, though badly damaged, makes it clear that she rebuilt and beautified many temples and shrines in this neighbourhood, and of the actual Speos she says: "Pakht the Great, who traverses the valleys in the midst of the eastern land, whose ways are storm-beaten. I made her temple as that which was due to the Ennead of Gods. The doors were of acacia wood, fitted with bronze; the offering-table was wrought with silver, there was gold, chests of linen and every necessary vessel."

V

TEL EL AMARNA

THE temple of Tel el Amarna can be reconstructed only from the scenes in the tomb-chapels of Akhenaten's courtiers, for the building itself is so utterly destroyed that there remain only parts of the foundation of the girdle-wall and of the main gate and a mass of broken stones and masonry. Fortunately the royal officials, who were converted to the new religion and thereby obtained riches and honours, obtained also that most coveted of all possessions, a tomb decorated at the royal expense. The King, who was also the chief missionary of the new religion, lost no opportunity of recording the appearance of his chief temple to the new god, and all the principal tombs of Tel el Amarna have scenes of the cult in the temple.

The temple was double (pl. IX, 2), and stood in an enclosure which was about half a mile long. The building was at the east end of the temenos, and was orientated by the river. The main temple, known as the "House of Rejoicing," was for the worship of the Sun-disk, called in Egyptian "Aten"; at the back was another and smaller temple, "the House of the Benben." The Benben is, strictly speaking, the pyramidal top of an obelisk, and was essentially a symbol of the sun. Both temples are entirely different from any other Egyptian temple; there were no roofs, therefore there was no darkness, no mystery, no special shrine, for the god was present to all and hidden from none.

A remarkable point about both temples is the arrangement of passages and entrances, especially those leading to the House of the Benben, they appear to have been designed to resist attack. As a fanatical iconoclast himself Akhenaten understood the importance of securing the sacred places from those who dissented from the religious dogmas and practices in any given sanctuary, consequently the buildings suggest that they were designed to be held by a few determined men against an army.

Between the great outer wall and the wall of the main temple was a narrow passage, entered from the outside by narrow doors, one on the north, the other on the south, of the main door; the passage ran the whole length of the temple on the north and south sides, and was intended solely as the entrance to the House of the Benben; there is no means of access from it into the main temple. Doors and passages could have been defended with a very small band of armed men.

The main gate has the same form as all the other gates and doors of the temple; two flanking towers with cavetto mouldings, between the towers is the high gate which opens under an overhanging cavetto cornice. The main gate gave access to an outer court, which admitted to an inner ambulatory as well as to the temple. Within the precincts was a priest's house on either side of the gate, possibly the priests had also to act as guards. To the north lies the slaughter-house, where the sacrificial animals were killed and cut up.

The House of Rejoicing was entered by a magnificent gateway (pl. IX, 1), consisting of the usual two flanking towers, in front of which was a colonnade of eight pillars in two rows of four on either side of the gate. Against each tower stood five tall slender flagstaffs with long red pennons; the pennons are shown streaming in the wind, and these, combined with the lines of the sun's rays across them, give the effect of fluttering dancing motion. The flagstaffs were either held to the stonework by metal clamps, or were passed through holes in stone blocks which jutted out from the masonry. There were two sets of folding doors; the large massive pair was probably kept closed except on great occasions, the smaller pair was set within the larger, and was the door commonly used; this is again a suggestion that an attack might be feared.

The temple consisted of six axial courts, with numerous little chapels or store-rooms at the sides; small altars were set along the sides of each court, and are represented as covered with food and flowers, and on or beside each altar is a burning lamp. In the centre of the great first court was the main altar, which was so high as to be approached by a flight of nine steps; lamps burned beside it, and it was heavily loaded with food offerings.

The second court was merely a passage-way to the third court, and calls for no special mention. The third court was subjected to many alterations; when first built it had a double colonnade of eight pillars at the east end, joined by screen-walls, and possibly roofed; a small doorway gave admittance to the colonnade from the main axial doorway. Later, the court had colonnades on all four sides, with statues of Amenhotep III, Akhenaten and Queen Tyi set between the pillars. The colonnade on the north was known by the peculiar name of "Shadow of Ra." The last three courts had no special features beyond a heavily-laden square altar in the centre.

The House of the Benben could be entered from the main temple or from the inner ambulatory. From the main temple an axial gate led into an open area; in front of the gate were "lavers," perhaps for ceremonial ablutions. The other entrance was more complicated; although axial it could only be reached from the far end of the temples, and admission was by small doorways through a series of narrow chambers.

In the open area within the precincts stood a great round-topped stele, a priest's house, and a slaughter house. The entrance to the temple itself was through one of the usual towered gates with a colonnade as in the great temple, statues of the King standing in front of each column; the colonnade was protected by a wall and entered by small doors. The entrance to the inner court was by a passage which turns on itself.

The wealth of the temple is indicated by the quantities of food represented, jars of wine, loaves and cakes, joints of meat, fish, trussed birds, vegetables and fruits. It is, however, possible that the great stocks of food were, like the fortress-like arrangement of the temples, really the preparation for an attack or siege, in which case the "lavers" might have been for the practical purpose of storing water. The utter ruin of the temples and the vindictive breaking of the royal statues in the House of the Benben suggest that Akhenaten's fears were well-founded, and that his city, and especially his temples, were subjected to deliberate and systematic destruction.

VI

ABYDOS

Temple of Sethy I

THE most beautiful temple in all Egypt is the one which Sethy I of the XIXth dynasty built for the worship of his ancestors. The plan is peculiar, and is probably due to the fact that an underground spring of water made the foundations unsafe; this spring was afterwards enclosed by the building now known as the Osireion. The insecurity of the ground forced a change of plan upon the architect; and the chambers which should normally be at the back of, or round, the sanctuary were put to the side. The ground-plan is therefore like a capital L in shape, the head of the L pointing to the north, and the base running east and west. Another peculiarity of the temple is that, instead of only one shrine to the god or gods of the temple, there are seven; these are, however, more correctly described as chapels rather than shrines. The dedications in order from east to west are to the King, Ptah, Harakhti, Amon, Osiris, Isis, and Horus.

The temple is orientated by the river, and therefore runs only approximately north and south, the entrance being at the north (pl. X, 1). The approach is through two courts, both hypæthral; and originally there was as in other temples of the period a great entrance pylon. The foundations of the pylon are left, and also part of the wall, showing niches for the royal or divine statues. The walls of the first court are destroyed to within a short distance of the ground; the sculptured scenes of the Hittite campaign indicate Rameses II as the decorator and the probable builder of this court.

A second pylon, now ruined, separates the first court from the second (A), of which only the outline can be traced. At the west end an inclined way leads up to a terrace, where stood a colonnade of square pillars; in the wall at the back are seven doors, corresponding with the seven shrines within the temple. The whole temple is built on a rising slope; the second court and the two hypostyle halls rise steadily by ramps or steps from the entrance to the chapels, suggesting in this way that the gods were on a higher level than the inhabitants of the earth.

In the first hypostyle hall (B) the pillars are arranged in pairs, so as to make seven aisles leading through doorways in the west wall, which, in their turn, lead through seven similar aisles in the second hypostyle hall (C), (pl. X, 3), and so to the seven chapels which stand in a row opening out of the highest terrace of the building (pl. X, 1).

The axis of the temple from the pylon, and through the two courts and the two hypostyle halls, leads direct to the central chapel, which is dedicated to the god Amon, at that period the supreme god of all Egypt and her dependencies. All the chapels, with one exception, are blocked at the west end by stone walls, carved to represent a shut and bolted wooden door with panelling above and rolled-up mat-hangings over the closed door. Although the chapel of Amon is the largest as well as the axial shrine, it is not the most important. Pride of place was given to the great Theban god as the supreme deity, but the true god of Abydos was Osiris; and although his chapel does not lie in the axis of the temple it is the only one through which there is a passage. The doorway at the end is not barred to the suppliant by hard cold stonework like the chapel of Amon, but stood always open. In each chapel is represented the royal ritual when the King performed the daily religious ceremonies; he is seen opening the door of the shrine to disclose the image within; he performs the toilet of the god, draping the robe round the divine figure, adjusting its crown and jewels, and perfuming it with scented ointment; he then makes offerings of incense, food, and especially flowers, for the gods were believed by the Egyptians to be as passionately fond of flowers as they were themselves. In almost every offering which Sethy makes flowers form a large part. In each chapel the ritual varied slightly, for the functions of the different deities were not always the same, and the ritual had to be altered to suit the god to whom it was addressed. In each chapel there is a representation of the sacred boat-shrine, in which the god was carried processionally round the temple on festival days.

The chapel of the King is partially ruined, and the colour on the reliefs has been destroyed, therefore the sculpture can be more clearly seen. As the Pharaoh was still living, his sacred boat is empty, though the royal head is shown at prow and stern; but the king himself as the incarnate god is carried in a litter by six masked priests, three with falcon heads, and three with jackal heads, symbolising the spirits of Nekheb and Pe, the primitive deities of the north and south. In front of the royal god walks his son, the young Rameses, burning incense before his divine father. Of all the beautiful heads in this temple, and they are many, the head of the young Rameses in this scene is perhaps the most beautiful. Rameses II was when young one of the handsomest men whose portraits have survived. The profile is fine and delicate, and the big nose saves the face from weakness; later in life, when the features were heavier and not so clearly cut, the beauty still remained, for there came then an expression of conscious power not found in the face of any other Pharaoh.

TEMPLE OF THE ATEN
(1)

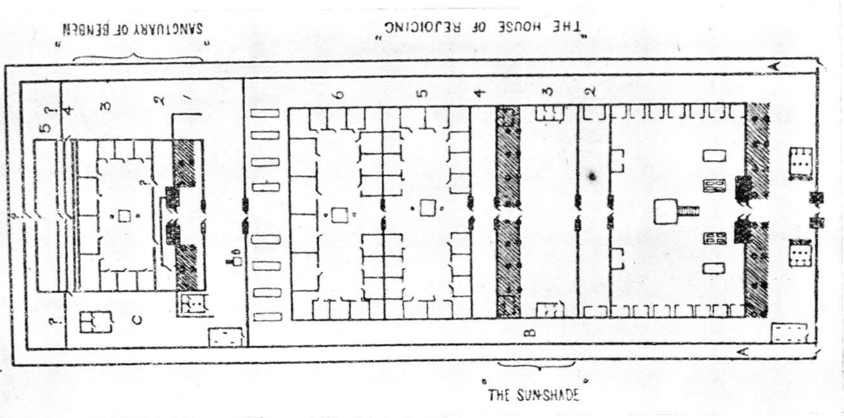

TEMPLE OF THE ATEN (PLAN)
(2)

[*Egyptian Exploration Society*

[*Face page* 38

Plate X

Abydos—Temple of Sethy
Corridor in Front of Chapels
(1)

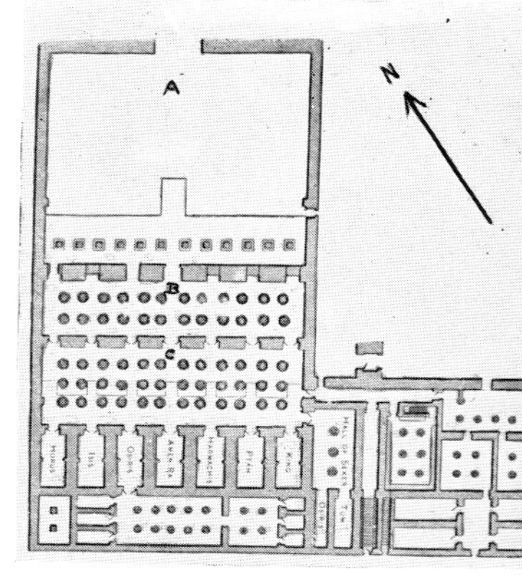

Abydos—Temple of Sethy
(2)

Temple of Sethy: Hypostyle Hall
(3)

Abydos
Temple of Rameses II
(4)

In the chapel of Ptah the roof has disappeared, and again the sculptures are without colour. The sacred boat has a special form of figurehead in the shape of two falcons standing on the emblem of Osiris; the standard of the standing sphinx, which is a feature of this boat, occurs also in some of the other chapels and is perhaps a royal emblem. In the centre of the boat is a shrine in the form of a primitive temple, obviously a highly decorated wooden structure; drawn across it is a white curtain which billows out in front and completely hides the image of the god within; similar shrines are shown in all the sacred boats. The boat is set on a stand to which poles are attached, showing that it was an object which could be carried by bearers.

Harakhti was a god to whom the Pharaohs of the XIXth dynasty seem to have paid a considerable amount of reverence. The name means the Horizon-Horus, and he appears to represent the sun both at its rising and its setting, with a consequent underlying idea of duality. The sacred boat gives expression to this idea by being represented as two in one, with two prows and two sterns. As the sun-god, Horus is accompanied by Shu, whose figure upholding the sky is set at the stern.

The centre chapel has the roof intact, and the colours on the reliefs are almost completely preserved. As this was the chief chapel the detail of the ritual is given fully; more so than in the slightly smaller shrines to left and right. The sacred boat bears the head of a ram at prow and stern decorated with the wide collar worn by human beings and gods alike. The ram was the original form of Amon, but, except on the boat, he is represented throughout this chapel in the form of a man wearing the high upstanding feathers which were the peculiarity of his costume.

The chapel of Osiris is by far the most interesting of the seven, for the ritual was the most elaborate, and had all the mystery and secrecy required to rouse devotion and interest in the worshipper. The sacred boat bears at the prow the head of Osiris wearing the feathers and horns, and at the stern is a lotus. The shrine in the centre of the boat is surmounted by the representation of the great reliquary of Abydos, which is in the form of a human head mounted on a pole; here the head is shown in profile and wears a long wig. The crew of the boat consist of figures of the king and of various gods. On the opposite wall the reliquary is represented again, but as seen from the back; the long wig is shown in detail with its ribbon bands. The pole is set on a stand ready for carrying.

The chapel of Isis is remarkable for the exquisite faces of the goddess; the artist clearly had more than one model, for they are evidently portraits from life, and range from a young girl to a woman in the fullness of mature beauty. At the prow and stern of the sacred boat of Isis is the head of the goddess wearing the disk and horns. In this chapel the ritual gives the effect of more intimacy than in the other chapels, for the King always regarded himself as the child of the goddess, and treats her as a loving son would treat a fond and adored mother.

In the last chapel the god is Horus, and should be represented as Harpocrates, i.e. Horus the Child, the third in the Osirian Triad, and like the other members of the Triad he should be entirely human. But there seems to have occurred here that confusion which makes the two Horuses difficult to disentangle; and he is shown as a falcon-headed man, a form which belongs to Horus the Elder, whereas Horus the Child, son of Isis and Osiris, is invariably human. The falcon head wearing the disk and horns is at the prow and stern of the sacred boat.

The temple is arranged for the celebration of the mysteries of Osiris. The chapel of Osiris admits to a small pillared hall which stands at the back of the seven chapels, and cannot be reached except by the one door. At the north and south ends of the hall are three small chapels, all six dedicated to the worship of the King as Osiris, thus identifying the Pharaoh with the god. The scenes on the walls of the hall show the celebration of some of the mysteries; the great reliquary occupies an important place, the pole is planted firmly on the ground, and the Holy Head is turned to face the worshipper; the front view of a face is extremely rare in Egyptian art. In another scene the King and Isis raise the *Dad*-pillar, the last act in the drama of the death and resurrection of Osiris when enacted at Busiris; and, like the Maypole, the *Dad*-pillar is decked with ribbons when raised. The Cow-goddess Shenty has an important place in the sculptures; this is the goddess in whose sanctuary, according to the Ritual of Dendera, the whole mystery of the burial and resurrection of Osiris were performed. Thoth, as the god of magic and mystery, is represented by the *kherp* sceptre with two eyes on the blade; a peculiar emblem for which there is as yet no explanation. It was to this hall, perhaps, that the candidate was brought, when at the end of the initiatory rites, he had to answer the Catechism of the Door.

To the north of the hall, beyond the three small chapels of the Osiris-king, is a chamber to which there is no opening, neither door nor window; but as the roof is destroyed it is possible that the entrance was from above. This strange chamber, which has no apparent use, may have been for the candidates who had to spend a certain time in solitude before the final ceremony of initiation. Apuleius speaks of the visions which he saw in his night vigil with the priest, visions which he beheld with his mortal eyes: "I drew nigh to the confines of death, I trod the threshold of Proserpine, I was borne through all the elements and returned to earth again. I saw the sun gleaming with bright splendour at dead of night; I approached the gods above and the gods below, and worshipped them face to face". This chamber, however, is not so mysterious as the one which lies below it; and to which there is no means of access either by door or window; and the floor of the upper room, which forms the roof of the lower, is built of solid immovable blocks of stone. It was probably for hiding some of the temple treasures; but, unfortunately, when Mariette excavated the temple, he also cleared this chamber, and left no record of anything which he may have found there.

From the terrace on which the seven chapels open, a passage leads southwards to that part of the temple which forms the base of the L. On the west wall of this passage is a list of all the Kings of Egypt from the first historic King, Mena, down to Sethy I, who is represented with his son Rameses II worshipping the names of his ancestors. This list is of great historical importance as giving the names in sequence, and it is also interesting in the omission of certain names which might reasonably have been expected to be inscribed on the document.

From this passage a staircase turns off to the west under a stone roof, of which the blocks have been cut in imitation of a vaulted roof. The stairs lead to the roof of the temple, and form part of a system of passages and stairs, by which a priest could go from one part of the temple to another without crossing in front of the sanctuary.

In late times there was an oracle of the god Bes in a chamber adjoining these stairs and the passage leading to them; and the walls of both passage and stairs are covered with graffiti in hieratic, Phœnician and Greek. It is probable that the people, who came to enquire of the god, passed the night in the passage and on the steps while waiting for the dream in which he answered their prayers.

All parts of the temple, with the exception of the storerooms, are covered with sculptures. The work of the time of Sethy I is perhaps the finest temple-sculpture in the whole of Egypt, and scenes of ritual and worship are not found in such profusion elsewhere. Sethy's sculpture is in low relief, characterised by a wonderful delicacy of line and of detail; the technique of his artists was unsurpassed. The outer courts appear to have been still undecorated at the time of his death, and they were completed under Rameses II. Whether the style of art had changed in the time, or whether Rameses was employing inferior artists, is uncertain; but it is very noticeable that the work of Rameses is greatly inferior to that of Sethy; it is in hollow relief, too deeply cut, and is entirely without the delicacy and finish of the earlier period.

The connection of the temple with Osiris is shown, not only by the sculptured scenes and by the existence of the Osiris-hall and the representation of the King as Osiris, but also by the fact that in its axis lies the underground structure known as the Osireion, for the worship of the dead and risen god. Continuing the axis across the Osireion, and through the pylon which leads out on the desert, the Royal Tombs will be reached. These are the tombs of the Kings of the Ist and IInd dynasties, and the direction of the axis shows that the temple was built for the worship of the royal ancestors.

Among the ceremonies for the worship of Osiris were mystery-plays, representations of the passion and death of the god. The legend as given by Plutarch shows that Osiris was killed by his brother Seth, that he was brought to life by Isis and her son Horus, and that later Horus fought with Seth and destroyed him. An inscription of a certain I-kher-nefrut of the XIIth dynasty is still extant, in which he describes how he was sent by King Senusert III to Abydos to make and decorate the sacred objects used at the festival of Osiris, all of which were to be fashioned of sweet-scented woods, of gold and of lapis lazuli; he was also commanded to take part in the representation of the divine mysteries, and he states that twice he overthrew the enemies of Osiris. In another mystery play, of which the words have survived, the play concludes with the binding and killing of Seth. It is not unlikely that in these plays a human victim was forced to be the enemy of Osiris, and was slain by the man who impersonated Horus.

The south part of the temple, to which the Corridor of the Kings leads, consisted of storerooms and was used in Christian times as a nunnery. Mariette, in his usual drastic manner of clearing, cast away without record everything that he found in the temple except inscriptions and statues; his rubbish heaps have yielded many objects of the Christian period, but without any means of dating them. All that can be known of the nunnery, which was housed here, must be gleaned from literary sources and from the contemporary inscriptions in the temple itself. These inscriptions are scrawled in red paint on the walls, and are mostly lists of saints and the names of nuns; the most interesting is the record of the height of the Nile. From literary sources it appears that the nunnery was founded by the celebrated Apa Moses of Baliana; he was that "monastic hero" who destroyed the heathen temple at Abydos, and who lived in the latter half of the fifth century A.D. It is to be hoped that he was more merciful in his destruction than the great Apa Shenudi, who shut up the heathen High-priest in his own temple, and then consigned both the building and the man to the flames.

VII

ABYDOS

Temple of Rameses II

THIS temple has suffered more than any other in Egypt from the hand of the deliberate destroyer. Mariette records that the old inhabitants of the villages nearest to the temple told him that they remembered how Selim Pasha, the proprietor of the villages, systematically demolished the temple, using the limestone blocks for building and for burning for lime. Consequently the temple, which a century ago was nearly complete, is now wrecked and desolate.

The dedication of the temple was to Osiris, though other gods also had shrines; Osiris, however, was the chief god of Abydos, therefore his shrine is in the axis and much larger than those of the co-templar deities (pl. XI). The entrance pylon is almost entirely destroyed, the plan shows that there were grooves for flag-staffs, two on either side of the gateway as in other pylons of the period. The pylon was of limestone with a gateway of granite; the inscription on the jambs of the gateway says that the gate was of granite, and that the actual doors were of bronze. The exterior of the walls of the temple was richly sculptured; on the north were scenes of the battle of Kadesh, and the whole poem of Pentaur was engraved also; unfortunately the greater part of the epic has been destroyed. On the south side is a description of the temple and its endowments; Rameses II was always proud of his achievements in building, and in this case he had great reason for pride; he says that the building was "of fine white limestone of Ayan, the doorways of granite, the doors of bronze worked with figures in fine gold, a Great Place in alabaster mounted on granite. The granaries were filled to bursting, the grain-heaps reached the sky. He [the King] planted many gardens, set with all kinds of trees, all sweet and fragrant woods, the plants of Punt."

The granite doorway leads into a square court (A), on every side of which was a row of colossal Osirids of the King, sculptured in sandstone; the whole of the upper part of each statue has been destroyed, so that they are no higher than the partly demolished walls (pl. X). Only the lower parts of the walls remain; these are decorated with lists of the peoples conquered by Rameses in his victorious campaigns, and in all probability the upper part also showed scenes from the campaigns. Representations of a great procession show priests and temple-officials leading sacrificial animals and carrying offerings, while soldiers and prisoners of war escort the royal chariot. The animals are drawn with great spirit and accurate observation, the fat oxen with up-curved hoofs and the *majok*-ox with one artificially-crumpled horn are worth noting.

At the far end of the court three sets of steps lead up to the usual platform; this was probably roofed to form the portico of the first hypostyle hall (B), for behind the Osirids is a row of square columns which would be unnecessary unless as supports for a roof. The central doorway which opens into the hypostyle hall was dedicated to Osiris and is said in the inscription to be "of black granite, the double doors of bronze worked in gold". On either side of the hall are two chambers entered from the portico; of these chamber N was obviously of some special importance, for a side door was cut at some unknown period to serve as an entrance into the first hypostyle hall; the door was most carefully cut so as to injure the sculptures as little as possible. It was from this chamber that the list of Kings, now in the British Museum, was obtained;

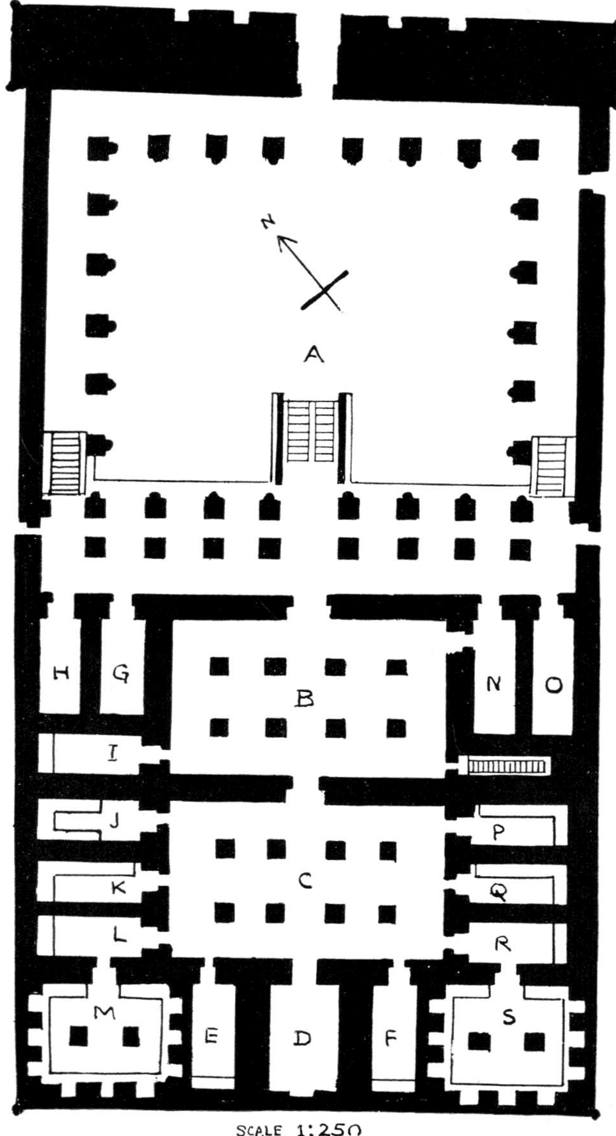

Abydos—Temple of Rameses II

[Face page 46

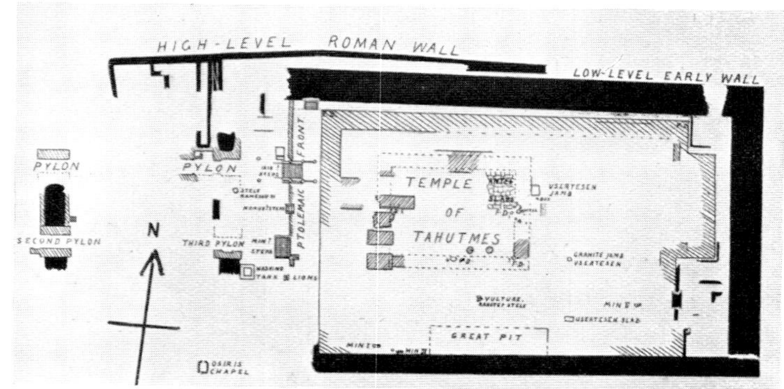

[The Plan by Sir Flinders Petrie

KOPTOS—TEMPLE OF MIN

(1)

KOPTOS—TEMPLE OF MIN

(2)

as in the list in the neighbouring temple of Sethy I no mention is made of Akhenaten and Tutankhamon.

The first hypostyle hall has eight square pillars, and must have been richly decorated with painted sculpture, but the walls are now only of sufficient height to show one register, which contains a list of the nomes of Egypt personified as men with the appropriate nome-symbol on the head, kneeling and offering flowers and vessels of water.

The second hypostyle hall (C) also had eight square pillars, and had chambers on either side. The roof was of sandstone sculptured with astronomical figures; many of the stars are personified, and each is said to give a special blessing to the King; it is possible that this sculpture recorded a horoscope.

Room G appears to have been of some importance, as it was specially dedicated to the divine Ennead of Abydos and the doorway was protected by the three members of the Osirian triad, Osiris, Isis and Horus. The chamber was evidently a chapel for the worship of the deified King, and the remains of the walls are sculptured with the divinities who inhabit the Other World, among them being Amenhotep I and Queen Aahmes-Nefertari of the XVIIIth dynasty, and Rameses I, Sethy I and Queen Tuy of the XIXth dynasty, the last three being the grandfather, father and mother of Rameses II. The stairs on the south side of the court led up to the roof.

The other chambers at the sides of both hypostyle halls are dedicated to various gods, but are of little interest except for the beauty of the sculpture and the brilliance of the colouring (pl. XI). It seems certain that the artists who decorated the temple of Sethy worked for Rameses also; if so, the temple must date to the beginning of Rameses' reign.

The sanctuary (D) was the most magnificent and costly of all the chambers in the temple; the lower part of the walls is of fine sandstone, the upper of alabaster, and the roof of rose granite. A fragment of the roof gives the dedication of the sanctuary, which "the Son of the Sun, Rameses, beloved of Amon, made as his monument for his father, Osiris, making for him a Great Place in pure alabaster".

On either side of the sanctuary is a subsidiary shrine (E, F); both of these are curiously dedicated. The portal of E bears the names of Isis and Horus; while the shrine itself belonged to Thoth. The door of F was also protected by Isis and Horus, but the shrine was dedicated to Horus the Avenger.

For sheer beauty, artistic merit and costly material this temple is the finest monument which Rameses built; but of all the beauty and splendour and delicate workmanship nothing remains now but a few walls and some fragments of inscribed stones.

Abydos was not behind Thebes in its record of miracles, for on a stele found there, though not actually in one of the temples, is recorded a miracle performed by Neb-pehti-Ra (King Aahmes I). The scene represents the boat-shrine of the deified Pharaoh borne by eight priests, the prophet Pa-yri walking beside them. The inscription says, "The 14th year, the 25th day of Paophi, in the reign of User-Maat-Ra (Rameses II), the day when the priest Pser and the priest Thay arrived to obtain (the oracle) of Neb-pehti-Ra. The priest Pser arrived at the field of my son. He heard the claims of the bereaved (lit. naked) children. The god was to establish the right. The god arrived saying, 'It belongs to the priest Pser, the son of Mes.' Then the god became extremely heavy in the presence of the priests of the King Neb-pehti-Ra, the priest Pa-yri, the priest of the front Inzabu, the priest of the front Tha-nefer, the priest of the back Nekht, and the priest of the back Tehutmes."

This was one of the chief ways by which an oracle was given; the shrine became too heavy for the bearers to continue their march. The phenomenon is recorded still in Egypt, when the dead on the way to burial indicate where they wish to be interred.

VIII

KOPTOS (QUFT)

THE ancient Koptos was one of the most important cities of Egypt from the earliest historic period until after the Moslem invasion. It lies near the Wady Hammamat, which was the regular caravan route to the Red Sea and the course by which all the Eastern trade passed into Egypt. As late as Roman times it was worth while to have a customs post at Koptos, and a list of customs dues has been found inscribed on a stone slab which had been set up half-way between the town and the desert.

The god of Koptos was Min, one of the chief gods of fertility in Egypt. But Isis was also as closely connected with Koptos as Min, and tradition states that it was at Koptos that she heard of the death of Osiris; and as she feared to leave her young son Horus in the Upper Country, so near to her enemy Seth, she departed from Koptos and placed the child with the goddess Buto in the Delta, while she herself went in search of her husband's body. In the demotic story Nefer-ka-Ptah journeyed to Koptos to search for the means of finding the hidden Book of Thoth, which contained all the magic in the world; at Koptos he met a priest of Isis, who was highly skilled in magic, and by his help and at the cost of three lives was able to carry off the book.

Min was so essentially a god of fertility that he was equated by the Greeks with Pan. Originally he was the sole deity of Koptos, but in the New Kingdom the theologians had a passion for uniting deities, therefore Isis and Horus were given to him as wife and child, though elsewhere they were in no wise connected with him. Even in the story of Nefer-ka-Ptah the priest of Isis is spoken of as though he were the priest of the only deity of the city.

The ritual of Min included a running dance performed by the Pharaoh in front of an image of the god; in this dance the King bore an oar and an object which has the same phonetic value as the oar. The meaning of these two objects has not yet been explained satisfactorily; but, as the dance appears to have been performed as part of the coronation ceremonies, it must have had some important and significant meaning.

The temple as it now stands was built in the Roman period (pls. XII, 2, XIII, 1) and presents no particular feature of interest; the walls are of stone and entirely undecorated. The objects found in the temenos show that the spot had been sacred since the beginning of the historic period, and that a temple stood here in the Middle Kingdom, replacing a still earlier structure (pl. XII, 1). The colossal statues of the god himself, which can be dated to just before the Ist dynasty, were found within the temenos, and must have belonged to a building devoted to his cult; they are of heroic size and were therefore too large to be for private worship. In one corner of the ruins of the XIIth dynasty temple was found a small limestone head of Khafra, probably a dedicated statuette in the Old Kingdom shrine. In the same part of the temenos were slabs of the Middle Kingdom turned face downwards and used as paving stones by a later builder. The sculpture on the slabs was preserved by their position; one of them shows Senusert I performing the running dance; the gallant figure and the spirit and energy of the living dancer, contrasted with the lifeless image of the god, make a fine composition. Still of the Middle Kingdom is the decree of King Antef, which was set up at the door of the temple. This decree is a fine example of an ancient and comprehensive anathema; it was promulgated against a certain Teta, "blasted be his name. Let him be cast out upon the ground from the temple, let him be driven from his office in the temple, to the son of his son and the heir of his heir; may they be driven forth on the earth, let his priestly portion be seized, let his name not be remembered in the temple, let his writings in the temple be destroyed and in every government office on every roll likewise". This meant that the wretched man was practically annihilated; without even a name, neither God nor man could know him. The curse also included any Pharaoh or governor who should pity or help the culprit or his unhappy relatives or descendants.

The entrance to the temple of Min suggests that, in the XVIIIth dynasty and possibly earlier, there were actually two temples within the encircling wall, one dedicated to Min and one to Isis, as there are two sets of pylons and two sets of entrance steps. Isis was essentially a goddess of magic, and miracles performed by her are recorded in many places. These are usually miracles of healing. The small flight of stairs between the steps to the Min-temple and the steps to the Isis-temple may possibly be the entrance to a small shrine of Horus.

As the giant figures of Min are the earliest images of a god known in ancient Egypt, so the slab dedicated to Min by the emperor Nero is one of the last representations of an Egyptian god. Although few Roman emperors set foot in the country, yet they are constantly represented as making offerings in person to the deities in the temples; and on this stele Nero is shown with a vase in one hand and a tray with a bowl on it in the other, offering them to two figures of Min; one of these is drawn in profile in the usual manner; the other is represented in front view standing in a shrine to which there is a sloping ascent, possibly a representation of the actual shrine of Min in the temple. An official of the temple, named Neb-nekht-tuf, records in the reign of Rameses II a miracle of an unusual kind performed by Isis of Koptos. The record is on a stele, which was set up in the temple. At the top of the stele is a representation of the boat-shrine of the goddess carried by twelve priests marching by threes; at the side of the shrine is the chief priest robed in a leopard-skin, while Rameses II heads the procession burning incense before the shrine. The inscription says: "This humble servant reached his city in order to give praise to Isis, to glorify the great goddess daily. She stopped at the chief of the *mezay*, she beckoned to him, she put me beside him. I adored her, saying, 'Thou hast made Neb-nekht-tuf. Behold, I will make a record of it on a tablet.' For all her ways are established well, and her hand is not stayed. All that happened to him has happened to me. I was made governor of foreign lands in the north, I officiated as chief of the *mezay*, charioteer likewise of His Majesty and royal ambassador to every land."

IX

DENDERA

At Dendera, as at Karnak, one great temple with a group of subsidiary temples stand within a girdle wall. The dedication of the great temple is to Hathor, and the name "Dendera" still retains the appellation of the cult object or fetish worshipped in the primitive shrine, *Ta-ynt-netert*, "She of the goddess-pillar."

The cult of the pillar is not so common in Egypt as in the other countries of the Eastern Mediterranean; the three chief Egyptian deities so worshipped are Hathor, Osiris, and the sun-god, and of these three Hathor is the only indigenous deity. The pillars of the two gods are entirely different in form and origin, the pillar of Osiris has proved to be derived from a bundle of reeds or a sheaf of corn, but later the form was copied in many different materials, and the origin was lost. The sacred part of the obelisk, the pillar of the sun-god, was the pyramidion on the top, and it is possible that the square shaft, on which it was set, was merely the necessary support for raising it high above the ground; the hieroglyphs of the Old Kingdom show the obelisk with a short shaft standing on a high square base and with a disk above the pyramidion, while in the sun-temple at Abusir there are still the remains of the square base of the great obelisk of Ne-user-Ra.

"Hathor, Lady of the Pillar" is known in the Old Kingdom, but in still earlier times she appears to have been a cow-goddess, for the earliest representation of her is on the slate palette of Narmer, where she has a woman's face, and the ears and horns of a buffalo-cow. Throughout the historic period she is represented as an actual cow, as a woman with a cow's head, as a woman with cow's horns or cow's ears or both, or as a woman with a horned head-dress. She was regarded as the great mother-goddess, and in late times she was fused with all the other great goddesses, more particularly with Isis. The seven Hathors, who decided the fate of the new-born infant, have no temple, and are mentioned only in religious legends; though they bear the name of the goddess it is possible that they are not really connected with her; it may be that here the name is a generic term for " divine," or in its more restricted sense, " diviner " or " prophet."

Hathor the Mother was identified with the goddess Nut, the all-embracing sky; but her fusion with the fierce goddess Sekhmet is difficult to understand, unless as seems probable Sekhmet was regarded as the northern form of Mut, the " Mother " at Thebes. The worship of Hathor seems to have been essentially joyous, degenerating in later times into license, as was the case with the Syrian Mother-goddess cult and the cult of Isis at Rome.

The number of hidden and secret chambers in the temple of Dendera suggests a mystery-cult; at the period when the temple was built Hathor was, in the eyes of the rulers of Egypt, merely another form of Isis, and according to Diodorus the mysteries of Isis and the mysteries of Eleusis were alike in every detail except the names of the respective goddesses. The mystery-cult of a goddess differs fundamentally from that of a god; the one is the mystery of birth, of life coming forth from life, the eternal unbroken chain; the other is the mystery of death, of life issuing from death, the chain eternally broken and eternally re-united.

The great temple of Dendera is the most magnificent and imposing of the Ptolemaic temples of Egypt. It

Koptos—Temple of Min
(1)

Dendera: Pillars of Portico
(2)

[*Face page* 54

Plate XIV

Dendera Temple

Face page 55]

would seem that the goddess inspired a passion of religious fervour unknown in the worship of other deities; nothing was too grand, nothing too beautiful for her abode. Though the temple is not so well preserved as Edfu, even in ruin it is a more splendid and impressive pile.

The axis runs from north to south, the entrance being to the north; the whole structure was enclosed by a wall, which also surrounded the outer court (A) and formed an ambulatory (B) completely round the temple proper. The precincts were entered by a stone gateway in the wall; of the gateway some part is left, but the colonnade which led from it to the portico is no longer to be seen. The Great Portico (C) is perhaps the most stately building in the world (pl. XIII, 2, XIV); it consists of a lofty hall, the roof supported by twenty-four great columns, twelve on either side; the pillars of the façade are connected by screen-walls. The massive over-hanging entablature bears a winged disk as its chief decoration. In the midst of all this solemn grandeur it is interesting to find a human touch in the inscription along the cornice, which records that the cost of the portico was met by local subscriptions: "For the Emperor Tiberius, the young Augustus, son of the divine Augustus, under the prefect Aulus Avillius Flaccus, the governor Aulus Fulvius Crispus, and the district-governor Sarapion, son of Trychambos, the inhabitants of the capital and the nome dedicated the Pronaos to the great goddess Aphrodite and her fellow-gods."

The pillars give the effect of immense size; they are about fifty feet high, and over thirty-five in circumference; the shafts are circular with four-sided Hathor-headed capitals. The shafts are sculptured in horizontal registers of varying widths, the subjects being religious scenes, figures of gods, inscriptions, and emblematic signs. Laid across the columns are deep stone architraves sculptured on every face; in short, wherever there was a space on which the sculptor could put any decoration, he never missed his opportunity, for even the vertical sides of the pillar-bases were sculptured. The architects appear to have followed the ancient Egyptian rule of contrasts, joining the massive simplicity of the architecture with the small and crowded detail of the decoration. The whole interior—walls, columns, ceiling—was once brilliantly painted, now only a few traces of colour remain. The decoration gives a rich effect though the detail is unpleasing, owing to the smallness and awkward arrangement of the figures and the dumpy little hieroglyphs. The scenes are, however, very interesting, they show the ceremony of a royal visit to the temple, and the presentation of estates (typified by the sign of a field) to the goddess. The ceiling decoration is entirely astronomical, with pictures of the zodiac, star-boats, dekan-stars, and the phases of the moon; quaintly interesting, too, is a scene of the sun shining on the temple, here typified by the head of Hathor.

The south wall of the portico was the original front of the earlier temple; it was not altered when the portico was built and therefore retains all the characteristics of a temple façade. The central doorway leads into the hypostyle hall (D), and beyond in the axis lie two vestibules (E, F), and the shrine (G). The hypostyle hall contains six columns with foliage capitals, above which as a kind of abacus are heads of Hathor; the bases and two lowest drums of the pillars are of granite, the upper parts of sandstone. The roof is intact, light and air being admitted from eight openings in the stonework. The sculptures deal with the foundation of the temple; on one side of the hall the King is seen setting out in state from his palace, he breaks the first sod, he shapes the first brick, he lays the first stone, he presents the whole temple to the goddess, and finally inaugurates the religious rites by the burning of incense. On the opposite wall the King performs another dedicatory ceremony after coming in full regal state from the palace; he presents ingots of precious metals to Hathor, he casts balls (perhaps of perfume) over the temple, he presents the building to Hathor and Horus of Edfu, and finally obtains an introduction to the two deities and their little son by the good offices of Ptah of Memphis.

Three chambers open from each side of the hall; some of these are lighted by openings in the roof, others are entirely dark, but all are sculptured and named. Here as at Edfu some of the names have a poetic turn, though most are severely practical. The "Silver Room" (H) was for the storage of treasures, gold, silver, lapis lazuli, malachite, and "all the costly stones of the mountain." Opposite to the Silver Room was the chamber (I) where the priests prepared the incense and other perfumes of which the goddess was supposed to be inordinately fond. The rest of these rooms were for storing jars of water, and for perishable and non-perishable offerings.

The first vestibule was known as the "Hall of the Altar," where the sacrifices were made. The scenes are entirely of the King making offerings to Hathor and her son Hor-samtaui; and it is perhaps worth noting that the greater number of the offerings are of the fruits of the earth and not of slaughtered animals. On the west is a chamber called the "Chamber of Purification" (J) where probably the offerings were ceremonially sanctified before presentation. To east and west are stairs leading to the roof.

The second vestibule is the "Hall of the Divine Ennead". Though in some ways little more than a passage room, it was the chamber in which some of the mysteries of the cult were celebrated. The sculptures indicate that as Hathor embodied in herself all other deities she alone was the source of all life. A small chamber, known as the "Linen Room" (L), opens from the east side of the second vestibule; here were kept the robes with which the image of the goddess was decked on great festivals. These garments were of linen, woven or embroidered in patterns and presenting a wonderful combination of colour.

The door on the west leads into a second "Silver Room" (K) which gives access to a small hypæthral court (M) standing parallel with the sanctuary. At the far end of the court is a small kiosk or chapel with two Hathor-headed columns which form the façade and support the roof. The purpose of the chapel was for the services attendant on the birth of the divine infant, which were performed annually on "the Day of the Night of the Child in the Cradle". This great day was the ancient New Year, the day of High Nile, a festival which was kept with rejoicing throughout Egypt as the greatest of all festivals. Even at the present time the Coptic New Year, or Day of Nawruz, is still marked as a public festival and kept as a time of rejoicing. On the ceiling of this small chapel is one of the most interesting sculptures in Egypt; the figure of the sky-goddess Nut, in her conventional position of making the arch of heaven with her body, covers the whole space; she stands on water and is clothed with water, and from her issue both sun and moon; she is therefore the primeval source of moisture, light and heat, without which earth would be barren; and her name is given as "Nut the Unknown". Her identification with the goddess of the temple is indicated by the shrine of Hathor which stands beside her.

In the axis of the temple is the shrine, leading out of the second vestibule. This chamber is completely dark, and its name was "The Dwelling-place of the Golden One". The sacred boat stood here, and in it was set the most holy image of the goddess; the doors were kept shut and sealed, and the seals were solemnly broken and the doors opened only at the great festivals. Even then it was only the High-priest and the Pharaoh, who by right of his position could officiate as High-priest in every temple, who might enter into the Holy of Holies. The sculptures show the whole ritual of the Pharaoh's visit to the goddess; he mounts the steps, breaks the seal, opens the door, gazes on the image, makes his offerings, and worships the divine Mother.

A corridor (N) surrounds the shrine, and from it open eleven small rooms, the "hidden secret chambers". These are called by various names, as the "Flame-room", "the Throne of Ra", "the Union of the Two Lands", "the Birth room", and "the Room of the Resurrection". The purport of these rooms cannot now be explained, the meaning of the names is lost; it is perhaps possible that the Flame-room is the same as the House of Flame referred to in the "chapter of making remembrance" (the 25th) in the Book of the Dead, "My name is given to me in the great Shrine, my name is remembered for me in the House of Flame on that Night of the Counting of Years and the Reckoning of Months".

The staircases to the roof of the temple are decorated with representations of the procession of the goddess, when she was carried with great splendour to feast her eyes on her great possessions and to "be united with the rays" of the sun-god. A long row of priests headed by the Pharaoh bear the sacred objects, the shrine itself being carried by eight stalwart priests; at stated intervals the procession stopped and the Pharaoh burnt incense before the image. Priestesses also appear in the procession holding garlands and sprays of leaves; and as one of the names of the goddess is Hathor of the Roses, they bear garlands of flowers as well. The procession is seen mounting the stairs to the roof, and then descending again.

The roof is flat, and is on two levels, for the portico is higher than the main temple. On the lower level are several shrines or chapels, the largest is in the south-west corner at the extreme end of the roof; it is hypæthral and has twelve Hathor-headed columns. At the north-east and north-west angles, abutting on the wall of the portico, are three small chapels on either side; these were for the worship of Osiris and the sculptured scenes show forth his death and resurrection. Inscribed on the walls is the famous "Ritual of Dendera", which gives the whole service as performed in the two "lands" of Egypt, the south and the north. At Dendera the Ritual was performed as a mystery play with puppets; the size and material of each figure is given in full detail, and the prescribed attitudes shown, beginning from the time when the body of Osiris lies stark and dead upon the bier till the moment when the god springs to life protected by Isis, who shields her eyes from the exceeding great glory of the risen deity.

In one of the north-east chapels is a procession of twenty-nine priests wearing striped robes and carrying standards of sacred emblems; they are preceded by the King burning incense. The last two priests are the most interesting; one wears a mask of the jackal-god Anubis, the man's head and shoulders being depicted as though the mask were transparent, but it is obvious that he was unable to see for he is being led by another priest who holds him by the arm. A pottery mask of Anubis, large enough to fit over a man's head and shoulders, is now in the museum at Hildesheim. Apuleius in "The Golden Ass", describing the procession of Isis, says, "There came forth the gods themselves, deigning to walk with human feet upon the earth. First came the dread envoy that goes between the lords of heaven and of the nether world, even Anubis. Lofty he was of stature and his face seemed now to be black, now golden bright; high he held his dog-like neck, in his left hand he bore the herald's wand, in his right he brandished a green branch of palm." The mask and the sculpture, in addition to the literary evidence, prove that ritual masking was practised in Egypt and that the grotesque animal-headed gods were in reality masked men.

In the centre chapel of the three on the north-east was found the great zodiac, now in the Bibliothèque Nationale in Paris; it has been replaced in the temple by a plaster cast. The reason for such a form of sculpture can only be explained by the identification of Hathor with the sky goddess.

The secret chambers or crypts are more numerous here than elsewhere; they were constructed in the thickness of the walls and under the floors, and the entrances to them were by movable slabs, so that they were entirely hidden. They are all sculptured and painted, and the colours having been preserved from the light are wonderfully fresh and brilliant. Some of the crypts were for the secret rites of the goddess, others were for the more mundane purpose of keeping the temple treasures, which according to the inscriptions must have been of great value. The huge necklace of the goddess—consisting of the *usekh*-collar and four totems of Hathor, all connected by chains with the *menat*, the so-called counterpoise—was of gold encrusted with precious stones. And this was only one of the many objects used in the ritual.

The temple walls are sculptured on their outer faces with figures of various deities and scenes of their worship. Among these figures is Cleopatra as Isis, wearing the disk and horns of the goddess; there is no doubt of the truth of the portraiture if the face is compared with the statue of her father, Ptolemy Auletes, now in the British Museum. The figures of Cleopatra's young son, Cæsarion, are of pathetic interest for the boy at the age of seventeen was, after his mother's death, betrayed into the hands of Augustus and murdered.

The Sacred Lake (R) is to the south-west of the Great Temple; it is rectangular, and has a flight of steps at each corner. It was still in use in the time of Abu Salih (*circa*

A.D. 1200) by whom it is described, "There is here a well, square in form, the opening of which measures 100 cubits on each side; the entrance into it is by steps, which can be descended by camels, oxen, horses, sheep, and all other beasts which drink the water of the well. In this district there is the most wonderful ancient temple, such as has never been seen elsewhere; and it is said that the giants who built this temple also planned the construction of the well."

The tradition of a horned deity in the temple still remained in the time of the Arab author Maqrizi, "The spirit which haunts this temple appears in the form of a man with a lion's head on which are two horns." The horns were characteristic of Hathor, and the feline deities were usually feminine in ancient Egypt, it is therefore interesting to note that the ghost of the goddess has changed its sex.

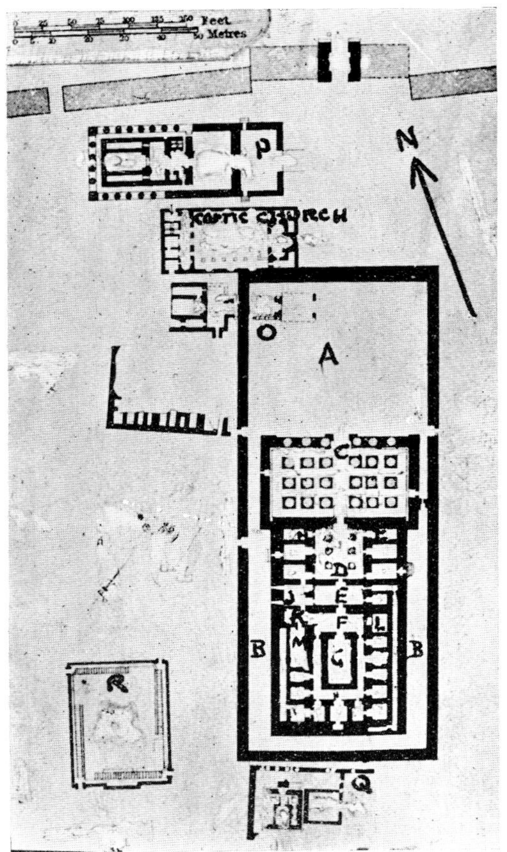

DENDERA
(1)

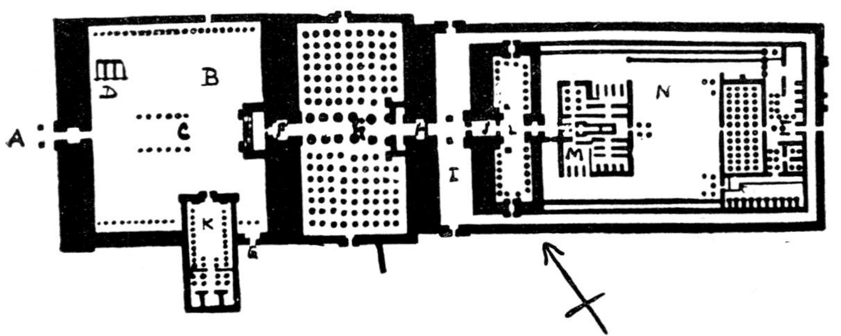

KARNAK: GREAT TEMPLE OF AMON
(2)

[*Face page* 62

KARNAK: GREAT TEMPLE [Photograph by Mr. Percive

Showing Quay, Sphinx Avenue, and Entrance Pylon

(1)

KARNAK: AVENUE OF SPHINXES

(2)

X

DENDERA

Dendera—The Smaller Temples

Birth-House of Nectanebo I (O). When Nectanebo I built this birth-house the temple of Hathor was of much smaller dimensions than at the present day; and the birth-house lay outside the outer court. But when the Ptolemies decided to rebuild the temple on a grander scale, the new outer court with its encircling wall cut across the birth-house; all that interfered with the new building was pulled down, the sanctuary of the birth-house was preserved only because it happened to lie outside the wall.

Part of a colonnade survives, this leads to a transverse chamber, out of which open the sanctuary and two side chambers. In the sanctuary the whole story of the birth of the Divine Child is represented on the walls. The mother is Hathor, but the father is not her official consort Horus of Edfu, but Amon of Thebes; and the fruit of the union is Nectanebo himself. This carries on the tradition of the divine birth of the Pharaoh, of which the earliest examples are found on the walls of Hatshepsut's temple at Dêr el Bahri and Amenhotep III's temple at Luxor. The traditional father even at this late period is still the Theban god, who was nearer to Hathor geographically than Horus of Edfu, and may therefore have been her original consort.

Birth-House of Augustus (P). This lies outside the precincts of the Great Temple, to the north-west of the outer court. Though it was built by Augustus the names of Trajan and Hadrian are found throughout the inscriptions.

It is entered by a sloping way which leads into an outer court; an inner court and two antechambers lie between the outer court and the sanctuary. The enclosing wall ceases before reaching the level of the sanctuary and is replaced by a colonnade which forms an open gallery at the sides and back of the sanctuary. The columns have flower capitals, and the abacus above each column has on it the figure of the god Bes, the protector of new-born infants. The reliefs in the sanctuary refer to the birth of the Divine Child, who in this case is not identified with the Pharaoh.

Temple of Isis (Q). This temple stands to the south of the Great Temple, and is built on a terrace. Though within the great girdle-wall it is distinct from all the other temples in the enclosure, having its own sacred precincts surrounded by a wall which runs almost parallel with the outer wall of the Great Temple. The axis runs east and west, with the sanctuary to the east; the greater part of the building has disappeared, only a few chambers being left. The chief interest of this temple lies in the fact that it was built by the cold-blooded Augustus within a few yards of the walls which bear the portraits of his victims, Cleopatra and Cæsarion.

It is perhaps worth noting that the axes of the smaller temples of Dendera run at right-angles to the axis of the Great Temple.

XI

KARNAK

THE great city of Thebes was the capital of ancient Egypt from the sixteenth century before Christ till the Assyrian armies sacked it more than eight hundred years later. Even as early as the Middle Kingdom its chieftains had made themselves rulers of Egypt, and incorporated the name of the Theban god in their own names; four Pharaohs of the XIIth dynasty were called Amon-em-hat (Amon in front). But when the "impure foot" of the foreign Hyksos invaded the country, Thebes retired into the obscurity of a small provincial town. After many generations there came a great rising against the invader, and the Theban royal family produced one military genius after another. Under these great generals Egypt became united, with a Theban prince as Pharaoh; step by step the Hyksos were driven out, the Egyptian kindgom being steadily consolidated as the invaders were expelled. Then the military genius reached its highest point in Tehutmes III, who carried the arms of Egypt beyond her borders, and made her the great world-power for many centuries. The glory of Thebes increased with the increasing power of her princes, till the small provincial town—originally nothing more than a collection of lattice-and-mud huts —became "hundred-gated Thebes", the capital of a mighty empire.

The god Amon shared the fortune of his city. At first only an obscure provincial deity he blossomed out, not only as the chief god of Egypt but as the conqueror of those deities whose countries were subject to Egypt. He thus became the Supreme God of the world, hence his title "King of the Gods". Even when Egypt lost her supremacy and Thebes was reverting to its original condition of a lattice-and-mud village the Greeks still called the Theban god by the name of their own supreme deity Zeus. It is not surprising therefore that the ruins of Thebes should contain more temples than any other site in Egypt.

Thebes was divided into two distinct parts; on the east bank of the Nile were the dwelling-places of the living, the palaces of the Kings, and the temples of the living Gods. On the west bank were the homes of the dead, the burial-places of Kings and nobles, and the funerary temples of the Pharaohs. This division has continued to the present day. The modern town of Luxor lies on the east bank, while only a few scattered villages have risen among the ancient tombs on the west. The contrast between the bustling modernity of Luxor and the unchanging mentality of the western villages is still very marked.

On the east bank of the river, about a mile to the north of modern Luxor, there lies a group of temples known at the present day as Karnak. The name was given to the village which grew up over the ruins of the ancient city and temple. The debris of succeeding generations of villages buried the whole temple, leaving only the highest portion of the nave of the hypostyle hall above the ground, the clerestory alone remaining visible; hence the name given to the village, "the town of the Windows". Now that the site has been extensively excavated it will be seen that there are at least twenty temples in the group; the greater number being dedicated to Amon, but there are also temples to Mut, Khonsu, Ptah, Sekhmet, and others, besides chapels to minor deities which occur in several places within the walls of the main buildings.

The earliest temple of which remains have been found

was situated between the Great Temple and the so-called Festival Hall of Tehutmes III (N). It dates to the XIIth dynasty, but its extent is not known, nor is the dedication; it was perhaps not more than a chapel, for Thebes was not then so important as Memphis, Abydos or many other places where the Pharaohs of the Middle Kingdom erected temples to the local deities. It is, however, evident that the Kings of the Middle Kingdom honoured the god of Thebes, for their statues have been found in various parts of the sacred precincts, and portions of an inscribed wall bearing the cartouches of Senusert I were used as the filling of the pylon of Haremheb in the XVIIIth dynasty.

The Great Temple

The Great Temple was dedicated to the local god of Thebes, Amon, called in the XVIIIth dynasty Amon-Ra. Originally he was worshipped in animal form as a ram, and even to late times the recollection of his early form was retained with some vividness. Herodotus describes the ceremony of the sacrifice of a ram to the god, and states that the fleece of the slaughtered animal was wrapped round the divine image. From the XVIIIth dynasty onwards Amon was represented in human form, but usually with the curving horns of his sacred animal. The Theban breed of sheep appears to have been peculiar to that district; the ordinary Egyptian sheep had straight horizontal horns, whereas the Theban breed had horns curving forwards and downwards.

The present condition of the Great Temple of Amon is deplorable, owing to natural causes. M. Pillet's report in 1922 states: "Every year water appears in the court of the Temple about October 5, then it rises gradually until the end of the month, when its height in the great hypostyle hall reaches 1·35 metres on an average, sometimes more. It then decreases and disappears completely towards the middle of November, leaving on the ground and on the stones of the temple a thick deposit of saltpetre which gives the ruins the aspect of a vast field of salt. The water comes by infiltration through the cultivated land from the canals and lakes formed on the east of Karnak long after the Nile has gone down. In ancient times the bottom of the river was four or five metres below its present level, but the accumulating ooze has gradually raised the river-bed. The temples at that time were preserved from the inundation and also from the infiltration from the canals whose level has been greatly raised by the present dam. . . . When it is not the water itself which attacks the granite and sandstone of the temple, it is the treacherous humidity which rises by capillary attraction in all the buildings. It reaches a point where evaporation is sufficient to stop it, then comes disaster, the saltpetre crystallises and splinters the hardest granite. Thus all Karnak is being devoured by this terrible leprosy. The inside of the sanctuary of the sacred barque is almost entirely eaten away, its reliefs break off in great flakes which fall every year owing to the crystallisation of the saltpetre; the disease is reaching the highest part, and a few years hence nothing will remain of the reliefs. The feet of the admirable colossi of Tehutmes III, which decorate the southern façade of the VIIth pylon, are eaten as though by an ulcer; the inscriptions, which ornamented the upper part of the pedestal are now nothing more than red gravel."

The ruin of the temple is also partly due to the ancient architects' method of building, which M. Pillet describes: "after digging to a slight depth they arranged, on a shallow bed of sand, blocks of different dimensions, coming as a rule from the buildings of their predecessors. Sometimes these blocks were held together by a layer of plaster; more often the interstices were masked by pieces of stone mixed with earth; then without taking any further trouble they raised their formidable pylons and gigantic hypostyle halls. The hypostyle hall is thus erected almost entirely on a foundation of small blocks measuring a royal cubit, piled up in five layers without mortar. The sandstone eroded by saltpetre is transformed into sand, which the waters gradually wash away." Since the disaster of 1899, when eleven columns crashed to the ground, the Department of Antiquities has used all modern methods to repair the faults in building-construction committed by the ancient architects; but the danger from natural causes is irremediable.

The Great Temple of Amon dates probably to the beginning of the XVIIIth dynasty, when the XIIth dynasty shrine had fallen into decay. The continual additions and alterations to the original structure by succeeding generations of Pharaohs show its importance and the veneration in which it was held. Though it was begun in the early part of the XVIIIth dynasty it was not until the third King of the dynasty, Tehutmes I, that any exact dating can be obtained. In his reign the temple was little more than a quarter of its present length, his pylons (pylons IV and V) and obelisks marking its extreme western limit. There are three pylons between the so-called Central Court (I) (which in the time of Tehutmes I was open ground) and the actual shrine (M), and confusingly enough, they are later in date the nearer they approach to the Holy of Holies. Tehutmes I's name occurs on two of these great gateways, and in the space between them Hatshepsut set up her obelisks. As a pair of obelisks always indicated the entrance to a temple this is clearly the original entrance.

All the monuments of Queen Hatshepsut add to the mystery which surrounds her. Did she erect the obelisks in front of the pylon of her father, Tehutmes I, thus claiming his gateway for her own? Then there is the mysterious fact that the obelisks of Hatshepsut were partially walled up with blocks bearing sculpture reft from some building of hers, and so arranged as to hide her name on the obelisks without entirely covering them. Her successor, Tehutmes III, is credited with having tried to destroy all traces of her memory after having pushed her from the throne or perhaps having murdered her. There is no proof of such a supposition, though it is often stated as an ascertained fact; and it is at least noteworthy that the obelisks are covered only where the inscription might have been considered private, while the upper part, which was of public interest, was left visible. These are the celebrated obelisks which were completely finished in seven months from the date of the order for their making. The Queen appears to have realised that even for Egyptian quarry-men, stone-masons, and architects, it was a remarkable feat, for she records the fact on her inscription on the obelisks. The full form of the great royal oath is worth noting, the shortened form is often found in the inscriptions of other Pharaohs.

"I sat in the palace, I remembered him who made me, my heart led me to make for him two great obelisks, whose points mingled with the sky, in the splendid colonnade between the two great pylons of the King Tehutmes I. I swear as Ra loves me, as my father Amon favours me, as my nostrils are filled with satisfying life, as I wear the White Crown, as I appear in the Red Crown, as Horus and Seth have united for me their portions, as I rule this land like the son of Isis, as I have become strong like the son of Nut, as Ra sets in the evening Barque, as he rises in the morning Barque, as he joins his two Mothers in the divine Barque, as heaven abides, as that which he has made endures, as I shall be to eternity like a never-setting star, as I shall go down in the west like Atum, [so surely] these two great obelisks, which my Majesty has wrought with fine gold for my father Amon, are of one block of enduring granite without seam or joining. My Majesty

KARNAK: TEMPLE OF AMENHOTEP II
(1)

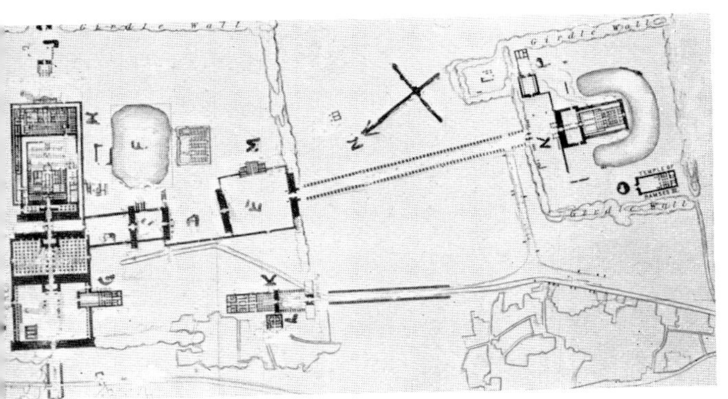

KARNAK (PLAN)
(2)

[*Face page* 70

PLATE XVIII

[Photograph by Mr. Perciv

KARNAK: FESTIVAL HALL OF TEHUTMES III
Showing Clerestory Windows and Tent-pole Pillars
(1)

[Photograph by Mr. Perciva

KARNAK: TEMPLE OF PTAH
(2)

Face page 71]

exacted work thereon from the first day of Mechir until the last of Mesore, making seven months of work."

Tehutmes III built the inner gateway (pylon VI) and so enclosed the shrine within three gates. The actual shrine is of late date, being of the reign of Philip Arrhidaeus, the half-brother of Alexander the Great. On the walls of the ambulatory which surrounds the shrine are the inscriptions of Tehutmes III recording his campaigns and victories in Syria. The celebrated campaign against the coalition of Syrian princes, whose headquarters were at Megiddo above the plain of Esdraelon, is given in full detail. The account is evidently copied from a diary kept by the King's own secretary, and sets forth the events of the campaign from the departure of the Egyptian army from Egypt till the capture of the stronghold of Megiddo. Quite unintentionally the scribe has drawn so lifelike a study of the King's character, and made the reader of the record see so clearly the reckless courage of Tehutmes, his hot temper, his magnificent generalship, and his merciful disposition towards the conquered, that this great Pharaoh becomes the most human and lovable of all the Kings of ancient times. The scribe notes that he made the record "upon a roll of leather in the temple of Amon". The leather has perished long since, but the copy inscribed on the stone walls of the ambulatory is still in sufficiently good condition to permit of transcription. When the Egyptian army reached the south side of the Megiddo hills, Tehutmes called a council of war, and the generals advised extreme caution. "How should we go upon this narrow road while they come and say that the enemy is there waiting, holding the road against a multitude? Will not horse come behind horse, and man behind man likewise? Shall our vanguard be fighting while our rearguard is standing at Aruna without fighting? Behold, there are two other roads, one comes out at Taanach, the other will bring us to the way north of

Zefti, so that we shall come out to the north of Megiddo. Let our mighty Lord proceed on the road he prefers, but do not let us go by that difficult road. [The King replied :] I swear as Ra loves me, as my father Amon favours me, as my nostril is rejuvenated with life and power, my Majesty will go upon this road of Aruna. Let him among you who so desires go by those roads you mentioned, and let him among you who so desires follow my Majesty. Shall the detestable enemy think, 'Does his Majesty go by another road? Then he is afraid of us.' [The generals agreed to follow the King.] Then his Majesty commanded the whole army to march on the narrow road. His Majesty swore, saying, 'Not a man shall go in front of my Majesty'. Then his Majesty marched at the head of his soldiers, showing the way by his own footsteps, while horse came behind horse, with his Majesty at the head of the army. [Then comes the description of the preparations for the battle and an account of the battle itself.] His Majesty went out in his golden chariot, equipped with his weapons of war. The south wing of the army was on the hill to the south of the Kina brook, the north wing was to the north-west of Megiddo, and his Majesty was in the centre between them. When the enemy saw his Majesty at the head of the army prevailing against them, they fled headlong to Megiddo in terror, abandoning their horses and chariots of gold and silver. They were hauled and pulled up by their clothing into the town, for the townspeople had shut the gates upon them, and had let down cloths to pull them up. Oh! if only the soldiers of his Majesty had not given their attention to plundering the things of the enemy, they would have captured Megiddo at that moment when the miserable enemy of Kadesh and the miserable enemy of Megiddo were hauled up hastily to get them into the town. [The King rebuked his army with severity] 'because every chief of every rebellious country is in that town, because the capture of Megiddo is the capture of a thousand cities. Capture it then completely'." Megiddo was then strictly invested, though provision was made for refugees leaving the town; the city finally made terms and surrendered. At the end of the campaign Tehutmes "appointed new chiefs to every town"; in other words, he removed the princes who had fought against him and set Egyptian governors in their places and so laid the foundations for the suzerainty of Egypt over the whole of Syria. Though Tehutmes was feared by his enemies as no other Pharaoh was feared, he seems to have held the love and confidence of his own people, especially of the army; and he had the respect of the peoples he had conquered. The campaign against Megiddo is the only one given in full detail; the rest are merely summarised, obviously because there was not space enough on the walls to treat each campaign on the same generous scale.

Though the temple was continually altered the axis was never changed, all the additions being made in the line of the first building, the vista lengthening with each successive addition. Amenhotep III built a pylon (pylon III) still further to the west, and increased the size of the earlier temple by enclosing a court between his own pylon and those of his predecessors. It is not unlikely that the great hypostyle hall was also his project, but as he was already concentrating on building the temple of Luxor he probably could not be too lavish with men and money at Karnak.

In the reign of the Heretic King the temples of Amon were not only neglected but ran great risk of being destroyed. Failing the utter destruction of the worship and temples of the hated god, Akhenaten had to content himself with changing his own name from Amenhotep to Akhenaten, and with erasing the name of Amon on every inscription where it occurred. Whether his fanatic zeal was inspired by religious fervour or by a political revolt against the ever-increasing power of the priesthood of Amon, is still uncertain. Whichever it may have been the result was the same; the two great powers—the royal and the priestly—were arrayed against each other, with consequent chaos in the government of the country. The opinion in which Akhenaten was held in later times by the people at large is shown by the epithet "the wicked one of Akhenaten" applied to him in the inscription of Mes in the reign of Rameses II.

Haremheb who reduced the country to order after the misgovernment of the Tel el Amarna epoch, was probably the builder of the great hypostyle hall (G), though the decorations were of later date. Haremheb also showed his hatred and contempt for the Heretic King by using the statues of Akhenaten as filling for his pylon. Rameses I, Haremheb's immediate successor whose very short reign gave no time for much building, erected a great pylon (pylon II) to the west of the hypostyle hall, thus making a new entrance and increasing the length of the temple. That great builder Rameses II did little at Karnak beyond setting up statues of himself, but the Bubastite Kings of the XXIInd dynasty and the Ethiopian Kings of the XXVth dynasty were responsible for the great outer court (B) and the immense entrance pylon (pylon I). Both court and pylon were probably erected on the site of earlier structures, for the splendid avenue of ram-headed sphinxes (A), leading up to the pylon, belongs to the time of Amenhotep III of the XVIIIth dynasty, several centuries earlier.

The apparent confusion in the building is due to the continual alterations effected through the centuries; but if the main facts of the increase in the length of the temple are borne in mind, the side-chapels and subordinate temples will be easily understood.

The main approach to the Great Temple was from the river, where the remains of a stone-built quay are still visible. From the quay an avenue of ram-headed sphinxes outlines the processional way to the western pylon (A). The sphinxes have the bodies of lions, but in honour of the ram-god they have the heads of rams. Between the paws of each sphinx stands a figure of Amenhotep III, who thus shows himself as under the special protection of the god. In any other art than that of Egypt this strange combination of lion and ram would be grotesque, but here the effect of the long double row of couchant animals is entirely majestic (pl. XVI, 2).

Though the entrance pylon (pylon I) is greatly damaged and has lost the overhanging cornice, it is still an imposing mass of building (A), and through the gateway the vista to the shrine is grand and impressive. In the axis of the Forecourt Taharqa of the XXVth dynasty erected a roofed colonnade of ten pillars (C), five on either side. This was the "Tirhakah, king of Ethiopia" mentioned in Isaiah xxxvii, 9; he was defeated by the Assyrian hosts under Assur-bani-pal and fled to his native Ethiopia, leaving Egypt to be ravaged by the fiercest and most savage nation of the ancient world. Assur-bani-pal recounts with pride the destruction he wrought in Thebes after the death of Taharqa; "Tirhakah fled to Ethiopia, the might of the soldiers of Assur my lord overwhelmed him, and he went to his place of night. Afterwards Tandamane, son of his sister, sat on his royal throne. He made Thebes his fortified city, and he gathered forces to oppose my army. . . . On my second expedition to Egypt and Ethiopia I directed my way. Tandamane heard of my expedition and that I had crossed over the border of Egypt. He abandoned Memphis and to save his life he fled to Thebes. I pursued my way after Tandamane, I went to Thebes his stronghold; he saw the approach of my mighty army, he abandoned Thebes and fled to Kipkip. In the service of Assur and Ishtar my hands took that city; silver, gold, precious stones, the furniture of his palace, many-coloured clothing, linen, great horses, people male and female; two wooden posts, tall, fashioned of bright *zahalu* [perhaps meaning 'overlaid with metal'], 2,500 talents their weight, standing at the gate of the temple, I plucked from their standing-place and brought to Assyria. Heavy booty beyond counting I carried off from the midst of Thebes. Over Egypt and Ethiopia I let my weapons rage and showed my might. With my hands full I returned to Nineveh, the city of my dominion, in good health." The doorposts were probably of the kind so often described in the Egyptian records as being made of some precious wood and overlaid with bronze. The prophet Nahum also describes the sack of Thebes by Assur-bani-pal; "Art thou better than No-Amon, that was situate among the rivers, that had the waters round about her; whose rampart was the sea, and her wall was of the sea? Egypt and Ethiopia were her strength, and it was infinite; Put and Lubim were her helpers. Yet was she carried away, she went into captivity; her young children also were dashed in pieces at the top of all the streets; and they cast lots for the honourable men, and all her great men were bound in chains" (III. 8–10). The colonnade of Taharqa, intended as a processional way, was probably the beginning of a more ambitious scheme of building; it remains now in ruin, the bases of the columns hardly above the level of the ground; one solitary pillar still stands to show what the beauty of the structure must have been. The pillar has struck the imagination of the local inhabitants, who connect it with the obelisk of Hatshepsut, the tradition of a great queen being handed down from generation to generation for more than three thousand years. According to the legend, the pillar is the spindle of the giantess Sarangouma, the obelisk is queen Sarangouma's needle for sewing the baskets and mats in which she placed her spun wool.

On the north-west of the colonnade there are three

chapels (D) dedicated to Amon, Mut and Khonsu respectively. These three deities form the Triad of Thebes, and shrines built in their honour are found in many Theban temples. Each member of the Triad was originally an independent divinity. The earliest was probably Mut, whose name means simply *Mother;* in early times she was represented by the vulture, whose wings overshadowing the Pharaoh became the symbol of protection; the vulture of Upper Egypt with the cobra-goddess of Lower Egypt form together one of the titles of the King as ruler of the South and North. Amon the ram-god appears to have superseded the vulture long before the temple was built, when he had already become the chief deity of Thebes. Khonsu was the moon-god, and as such is represented as a young boy wearing the plaited lock of youth. The theologians of the New Kingdom in a desperate attempt to connect all deities with one another, made the three previously independent local gods of Thebes into one family, with Amon as the father, Mut as the mother, and Khonsu as the child. The three shrines in the forecourt were the work of Sethy II, a king whose short reign has left few records in Egypt.

The temple of Rameses III (K) appears to have been an independent structure built outside the entrance pylon of his period. The Bubastite builders respected it, and merely enclosed the entrance and part of the outer court within the walls of the forecourt, and so made it one of the side-chapels of the main temple. It must have been still in good condition or peculiarly sacred, for no Pharaoh ever hesitated to pull down the ruined work of his ancestors, and to re-use the materials for his own buildings. The temple is dedicated to the Triad of Thebes, and was probably erected to commemorate the victory over the coalition of the Sea-peoples, and to show the piety of one of the most licentious monarchs of his time. As a monument of the last of the great Pharaohs the temple is of much interest.

The wall of the forecourt is pierced not only by the temple of Rameses III but by a pillared gateway or portico (E), which communicates also by a doorway with the forecourt of the Rameses temple. On the walls of this portico are the inscriptions of Sheshonk I, better known as Shishak, who raided Jerusalem in the reign of Rehoboam; "he took away the treasures of the house of the Lord, and the treasures of the king's house; he even took away all; and he took away all the shields of gold which Solomon had made" (I Kings. xiv, 26). Sheshonk has recorded his conquests in Syria, and gives a list of the captured towns, each town being represented as a fortified enclosure surrounding the name of the place, while the head and shoulders of a bound prisoner personifies the capture of the city. There is also an interesting suggestion of a change in the attitude of the Pharaoh towards the deity; here Amon leads the towns captive and presents them to the King, whereas Tehutmes III in the XVIIIth dynasty conquered Syria by his own strong arm and presented the plunder to the god as a freewill offering.

The entrance to the great hypostyle hall is through the pylon of Rameses I, (F) (pylon II) which originally had a statue of Rameses II on either side of the gate. The hall (G) is one of the most magnificent religious buildings in the world. The stone roof is supported on one hundred and thirty-four pillars arranged in sixteen rows. The pillars of the two central rows are nearly eighty feet high, and more than thirty feet in circumference; the other rows are lower, the pillars being only forty-two feet high, and rather over twenty-seven feet in circumference. This difference in height is part of the original plan in order to allow of a clerestory, which is formed by a vertical wall supported on the two rows of shorter columns next to the high central rows; the roof was carried partly on the central columns and partly on the walls, which were pierced with windows filled in with stone gratings. The

PLATE XIX

KARNAK: PYLON OF KHONSU TEMPLE

[Photograph by Mr. Percival Hart

[Face page 78

KARNAK: TEMPLE OF KHONSU (INTERIOR)
(1)

KARNAK: TEMPLE OF KHONSU
Roof showing aperture for lighting
(2)

clerestory windows were the chief means of admitting light to the hall, although doors opening to the outer air also allowed a certain amount of light to enter. All the columns are of the papyrus type, the two central rows have capitals of the same form as the colonnade of Haremheb at Luxor, which is a form probably derived from an original palm-leaf capital; the short columns have capitals of the late form of the lotus-bud. When first set up the columns were entirely plain, but before long the surfaces were covered with inscriptions incised and painted. When the eye became accustomed to the dimness of the Hall the colours must have taken on a brilliancy which is never seen in the full glare of the sunlight. The arrangement of the hall gives vistas in every direction, the rows of columns melting into the darkness, while shafts of sunshine from the clerestory windows cut the gloom with startling suddenness. The restorations, which have been recently carried out, have revived some of the ancient beauty of the hall; and its solemn grandeur remains as a lasting memorial of a splendid past. In the moonlight, when the little foxes play among the columns, the hall is perhaps more impressive than at any other time. Then, when all is silent, the visitor can imagine the shaven priests and the white-robed worshippers passing through towards the shrine to fall in adoration at the feet of the deity of the greatest temple in the world.

Following along the axis of the temple a doorway in pylon III (H) gives access from the Hall to the so-called Central Court (I), where the obelisk of Tehutmes I stands. At one time there were four obelisks here; what became of the others is uncertain, they were destroyed most probably in one of the many catastrophes which overtook the temple.

Beyond this point the remainder of the temple has suffered greatly from the hand of Time, from human depredations, and above all from the effects of the annual inundations. The pylon of Tehutmes I (pylon IV) (J), now in a ruinous condition, opens into a small hypostyle hall (L), originally roofed and decorated with Osirid statues of Tehutmes I. Hatshepsut appears to have removed the roof in order to set up her obelisks, and it is possible that the next pylon (pylon V) is really hers though Tehutmes I claimed it as his. Between the sixth pylon and the sanctuary are two small chambers of the reign of Tehutmes III, and the chapels and chambers surrounding the sanctuary are also his work. The actual granite shrine is of the Greek period and is of interest as being of the time of Philip Arrhidæus, the half-witted half-brother of Alexander the Great, who reigned only six years.

Leading southwards out of the Central Court there is a series of buildings forming a great processional way to the temple of Mut; these buildings consist of four courts and four pylons (plan, pl. XVII, 2).

From the Central Court a small doorway opens into another court (B), interesting only by reason of the inscription of Merenptah recounting his victories over the enemies of Egypt, among whom the Etruscans and Achaeans are mentioned. The court stands on the site where two shrines once stood, one of the Middle Kingdom, the other of Amenhotep I. To the south of this court Tehutmes III erected a pylon (pylon VII), perhaps as an entrance to his grandfather's temple; and inscribed on it a record of his own campaigns. The pylon leads to another court (C), and the doorway of the pylon is flanked in both courts by statues, chiefly of Tehutmes III. A broken obelisk of the same King stands in the south court near the doorway, and as an obelisk is always the sign of an entrance this is a proof that this pylon was in Tehutmes' time the main entrance for anyone coming from the temple of Mut. A small chapel of Tehutmes III is at the east of the court.

At the south end of the second court is the pylon of Hatshepsut (pylon VIII). The queen's names have been erased here as elsewhere at Karnak, and over them have been cut the names of either Tehutmes II or Sethy I. The reliefs on the north face are entirely religious; the south face was apparently left blank till the time of Amenhotep II, who found it a convenient space on which to depict himself in the act of smiting his captive enemies, a scene which probably represents pictorially the event recorded in words in the temple of Amada. Royal statues flanked the door on the south side.

The third court is merely an open area (D) and leads to one of the pylons of Haremheb (pylon IX). This pylon was built of materials torn from the temple which Akhenaten erected for his own god. Nothing that Akhenaten ever did could have been more daringly insulting than to build a temple to the arch enemy of the Supreme Deity of Thebes almost within the sacred precincts, and Haremheb marked his sense of such iniquity by "breaking down all the carved work thereof with axes and hammers", and using the stones for the filling of his two pylons. He clearly wished to annihilate all record of the sacrilege, so that it might be buried and forgotten, like the "criminal of Akhetaten" himself.

The IXth and Xth pylons are both the work of Haremheb, and between them lies an immense court, slightly irregular in shape as the east side is rather longer than the west (E). The court is merely a walled area without colonnades; Haremheb decorated the walls with reliefs of himself presenting prisoners of war to the Theban Triad, thereby showing that he was both a great conqueror and a generous benefactor to the temple. On the east side of the court is the temple of Amenhotep II (M) entered by a sloping way. The plan is not unlike the Festival Hall of his father, Tehutmes III, for the entrance is at the side and the sanctuaries are at right angles to the entrance. The façade has twelve square pillars, six on either side of the granite doorway; the entrance through this door leads direct into the hypostyle hall, which contained twenty square pillars arranged in two rows on either side, leaving a wide aisle up the middle of the hall (pl. XVII, 1). A small pillared hall or sanctuary, dedicated to Amon, is at the north; most of this sanctuary remains, including the greater part of the roof. A similar sanctuary in a more ruinous condition leads out of the south end of the hall. It is not unlikely that a corresponding temple lay on the west side of the court, though it has now disappeared.

The Xth pylon (often called the Pylon of Haremheb though the IXth is his also) is the last in the processional way, and was therefore for many generations the great entrance from that side into the precincts of Amon. The brick girdle-wall rose on either side almost to the same height as the stone work of the pylon, but the greater part has now fallen to ruin. In the repairs effected by the Department of Antiquities it was found that the pylon was built almost entirely of stones taken from the temple of Akhenaten; many of the blocks are inscribed with Akhenaten's cartouches, both before and after he changed his name; in other words, before and after his conversion to Atenism. Some of the sculptures retain traces of colour. In the court against the north face of the pylon is the famous stele inscribed with the account of Haremheb's work in restoring order after the chaos of the Amarna usurpations. From the pylon the avenue of sphinxes leads to the main portal of the temple of Mut.

Southwards of the great temple of Amon lies the Sacred Lake (F), and it was between the lake and the wall of the temple that the great *cache* of more than two thousand statues and statuettes was found in 1902. These range in date from the XIIth to the XXIInd dynasty, and are in so good a state of preservation that it is clear they had been intentionally buried. Their condition shows that they were not buried because of being broken or dilapidated, as at Hierakonpolis; they must have been put in the earth for purposes of concealment. This could only have been when Assur-bani-pal, that prince of looters, was marching up the valley of the Nile on his way to the sack of Thebes. These statues give many examples of royal portraits, besides those of great nobles, who are known to us otherwise only by name. The lake is rectangular, and was enclosed by stone walls with steps leading down to the water. It is filled by infiltration from the river, and in consequence the water is so brackish that the modern name is *Birket el Mellâha*, "Lake of the Salt-pit". Tehutmes III and "Tirhaka the Ethiopian" erected chapels on the north bank of the lake, probably for use in the water ceremonies of the god. These ceremonies were evidently of great splendour, for according to modern belief the golden barge can still be seen floating on the lake, filled with musicians and female singers. Legrain records that a native of Karnak sleeping in the temple was awoke by the strains of sweet music, and looking at the lake he saw the golden boat. The sight so amazed him that he ejaculated "Allah!" At the sound of the holy name a lady in the barge cut the mooring rope and the barge vanished from his sight. But when the lucky man went to the side of the lake he found the mooring-peg and mallet, both of pure gold.

It is a common belief that the temples are really covered with gold, but that being enchanted the gold is hidden from mortal eyes. English tourists are supposed to read in their magic little red-bound books the spells for disenchanting the gold, and that is why white men are so ready to buy old inscribed stones. Much of the ground in Egypt is enchanted; and where "this is the case it is useless to dig in it for ancient treasures, as they will be concealed from the digger. As fast as the treasure-seeker excavates, the treasure sinks into the ground away from him. Much of the land at Karnak and on the west bank of the river is thus enchanted."

At the north-west corner of the Sacred Lake is the giant stone scarab set up by Amenhotep III. The meaning of this monument is obscure; the scarab was the emblem of the resurrection and had no more special significance in the cult of Amon than in that of any other god.

LIST OF TEMPLES AT KARNAK

WITHIN THE GIRDLE-WALL

1. Great Temple of Amon, containing:
   (a) Sethy II's shrine of the Theban Triad.
   (b) Rameses III's Temple of Amon.

East of Great Temple.

2. Festival Hall of Tehutmes III.
3. Chapels of Tehutmes III.
4. Mortuary Temple of Tehutmes III and Hatshepsut.
5. Temple of Rameses II.
6. Temple of Osiris.

South of Great Temple.

7. 1st Chapel of Tehutmes III.
8. Chapel of Taharqa.
9. Temple of Middle Kingdom, altered by Tehutmes III.
10. 2nd Chapel of Tehutmes III.
11. Temple of Amenhotep II.
12. Temple of Khonsu, with separate avenue of sphinxes and pylon.
13. Temple of Ypt, the hippopotamus goddess.

West of Great Temple.

14. Chapel of Achoris.

North of Great Temple.

15. Shrines of Late Period.
16. Temple of Ptah and Sekhmet

OUTSIDE THE GIRDLE-WALL

NORTH OF GREAT TEMPLE.

1. Temple of Mentu, with entrance and separate girdle-wall, enclosing,
2. Ptolemaic Temple.
3. Six shrines of Ethiopian or Saite period.

SOUTH OF GREAT TEMPLE.

4. Temple of Mut, with separate pylon and sphinx avenue, with girdle-wall enclosing,
   (a) Temple of Amenhotep III.
   (b) Temple of Rameses III.

EAST OF GREAT TEMPLE.

5. Hall of Akhenaten.

TEMPLE OF MEDAMUT

[*Photograph by Mr. Percival Hart*

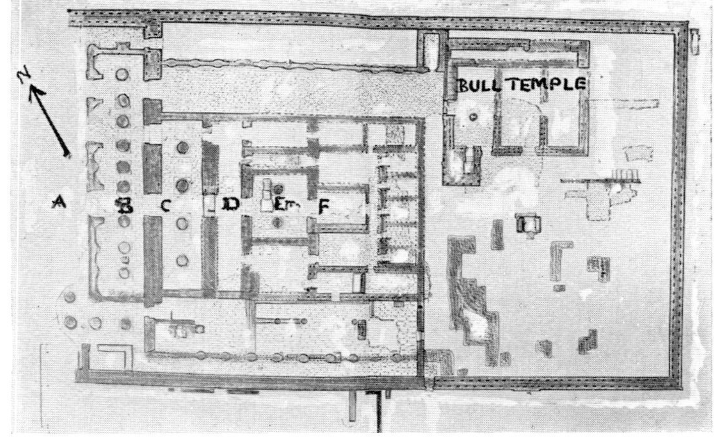

TEMPLE OF MEDAMUT (PLAN)
(1)

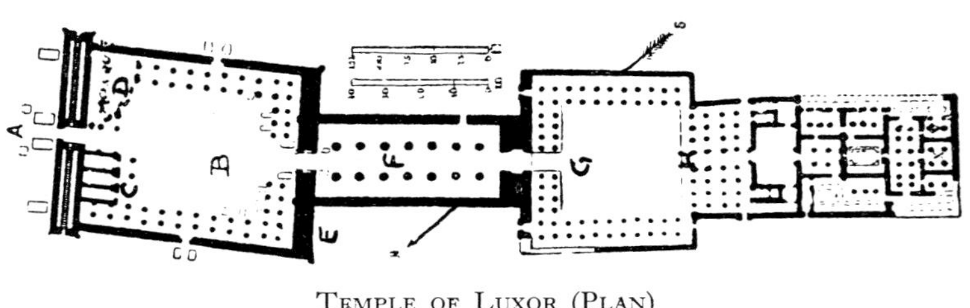

TEMPLE OF LUXOR (PLAN)
(2)

XII

KARNAK

Festival Hall

TEHUTMES III erected this temple in honour of the Triad of Thebes and in commemoration of his many victories. It stands to the east of the Great Temple (H); between the two was an open space where the shrine of the Middle Kingdom once stood (pl. XVII, 2). The shrine was probably in ruins, and Tehutmes cleared away the ancient building and made an open court with surrounding chapels, erecting his Festival Hall as the largest of the chapels.

Unlike the majority of Egyptian temples the entrance of the Festival Hall is not in the axis but at the side, and at right angles to the main part of the temple. The structure consists of a hypostyle hall, orientated north and south, with chapels and shrines leading from it to north, east and soutn; the entrance being at the south-west corner.

Two Osirid statues of the King flanked the entrance and two sixteen-sided columns probably upheld a portico, showing that the entrance was placed here intentionally. The hypostyle hall is the earliest of its kind, with a high central nave and lower side aisles. The nave consists of twenty columns in two rows of ten; the columns are unique in form, they are circular in section and have no contraction to the base like papyrus pillars, and the capitals are bell-shaped. As all columns and capitals are ultimately derived from the simple forms used in primitive and domestic architecture, the origin of these columns is easily found; they are copies in stone of wooden tent-poles, such as were used for the central supports of mat-shelters and other light structures. The temple is therefore only a great stone tent, probably an enlarged copy of the kind of shelter which Tehutmes himself had used in his campaigns and which he considered appropriate to commemorate his victories. On either side of the tent-pole pillars is a line of massive square columns which bear one end of the roofing slabs of the lower aisles as well as the wall, which rises to the height of the central pillars and carries the roof of the nave. The walls above the square columns are pierced with windows (pl. XVIII, 1). The outer wall of the temple, which bore the other end of the roofing slabs of the lower aisles, is destroyed, but when complete the lower aisles were lighted from the clerestory windows only. The square columns were decorated with painted reliefs of the King in the presence of various deities, chiefly Amon and Mut. The hall was used as a church by the early Christians, but the mutilation of the reliefs was not necessarily their work; Akhenaten rejoiced in destroying the figures of the Theban deities as inimical to his own religious ideas; the Christians contented themselves with covering the figures with paintings of saints and martyrs.

At the north end of the hall are three small chapels now ruined; they were dedicated to the Triad of Thebes. The figure of Mut is still visible, and in the most westerly is a colossal group with Tehutmes III as the third member of the Triad. At the north-east corner is a staircase leading up to a chapel in which stands an alabaster sarcophagus. The dedication is unknown, but it may have been for the worship of Osiris. At the south end of the hall are other chapels, in one of which was found the list of his predecessors set up by Tehutmes III and known to modern Egyptologists as the "Karnak Table of Kings". It was removed by the French and is now in the Bibliothèque Nationale in Paris. It is of great importance as giving the names of the Kings in historical sequence, like the Table of Abydos.

The chambers to the east are a wilderness of ruin and confusion, with here and there an oasis of beautiful architecture and interesting detail. A little chapel, of which only four columns are still standing, is unique in decoration; the columns are of the papyrus type with lotus-bud capitals; they stand in a row and the architraves are still in position though the roof has disappeared, the walls being broken down to within a few feet of the ground. All round the chapel on the ruined walls it is still possible to see the unique record of the plants, birds and animals which Tehutmes III brought from the foreign lands which he had visited in his campaigns, and afterwards presented to the temple. The plants are singularly interesting for the exquisite drawing and also for the scientific accuracy in the representation of the stages in the germination of a seed. Tehutmes may be claimed as the first founder of zoological and botanical gardens, and the artist who drew the plants was evidently a botanist also.

A little gem of architectural beauty is a small hypostyle hall, of which the outer wall is destroyed; the beautiful pillars are sixteen-sided with plain square abaci; and as the architraves and roof are intact it is possible to realise the full intention of the architect.

XIII

KARNAK

Temple of Rameses III

THE forecourt of the Great Temple of Amon was probably already laid out before the temple of Rameses II was begun; the wall of the court may not have been completed, but to break down a predecessor's wall was no hindrance to any Pharaoh who desired to erect a monument in any given spot. Why Rameses wished to build his temple at that particular place is unknown, unless it was built over an earlier shrine.

The entrance to the temple was from the forecourt of the Great Temple (G). Two statues of Rameses stood before the pylon flanking the gateway. The pylon itself is badly ruined, but a few sculptures are still visible; the scenes show the Pharaoh slaying a group of captives in the presence of Amon-Ra, a favourite subject for the decoration of a pylon, and perhaps explains the statement of Amenhotep II that he slew his prisoners-of-war " before the walls of Thebes".

The chief interest of the temple lies in the fact that it is a complete example of the temple of the period; though in miniature it has the correct number of courts and vestibules, the correct colonnades, and the shrine correctly set in the axis of the entrance. It is, therefore, a convenient building in which to study the plan of an Egyptian temple of the New Kingdom.

The axis of the temple runs north and south, with the entrance to the north. The gateway leads through the pylon to a hypæthral court, which is surrounded on three sides by roofed colonnades; the columns are square and are faced by Osirids of the King, now terribly mutilated by Christian or Moslem fanatics. The scenes on the walls of the colonnades are of religious ceremonies, and represent processions which probably took place in this court; on one side is the procession of the boat-shrines of the Triad of Thebes, on the other side is the procession of the god Min, the ceremony ending with the worship of the image when finally returned to its shrine.

As is usual in temples of the New Kingdom the end of the court opposite to the entrance is raised and forms a vestibule or portico, approached by a ramp. Two black granite statues of Sekhmet stand in this vestibule; it is worth remarking that the greater number of known statues of this goddess are made of black granite; it is not known why this should be so, whether this stone was used intentionally, or whether only the black granite statues have survived. Statues of the more kindly goddesses, such as Isis, are, however, rare in this stone, which would seem to point to an intentional use of black granite as suitable for the savage Sekhmet. The reliefs on the wall of the vestibule are of religious ceremonies and are of no great interest. On the jambs of the door leading into the hypostyle hall are figures of Rameses, these were originally overlaid with metal, gold or bronze; the sheets of metal had been fastened down with nails; the nail-holes are all that remain of this magnificent decoration. Undoubtedly the wooden doors of the temple were also overlaid with metal in the same way. When Solomon adorned the temple of Jehovah with "shields of gold" he was only following the example of the Egyptian Pharaohs in temple-decoration.

The hypostyle hall is very small and contains only eight columns; it leads into three shrines standing side by side and covered with reliefs, the scenes show that the dedication of the temple was to the Triad of Thebes. At the sides and back of the shrines there are several small undecorated chambers.

XIV

KARNAK

The Temple of Ptah

THIS little temple, though a separate entity, lies within the girdle-wall to the north of the Great Temple of Amon. The site was probably covered by a shrine as early as the XIIth dynasty, which was rebuilt in the XVIIIth dynasty by Hatshepsut and Tehutmes III, and was restored and enlarged by the Ptolemies.

The entrance is by six successive gateways; the first, third and fifth are certainly Ptolemaic, but there is a difference of opinion as to the date of the second and fourth, Weigall stating that they were built by Hatshepsut, Steindorff giving the credit to Shabaka the Ethiopian (pl. XVIII, 2). All the gateways have suffered greatly at the hands of Time and fanatics.

The fifth gate leads into a little court with four pillars with foliage capitals, screen-walls connecting the pillars with one another. A sixth pylon, smaller than the others was apparently the entrance to the temple proper; it was erected by Hatshepsut or by her successor Tehutmes III, and gives access to a hall, the roof of which is supported by two sixteen-sided pillars. Two of the three granite altars which stand in the middle of the hall are inscribed; the centre one by Tehutmes III, while that on the south is of Amenemhat I of the XIIth dynasty; this is the last remaining trace of the shrine of the Middle Kingdom. The sanctuary lies in the main axis of the temple and opens from the hall; in it stands a damaged statue of Ptah, probably of the same date as the temple itself. The reliefs on the walls are of scenes of worship of Ptah and Hathor by Tehutmes III.

Opening out of the sanctuary is another shrine, which is dedicated to the goddess Sekhmet. The lighting in this chamber was arranged by the architect to give a peculiar effect and to produce optical illusions. To anyone entering from the blinding glare of the sunlight the chamber appears totally dark; as the eyes get accustomed to the darkness a dark figure begins to be visible, growing darker while the chamber becomes lighter as though it drew the darkness into itself; at last the goddess stands revealed. The method of lighting and the fact that the figure is of black granite are the reasons for the illusion. The lighting is by an opening in the roof above the head of the statue, and the light pours down making the figure appear almost instinct with life. The statue represents a young woman with a lioness's head; the human part of the figure is a beautiful example of Egyptian work, the youth and symmetry of the rounded limbs is above the average of divine statues.

It is very certain that the priests of the temple realised the startling effect of the lighting of the figure, and also of another phenomenon which still occurs. Legrain records how, when he entered the shrine of Sekhmet on one occasion, he was startled to see a white gleam pass down the figure to its feet, then cross the ground towards him, and disappear before it reached him. These gleams or waves of light seemed to fill the whole atmosphere of the chamber, and must have had a terrifying effect in ancient times on the ignorant worshippers who entered the shrine to adore the goddess. Being a practical man, Legrain cast about for the explanation. He had observed before coming in that the sky was filled with racing clouds driven by a furious wind, and he came to the conclusion that the waves of light on the figure and the ground were a reflection from the clouds. He covered the opening in the roof until only a very small aperture was left, then he found the shape of the drifting clouds was projected faithfully into the chamber, as is done in any camera obscura. This phenomenon of reflection has been used in Egypt in all periods and in many places, and lasted down to modern times in some Christian churches. Père Vansleb, at the end of the seventeenth century, saw the same camera-obscura effect: "In the church of Gemiane (in the month of May) is the Festival of the Apparition of the Saints. One Chappel, . . . whited with Lime, namely that where the supposed Apparition happens, is on the North side. I found it (the Apparition) to be nothing else but the reflection of the objects that went by the Church at a convenient distance, which are carried into the Chappel by the Air, through two Windows that give light. . . . The people when they see the Shadow that represents a Cavalier they say that it is St. George. When they see a Woman carrying of an infant in her Arms, they say it is the blessed Virgin. When they see the Shadow of a man on foot of a reddish colour, they say that it is St. Menna, because they paint him with a red Habit."

The statue of Sekhmet bears an evil reputation among the inhabitants of the village of Karnak on account of a legend which is firmly believed. At some period (the date is not given) a certain European (the name is also not recorded in the legend) made an excavation in this chamber. He employed, as is usual in all Egyptian excavations, a number of boys to carry the baskets of earth. The legend relates that there came a fall of earth and stones from the roof and buried seven of the boys at the feet of the goddess. The terrifying part of the story is that neither bodies nor even bones were ever recovered; the obvious explanation being that the goddess

TEMPLE OF LUXOR
Colonnade of Haremheb looking towards entrance pylon
(1)

TEMPLE OF LUXOR FROM THE RIVER
(2)

LUXOR: COURT OF AMENHOTEP III
(3)

[*Face page* 94

PLATE XXIV

LUXOR: HYPOSTYLE HALL

[*Photograph by Mr. Percival Hart*

Face page 95]

had devoured them. This is perhaps a folk-memory of child-sacrifice to the statue, for Sekhmet seems to have been a deity to whom human sacrifice was offered; the only legend preserved of her is that of the Massacre of Mankind, in which she is said to have slain human beings, till even Ra, who had called her in to aid, was horrified, but could not stop her until a brilliant genius among the gods suggested making her drunk so that she could not see her unhappy victims. The plan succeeded to perfection, and mankind was saved. It is not unlikely that her epithet of "Crusher of hearts" refers to her bloodthirsty rites.

XV

KARNAK

Temple of Khonsu

THE temple of Khonsu is now the terminus of the processional way from Luxor to Karnak, and the Ptolemaic stone gateway which once stood in the wall is perhaps the best known portion of the temple (K). The main structure is of the reign of Rameses III, who dedicated it to the third member of the Theban Triad, the moon-god Khonsu. This was essentially a royal god, and not a deity of the popular religion, the people preferring to worship the moon itself without a name, or regarding Osiris or Thoth as the lunar deities. But to the king Khonsu was a definite deity, and it is not uncommon to find that the Pharaoh replaces Khonsu in representations of the Triad of Thebes; and even when Khonsu is shown as a separate entity he wears the royal lock of youth and carries in his hands the insignia of royalty. The identity of Khonsu is still a matter for investigation, and an intensive study of this god would throw light on some of the primitive cults and beliefs of the early Egyptians.

Chevrier, in his report on the temple to the Department of Antiquities, says "that the foundations are made of fragments of earlier works of different periods, some still retaining traces of colour; there is nothing later than Rameses III, so the general plan and the main part of the building is of his date, the decoration only was added by his successors." "Toute la superstructure est tellement farcie de matériaux remployés qu'on peut se demander si Ramses s'est servi d'un seul bloc vraiment neuf."

The temple was built in the axis of the sphinx-avenue from Luxor, and may have served as a gate-chapel to those coming on foot from the south. The last of the Ramessides erected an avenue of sphinxes from the gate in the main enclosure-wall to the entrance pylon: the pylon itself may have been the work of himself or of his immediate successor, the priest-king Herihor. The pylon is practically complete, and was decorated with religious scenes by one of the later priest-kings, Pinezem I, who is represented with his queen in the presence of various deities (pl. XIX).

The court to which the pylon gives access was decorated by Herihor, after the puppet-kings had passed away and the High-priest of Amon had seized the temporal as well as the spiritual power and made himself Pharaoh. A double colonnade of papyrus pillars with lotus-bud capitals surrounds the court on the east, north and west sides, on the north the pillars being on a higher level reached by a ramp. The court has seven doorways; on the south is the main entrance through the pylon, on both east and west there are two doors opening on the temenos of the Great Temple; to the north are also two doors, one in the axis of the temple leading to the shrine, the other rather more to the east may once have indicated the approach to a special shrine now destroyed (pl. XX, 1).

The northern doors lead into a hypostyle hall of eight columns built like so many of the Theban temples with a high central nave and lower aisles on either side. The decoration is of the reign of the last Ramesside Pharaoh, when Herihor, though actually wielding the royal power, had not yet assumed the royal title. Doors in the north wall of the hall give access into the ambulatory which surrounds the sanctuary and from which chambers and chapels open. From the ambulatory lead out the stairs to the roof.

The shrine itself is a passage with a door at either end so that processions could go either southwards through the hypostyle hall and the outer court and out at the main gateway, or could pass northwards through two small chambers and out into the precincts by a small gateway in the axis of the temple.

Several small chapels lie on either side of the axial halls beyond the sanctuary; these were decorated by Rameses IV, the immediate successor of the original founder of the temple, but it is obvious that the temple itself stands on the site of an earlier building, for stone blocks of Tehutmes III and Amenhotep III are found in the walls of the chapels. One of the larger of the chapels appears to have been dedicated to Osiris, who is represented lying dead on a bier with the two mourners, Isis and Nephthys, lamenting over the body.

The celebrated statue of Khonsu was found in this temple. It belongs to the end of the XVIIIth dynasty and is possibly a portrait of one of the kings. The beautiful face is reminiscent of Amarna work, so also is the rather stumpy effect of the figure, but the expression and technique point to a slightly later period, possibly Rameses II.

The temple is not only fine in itself but is interesting on account of the inscriptions it contains. The High-priest of Amon, Herihor, records that Khonsu appointed him King; this was done by the image, known as Khonsu in Thebes Nefer-Hetep, nodding with its head to Herihor. "The city went out as messengers [to Amon] to tell what Khonsu had said." Amon confirmed the appointment by nodding, and promised by word of mouth that Herihor should have twenty years, presumably of the supreme power. The High-priest said to Amon, " 'O my good lord, shall I make a record of this on stone?' And the god nodded his head exceedingly." The High-priest returned to Khonsu and asked, "'May a stele be made?' And the god nodded his head exceedingly." The name of the temple is probably indicated in the title of the image, which would be in English "Khonsu in the Theban Nefer-Hetep", there being possibly another Nefer-Hetep temple elsewhere.

The longest and perhaps the most interesting inscription was found in a small Græco-Roman temple adjoining the main temple of Khonsu, though it is of earlier date than the shrine in which it stood. It is inscribed on a stone stele; at the top are representations of two sacred boats; the boat to the right belongs to Khonsu in the Theban Nefer-Hetep, it is large and ornate, is borne by ten priests, two of whom are also fan-bearers, and in front walks the Pharaoh offering incense. The boat on the left belongs to Khonsu the Helper, it is smaller and much plainer, and is borne by four priests, while the chief priest of Khonsu offers incense. Both boats are ornamented with the hawk-head surmounted by the crescent moon at the prow and the stern. The inscription tells the whole history of the demoniacal possession of Bint-reshy, daughter of the prince of Bekhten and sister of the Queen of Egypt. When all remedies failed to cure her, as a last resource appeal is made to Khonsu in the Theban Nefer-Hetep to permit the image of Khonsu the Helper (literally: the Maḳer of Means) to go to Bekhten; twice he was asked, and both times he gave consent by nodding vehemently. "Then His Majesty commanded that Khonsu the Helper in Thebes should travel to a great ship with five barges and a multitude of chariots and horses to right and left." On arriving at Bekhten the god effected a cure and drove out the evil spirit, but the prince of Bekhten would not part with him, and kept the image there for three years and nine months. At the end of this time Khonsu the Helper appears to have become impatient. "The prince of Bekhten slept on his bed, he saw this god about to leave his shrine, he was a hawk of gold, and he flew up towards Egypt. The Prince awoke in a fright." He was so terrified that he returned the image at once with an abundance of rich gifts, which were presented by Khonsu the Helper to the more important image of Khonsu in the temple at Thebes.

XVI

KARNAK

Temple of Ypet

WHEN the French Expedition at the end of the eighteenth century reported on the ancient monuments of Egypt, they noted the fine preservation of this little temple, which was then as clean and fresh as if newly from the hands of the builder. Since that time it has been in turn a police-post, a prison, a cook-house, and its modern name of "The Castle of the Bats" testifies only too mournfully to the state into which it had fallen when the Department of Antiquities took it in hand.

The temple (pl. XVII, 2, L) was built by Ptolemy IX (Euergetes II); and in pursuance of the Ptolemaic policy of honouring the deities of the people he dedicated it to the hippopotamus-goddess of birth, associating with her the most popular of all gods, Osiris. The goddess was called Ypet in this temple, but the name she is usually known by is Ta-Urt, "The Great One", she was essentially a goddess of the people, not of the priests, and a shrine for her worship is excessively rare.

The temple is entered from the west directly into a pillared hall. The pillars have the usual Ptolemaic foliage-capitals, with the head of Hathor above as an exaggerated abacus; grated windows in the south wall admit light. The second hall has side-chambers where the ideas of death and life are represented emblematically by the dead Osiris on his bier and by Isis with the infant Horus. In another scene the hippopotamus-goddess is shown in company with a lioness-goddess protecting Horus, who as a falcon is standing among the reeds of the marshes.

In the sanctuary is a niche for the statue of the goddess, the sculptured decoration showing that the divinity in question was Ypet. Below the shrine is a crypt so arranged that the statue of the goddess must have stood immediately above the recess where a relic of Osiris seems to have been kept. As the temple of Ypet commemorated also the birth of Osiris, the position of the statue of the goddess of birth marked the exact spot of that joyful event.

XVII

KARNAK

The Temple of Mut in Asher

THE temple of the goddess Mut stands in that quarter of the city of Thebes which was called Asher (N). The goddess was probably the original deity of Thebes, and in her human form is possibly the personification of the Crown of Upper Egypt. In animal form she is the vulture, which, as a hieroglyphic sign, means "Mother". In all periods the symbolism of the mother-bird with wings outspread over its fledglings has appealed to all nations, and the vulture, being the largest bird in Egypt and having the largest spread of wing, became in that country the symbol of motherhood and maternal protection. The royal insignia of the queens of Egypt included the vulture head-dress, and from the earliest historical times the vulture is represented with outspread wings above the head of the king.

In the XVIIIth dynasty, when the god Amon became important and his priests endeavoured to make him the principal god of the capital city and of the whole Egyptian empire, they could not at first eliminate or even absorb Mut; all they could do was to make her the wife of Amon, with whom she was not originally connected. Later they succeeded in subordinating her to Amon, and reduced her to the position of second person in the Theban Triad. This was in the State religion; in the religion of the peasants the moon, the Peak of Thebes, and the cobra,

[*Photograph by Mr. Percival Hart*

LUXOR: EXTERIOR OF PYLON
Showing Obelisk and Statues
(1)

[*Photograph by Mr. Percival Hart*

LUXOR: HYPOSTYLE HALL
Showing Pavement and Bases of Pillars
(2)

[*Face page* 102

Qurna
(1)

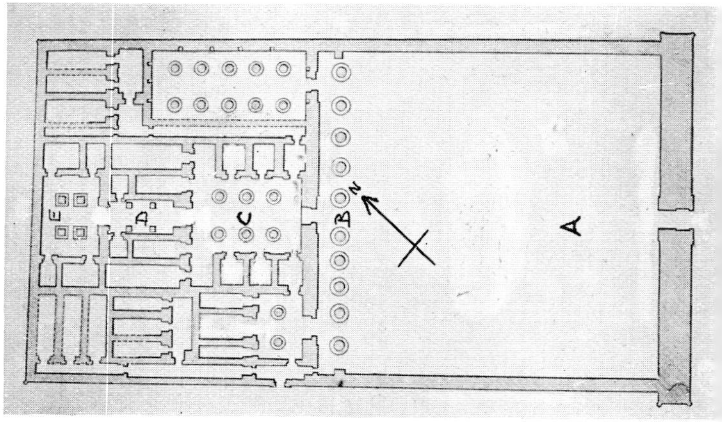

Qurna (Plan)
(2)

still held their primitive position as deities. As both the Peak and the cobra were goddesses, and the Peak at least essentially Theban, it is possible that their cult may have been fused in the end with that of Mut.

Few traces of the early shrine remain; the temple as it stands is of the XVIIIth dynasty, the same period as the Great Temple of Amon, with the precincts of which it is connected by an avenue of sphinxes. These were probably set up when Mut had begun to be overshadowed by the god of the powerful priesthood, for the sphinxes are ram-headed in compliment to Amon.

All the Pharaohs of the XVIIIth dynasty, with the sole exception of Akhenaten, delighted to honour the goddess Mut and to beautify her temple. Akhenaten on the contrary included Mut in his desperate crusade against Thebes, and persecuted her with the same virulence with which he persecuted Amon. But Tutankhamon erected a statue of himself in the temple, and other records of him have been found within the precincts; all this within a few years of the death of the heretic King, whose religion Tutankhamon had himself professed. The later dynasties were unanimous in showing their piety by restoring or adding to the temple. After the first sack of Thebes the great official Mentu-em-hat seems to have been the most active helper in restoring the sacred fane, and in proof of his pious endeavours placed his statue in the inner court. The great sack of the city by Assur-bani-pal utterly destroyed Thebes, and as the later dynasties fixed their capital at Memphis it never recovered. It still retained sufficient of its ancient splendour to induce the Ptolemies to restore and rebuild some of the ruined temples; and as these Greek rulers desired to be more Egyptian than the Egyptians the temple of the Mother was one of the chief objects of their piety.

Outside the main gateway are two statues of Amenhotep III, who was responsible for the greater part of the structure. The pylon is Ptolemaic, for the Ptolemies spent their energies at Thebes in building gateways and restoring decorations, not in building complete temples. From the pylon there runs a processional way straight along the axis of the temple to the shrine; through the outer and inner courts the way is marked out by a double row of columns, which must have supported a roof. Round the walls were ranged a row of statues of Sekhmet, the lioness-headed goddess. The connection between Mut and Sekhmet can only be conjectural, for the cults of the two goddesses have been so little studied that it is impossible to suggest any explanation; it is, however, certain that Sekhmet was here not as the consort of the Memphite god Ptah but as an entirely independent goddess. It is possible that she is the personified Peak of Thebes, for the Hymn to the Peak says: "The Peak is as a lion." The figures of Sekhmet are evidently votives dedicated by various Pharaohs, particularly Amenhotep III and Sheshonk I.

In the inner court there was a roofed colonnade on either side, supported by square pillars with Hathor-head capitals. In the spaces between the columns were statues of Sekhmet, and a row of figures of the goddess filled the raised passage between the pillars and the wall.

All the building beyond this point is greatly ruined, though sufficient remains to trace the plan. The hypostyle hall once had eight pillars; and on either side of the hall is a pillared chamber as well as a way out into the raised passage or "cloister" of the inner court. This passage has been blocked at the south-east corner by the little chapel of Taharqa, the last of the Ethiopian Kings of the XXVth dynasty. The triple sanctuary is reached by a passage and a vestibule with chambers on either side. In the vestibule are the remains of four large figures of dog-headed baboons, who as attendants on the sunrise are turned with their faces to the east.

A high brick wall surrounded the precincts, enclosing a wide space between it and the temple wall to form an ambulatory; and here again were many statues of Sekhmet. In Ptolemaic times the circuit of the temple was blocked by the building of a tiny shrine, consisting of two small rooms and a niche for the divine image. A flight of steps led from the shrine down to the lake so that when the water was high the approach was by boat.

The sacred lake is peculiar in shape; it spreads in a horseshoe round the sanctuary as though enclosing it in its two arms; this is unique as the sacred lakes of other temples are rectangular. Weigall notes that "it is perhaps not an accident that the lake is shaped like one of the hieroglyphics connected with womanhood." The lake is due to the infiltration of water from the Nile, rises with the inundation and subsides with the fall. As Miss Margaret Benson's donkey-boy graphically expressed it, "When Nile sit down he sit down by him."

The Temple of Rameses III

This little temple stands on the west side of the horseshoe lake within the girdle-wall (o). The orientation is north and south, with the entrance to the north, and the building consists of an outer court, a small hypostyle hall with lateral chambers, and a vestibule which leads to three shrines. The entrance was by a pylon, in front of which stood two colossi of the King, all greatly damaged. The outer court is large in proportion to the rest of the temple, and had a double row of sphinxes along its whole length from north to south. At the south end was a colonnade of four pillars standing at a higher level than the floor of the court and reached by a ramp, which starts at about a third of the way along the court. The hypostyle hall has four pillars arranged in a row from east to west; the lateral chambers are curiously unsymmetrical in plan, in shape, and in arrangement as well as in size.

The dedication to the Triad of Thebes is inferred from a relief sculpture of Amon in the axial shrine, and from the remains of an inscription mentioning Khonsu. The walls of the entire temple must have been covered with relief sculptures commemorating Rameses III's victorious campaigns against the Syrians and Libyans, but very few of these have survived.

The whole temple is in a miserable state of dilapidation and decay, this is due to natural causes induced by the parsimony of Rameses III in re-using stone from earlier buildings. When a stone freshly cut from the quarries is exposed to the air the silicates in suspension form a fine coating on the surface of the block, making an almost impervious "skin"; but if such a block is recut and exposed to damp—and every site affected by the inundation is so exposed—it simply crumbles to pieces by the action of the salts in the soil. Rameses III's desire to make a great show of piety and splendour at little cost did not result in a building of long duration.

XVIII

HALL OF AKHENATEN

OUTSIDE the precincts near the east gate Akhenaten built a place of worship for the Aten and himself. Very little of it has been excavated at present, only the corner and part of the side of a hall of statues. Twenty-four emplacements of statues have been found, with fragments of the broken figures scattered in every direction. The King is represented as Osiris, holding the crook and flail in his crossed hands; the figures are of heroic size and are of the most pronounced and hideous type of Tel el Amarna art. The statues and the whole building have been subjected to a fury of iconoclasm to which Akhenaten's own efforts in that direction are as child's play. The use of the stones in Haremheb's pylons point to him as the culprit, but there is no reasonable doubt that it was the priests of Amon who directed the destruction and wreaked their fury on the work of the Heretic. Haremheb must have given his consent, and to use another Pharaoh's buildings as a quarry was an ordinary custom; he does not appear to have been a spiteful man, and he had certainly received benefits from Akhenaten. But the priesthood of Amon had every reason to hate and fear the Amarna religion and would be only too rejoiced to obliterate every trace of the heresy.

XIX

MEDAMUT

The temple stands in the fields to the north-east of Karnak; it was erected under the Ptolemies, about the third century B.C., on the site of a temple which had its origin in the Middle Kingdom, and was rebuilt and added to in the New Kingdom. Of the older temples there remain a few blocks and three papyrus-pillars with bud capitals, and of the Ptolemaic temple there are only two pillars with characteristic Ptolemaic capitals, besides foundations and the lower courses of some walls.

The dedication was to Mentu, the god of war, of whom very little is known: the main point of interest concerning this god is that he shared his divine honours with a sacred bull. In all cases where both god and bull occur in the same place it would seem that the animal is the earlier deity. The anthropomorphic god was probably introduced from elsewhere, and ousted the local animal deity to a certain extent, though not among the common people. The temple might be dedicated to a god in human form, and the priests might perform magnificent ceremonies in his honour, but always within the precincts of the temple there would be a stable for the bull, to whom the people came for oracles, and whom they propitiated by offerings. The god and the bull never share the same name; at Medamut and Armant the god was Mentu, the bull Bukhis (Bekhi); at Memphis the god was Ptah, the bull Apis (Hapi); at Heliopolis the god was Ra, the bull Mnevis (Mer-wer). In all these instances of sacred bulls they were obviously the indigenous deities whose hold on the minds of the people was so great that their cult could not be disregarded by more civilised rulers and Pharaohs. The cult of Apis is more carefully recorded by classical authors than the other bulls, and the burial place of the holy animals is still to be seen at Saqqara. The importance of Apis is due to the fact that he was considered to be "the soul of Osiris", and was therefore connected with the Nile, as indeed his name shows.

The temple of Medamut is orientated east and west with the entrance to the west (pl. XXII, 1). A brick wall encloses the sacred precincts, which are entered through a gateway built by the emperor Tiberius. The façade of the temple was in the form of a pylon with three kiosks in front; behind was a colonnaded court (A), then came a vestibule (B), a small hypostyle hall (C), two ante-chambers (D, E) and the sanctuary (F). In the vestibule there are still five columns standing, two with foliage capitals, and three with bud-capitals, these last being re-used from the earlier building. There is very little left above ground besides the pillars and some of the walls (pl. XXI).

Behind the temple is a separate building which was for the worship of the bull; it seems to have been on the same plan as the temple of Apis at Memphis, in which the bull was kept in a stable of two compartments. The bull had liberty to walk about in the little building, and worshippers were admitted to make their offerings. Oracles were obtained by the behaviour of Apis when the offerings were presented, whether he accepted or refused food at the hand of the enquirer, and also which compartment he preferred during the interview. On the anniversary of his birthday he was led round the city in a splendid procession accompanied by a choir of boys singing hymns in his honour. Oracles could be obtained by listening to the talk of the children who accompanied him, and also to the words of the children playing round his stable, who, according to Aelian, poured out their predictions "in perfect rhythm". Herodotus says that in the court of the great temple of Ptah at Memphis Psamtek I built "a court for Apis in which he is fed whenever he appears." Strabo also gives some account of the bull, "Before the enclosure where Apis is kept is a vestibule where the mother of the sacred bull is fed; and into this vestibule Apis is sometimes introduced in order to be shown to strangers. After being brought out for a little while, he is taken back. At other times he is only seen through a window."

Aelian and Macrobius mention Bukhis, Aelian calling him by the name of Onuphis. "The Egyptians worship a black bull which they call Onuphis. Its hair turns the contrary way from that of other animals, and it is the largest of all oxen." "In the city of Hermonthis they adore the bull Bukhis, which is consecrated to the sun. It is remarkable for certain extraordinary appearances, according with the nature of the sun. For every hour it is reported to change its colour, and to have long hairs growing backwards; whence it is thought to be an image of the sun shining on the opposite side of the world."

DÊR EL BAHRI
Showing the two Temples

Plate XXVIII

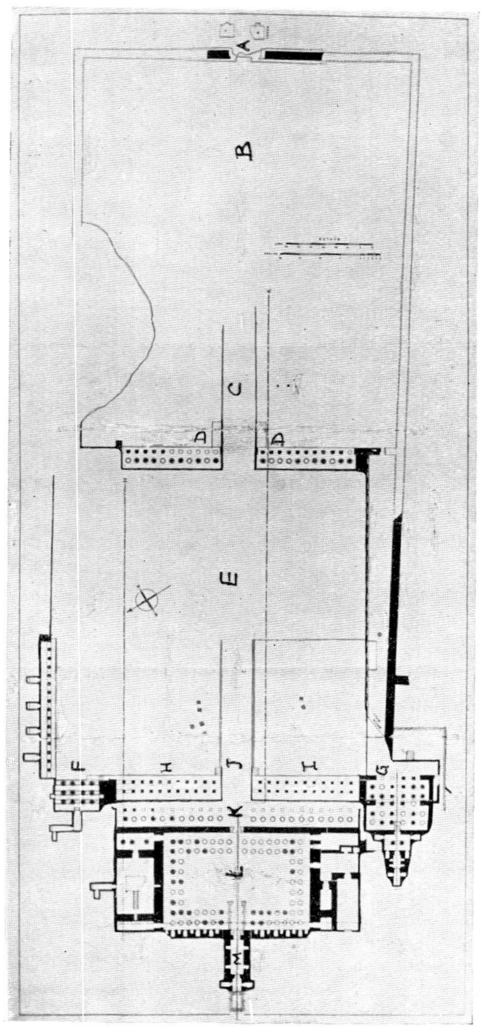

Egypt Exploration Society

Dêr el Bahri: Temple of Hatshepsut

Face page 111]

XX

TEMPLE OF LUXOR

THE modern town of Luxor takes its name from the ruins of the temple which stands in its midst. The course of centuries brought ruin and decay to the great building; it lost its sanctity, the village encroached upon it, and gradually mounds of debris rose round and within it. Houses were built on the mounds, and when these fell into decay they added to the rising heaps, on which fresh houses were erected, till at last only the tops of the colonnades and the architraves were visible above the accumulations of centuries. But the imposing grandeur of the ancient temple, seen here and there among the squalid houses, gave the village a fictitious importance, and it was called by the high-sounding name of El Uksor (The Castles). Sketches made by travellers in the eighteenth and nineteenth centuries show the ruins of the temple hardly discernible above the small huts crowding upon them; but now the temple is clear of all modern buildings, with the exception of the mosque in the outer court.

The temple was built along the river, from which it is now separated by a road. The best view of the building is from a boat on the river (pl. XXIII, 2), for then the eye can take in the whole extent, with its great courts and colonnades, from the pylon to the chapels behind the shrine. This is a view which was not permitted to the worshippers of Amon, for when the temple was in use it was jealously protected from staring eyes by a high wall.

Like all the great temples of Egypt it was built on the site of an early shrine; how early there is no means of knowing, but undoubtedly a holy place stood there in the Middle Kingdom, probably where the columns of the outer court now stand. In the early XVIIIth dynasty some small shrines and chapels were erected on the site, but the chief builder was Amenhotep III. The temple of Luxor was the great monument of this monarch, who reigned a century after Tehutmes III had made Egypt the great world-power, and while Egypt was still at the zenith of her prosperity. The very name of Tehutmes was still one to conjure with, and the traditional fear of his military prowess prevented attacks on the Egyptian Empire by any of the neighbouring states. The political supremacy of Egypt ensured her wealth; she received tribute from her own outlying provinces, and foreign rulers vied with each other in obtaining the favour of the Pharaoh by rich gifts. Precious metals and precious stones, costly woods and costly stuffs, perfumes and treasures of all kinds, poured into Egypt from every country within reach of her influence. She was probably the wealthiest kingdom of the ancient world; and the rising power of the priesthood caused a great part of her wealth to be expended on the temples and the endowments of the priests.

It is to this period of magnificence that the chief part of the temple belongs, for Amenhotep III built the beautiful colonnaded court, the hypostyle hall, the vestibules and the sanctuary. Haremheb, the last king of the dynasty, is credited with the erection of the double row of columns, which form the connecting passage between the outer court and the colonnaded court of Amenhotep III; and to Rameses II are attributed, though erroneously, the outer court and the entrance pylon. The later Pharaohs hardly interested themselves in this temple, a few small chapels and some restoration marking the extent of their activities. Alexander the Great made a considerable amount of alteration in the sanctuary, and built there a large shrine of stone, but under the Ptolemies the temple appears to have been entirely neglected.

With the advent of a new religion, the sacred site, with its decaying temple, took on a new lease of life, and the Christians used the ancient shrine as a place of worship; and built also a little church in the north-west angle between the colonnade of Haremheb and the great outer court in the space between the colonnade and the river (E). When a still newer religion entered the country the Christian church fell to ruin; but the sanctity of the site continued, and a Moslem mosque (D) was erected in the outer court to the east of the entrance pylon. It is interesting to stand in the temple and see at one glance the pagan, the Christian, and the Moslem places of worship, all within the same precincts. For over forty centuries the worship of the Divine has been carried on at this spot.

According to Abu Salih there was an avenue of ram-sphinxes leading to the pylon. "Before the gate of the town are idols standing like castles. Some of them have the forms of lions or rams and are standing on their feet in two rows, on the right and on the left. They are [carved] out of hard black stone without number." These have now disappeared.

The entrance to the temple is by a gateway through the pylon (pl. XXV, 1), before which stand obelisks and statues of the Pharaoh who claimed to be the builder (pl. XXII, 2 A). Though the colossi at the gate bear the name of Rameses II, it is very certain that the plan of this part of the building, including the pylon, was already drawn out and perhaps built under Tutankhamon or even earlier. A relief-sculpture on the south-west wall of the outer court shows the façade of the temple, either as it was in reality or as Tutankhamon intended it to be. There are seen the two towers of the pylon with a vertical doorway between, the flagstaffs on each side with fluttering pennons, the two obelisks, and the four statues, two standing and two seated facing inwards towards the gate. It is, of course, possible that this façade represented the original entrance to the temple, and may have been pulled down when Rameses II altered the outer court.

A double row of columns forms a colonnade round the outer court (B) broken only in the north-west corner, where stands a little chapel of three shrines (C), built by Tehutmes III and dedicated to the Triad of Thebes. The untouched condition of this chapel is strong evidence that the outer court was already in existence in the middle of the XVIIIth dynasty, and is not due to the energy of Rameses. If Rameses had really built the court, he would not have hesitated to destroy his predecessor's work where it interfered with the beauty and symmetry of his own.

In the north-east corner of the court is the mosque of Abu'l Haggag, built on mounds of debris within the colonnade (D). Abu'l Haggag is the patron saint of Luxor, and is regarded as having been a devout and holy Moslem; but part of the ritual connected with the mosque and with himself carries on the ritual of a far distant and almost forgotten faith, and shows the ancient god masquerading as a Muhammedan saint. In the days when Amon was worshipped, the image of the god was taken in his boat-shaped shrine on board a boat, and was carried down the river by torchlight to the temple of Karnak. There it was borne on the shoulders of priests up the sacred avenue of sphinxes into the temple, where it remained till the time for its return to Luxor. It appears to have been taken by road along the sacred way between Karnak and Luxor, the course being altered in order that it might pass round the fields and bless them, and so increase their fertility. Throughout its progress the image of the god was followed by crowds of the populace, both on the river and on land. The ceremony took place before the rise of the Nile, whose inundation has always meant the prosperity of Egypt. At the present day there rests on the roof of the mosque of Abu'l Haggag a boat, an ordinary Nile-boat. At midsummer, before the rise of the Nile, this boat, freshly painted, is placed on a carriage and is driven round the fields in the neighbourhood of the town, followed by the inhabitants of Luxor. The official cortège, which now takes the place of the procession of priests of ancient times, is composed of two officers of police, ten men on horseback and fifty foot-soldiers marching in line; then come seven camels covered with brilliantly coloured stuffs, hung with little bells and with feathers on their heads; each camel being led by a muezzin. After the camels, walk all the religious fraternities and the members of the family of Abu'l Haggag; and only when all these have passed can the populace take part in the procession. Thus does the god Amon still continue his ancient custom of blessing the fields, though under a changed name. The legend of Abu'l Haggag states that he married Tharzeh, the Christian princess of Luxor, who was converted from Christianity to Islam. This is surely an echo of that ancient custom whereby the princess of Thebes married the god Amon, who was represented by the Pharaoh dressed in the garments and insignia of the god.

The position of Amon in the hearts of his people is strikingly shown by the persistance of his cult. The fanatic zeal of the new religion failed to dislodge him from his temple, and under his new name he still remains the tutelary deity of Thebes. It is noteworthy that Abu'l Haggag is said to have died, or in other words to have received saintship, in A.D. 642, two years after the Muhammedan conquest of Egypt, when Islam first penetrated into Upper Egypt. Many and wonderful are the stories related to account for the extreme sanctity of this legendary being. He received the nickname of Abu'l Haggag (Father of Pilgrims) from a miracle which he performed when on the pilgrimage to Mecca; water ran short, and death threatened the caravan; Abu'l Haggag had a very little water left in his gourd; he offered a prayer to God, and at once the gourd was filled with an unfailing spring of water, and the pilgrims were saved. It is hardly necessary to call attention to the obvious connection between the god and the saint and their power over water. There is also a legend to account for the mosque in the temple. Abu'l Haggag was so attached to Luxor that he earnestly desired to die there, but his last illness came upon him at Armant, and he fell into the death-agony. But God gave him his heart's desire and sent angels, who bore the dying saint on their wings to Luxor. As they reached the temple Abu'l Haggag expired; the angels at once descended to earth and laid the body on the ground immediately below the place where his spirit had departed. The body was buried exactly where the angels had placed it, and the mosque was built over the grave. It is not improbable that there was a specially sacred shrine of Amon where the mosque now stands.

The columns of the outer court are of the papyrus type in its most decadent form, showing a plain surface with no ribbing; they should be compared with the earlier columns in the hypostyle hall. On the west side of the court are six royal statues standing between the pillars; they are of heroic size, and stand with one leg advanced as though they were striding forward from the cool shade of the colonnade into the glare of the sunshine; the effect by moonlight is still more startling and eerie. Some of the figures are of earlier date than Rameses II, who has removed the name of the original owner and substituted his own. Beside each large figure is a small figure of the queen, to whom the king owed his position. The outer court lies skew to the rest of the temple, possibly on account of some defect in the river-bank where the walls should have been built.

From the south side of the outer court the great colonnade of Haremheb (F) leads to the temple proper. This colonnade (pl. XXIII, 1) consists of fourteen pillars set in a double row, and constitutes one of the most imposing and magnificent parts of the temple, partly because it appears to stand alone and partly because the pillars are higher and larger than any others in the temple. The shafts are plain and cylindrical, and the capitals of the open-flower type. They once bore a stone roof, and the colonnade was enclosed with side walls reaching to the top of the pillars; making a dark passage between the two sunlit courts. Whether the contrasts of light and darkness had any symbolic meaning it is difficult to say; it is certain, however, that the contrast must have been impressive. The whole of the colonnade was at one time decorated with relief-sculptures brilliantly painted. The scenes represent the festivals of the god Amon, particularly the Midsummer festival; this was one of the greatest festivals in ancient Egypt; and both Tutankhamon and the Ethiopian Piankhy record with pride that they took part, as Pharaohs, in the procession of the boats.

The colonnade is in the direct axis of the temple, and leads into the famous court of Amenhotep III with its beautiful columns (G). It was once smoothly paved, and the colonnade which surrounds three sides of the court was once roofed (pl. XXIII, 3). The centre of the court was open to the sky; again affording that contrast of light and shadow so beloved of Egyptian architects. The columns have lotus-bud capitals, and still continue the ancient form, though the actual meaning appears to have been forgotten by this time.

At the south end of the court is the hypostyle hall (H), that wonderful mass of pillars, which in form and grouping suggests a grove of palms (pls. XXIV, XXV, 2). Whether these avenues of pillars are seen in full sunlight or by moonlight, whether at dawn or at sunset, the effect is equally striking and beautiful. It is almost impossible to imagine the condition of this hall when hardly a column showed above the mounds of debris, or to realise the amount of excavation required to bring this exquisite monument of the past to the light of day again.

The south part of the temple consisted of a vestibule and sanctuary with other small shrines and chapels; it is now greatly ruined, and was much altered in Roman and Christian times. The Romans made their changes to honour the god of the temple; the Christians used the building as a convenient place to worship the newer Deity, and covered the ancient sculptures with pictures of their saints, painted in the style which links Egyptian art with the Byzantine.

On the east side of the vestibule is a small chapel with pillars, once roofed but now open to the sky; the sculptures and inscriptions on the walls record the divine birth of Amenhotep III, whose mother was the queen of Egypt and his father the god Amon. Every Pharaoh claimed both royal and divine descent, being always the son of a human mother and of a god. Amenhotep's inscription is copied verbatim from the inscription of Hatshepsut at Dêr el Bahri, with the change only of the names of the royal mother and of the semi-divine child. There is no reason to believe that Hatshepsut's inscription was the first of its kind, but the original, from which both the copies were made, is still unknown. Hatshepsut's "Birth Colonnade" and this small chapel of Amenhotep III are the precursors of the stately "Birth-Houses" of the Ptolemaic temples.

DÊR EL BAHRI: CHAPEL OF ANUBIS
(1)

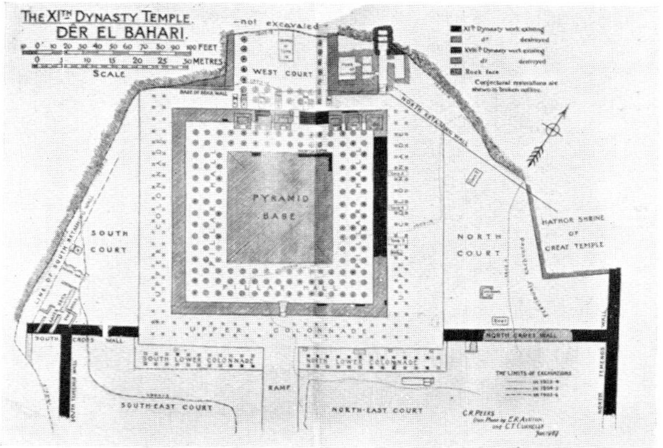

[*Egypt Exploration Society*

DÊR EL BAHRI: PYRAMID TEMPLE
(2)

RAMESSEUM
Showing High Nave and Clerestory Windows
(1)

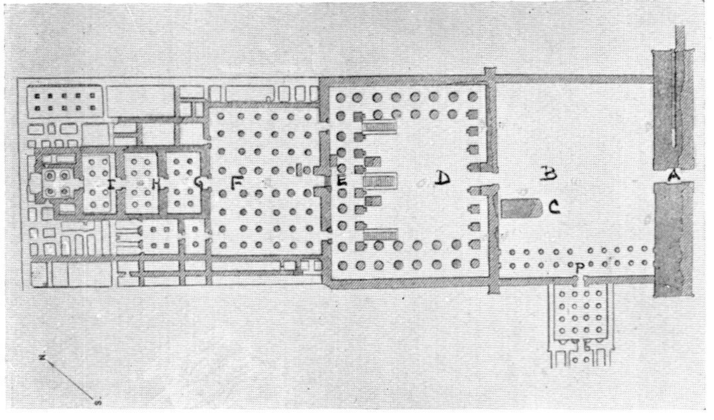

RAMESSEUM (PLAN)
(2)

Face page 119]

XXI

QURNA

THE temple of Qurna (Gourna) is one of the mortuary temples built on the west bank of the river and intended for the funerary and commemorative services of a Pharaoh, who lay buried in the Valley of the Tombs of the Kings. It was erected by Sethy I as a memorial to his royal father, Rameses I, and in honour of his divine father, the god Amon. Being unfinished at Sethy's death it was completed by his son, Rameses II, who included Sethy's and his own names in the dedication.

As late as 1861 the entrance to the temple was through a pylon bearing the cartouches of Sethy and Rameses II; then followed an avenue, one hundred and fifty feet long, bordered on either side by sphinxes, which even then were hardly distinguishable among the hovels of the little village of Qurna. A second pylon divided the first avenue from a second avenue of sphinxes which led to the façade. All this magnificent approach of pylons and sphinxes has vanished, fallen or pulled down, and much has probably been burnt for lime, a fate which has caused the destruction of so many buildings in Egypt.

The present entrance to the temple is by the colonnade of one of the hypæthral courts (B). The colonnade formed the entrance to the hypostyle hall; and, as in many of the other temples, stood on a raised terrace, now giving the effect of a verandah (pl. XXVI, 1). The pillars are of the papyrus type, with lotus-bud capitals of the later form.

The hypostyle hall (C) has lotus-bud capitals also, and here the sculptures are obviously by the same artists as those who decorated Sethy's temple at Abydos. Throughout this temple, as at Abydos, there is no difficulty in distinguishing the exquisite low-relief sculptures of Sethy from the coarse incised work of his successor. Rameses was, however, not at all averse to usurping the work of his father or any other of his predecessors; he had a sufficiently educated taste in art to appreciate good work when he saw it, and as the artists of his reign were unable to produce anything quite as fine as the old, he had no hesitation in adopting to his own glory a beautiful work of art no matter what its period. Sometimes the original owner's name can be made out below the cartouche of the usurper; but in many instances the stone-mason of the XIXth dynasty knew his work too well, the original name is entirely erased and nothing can be seen but the staring User-Maat-Ra of Rameses II. The best known and most glaring instance of such usurpation is the splendid "Tanis sphinx", and there is reason to believe that the statues in the temple of Luxor which bear the name of Rameses II are in reality portraits of a Pharaoh of the previous dynasty.

The temple followed the usual plan (pl. XXVI, 2); leading out of the hypostyle hall was a vestibule (D) and a pillared sanctuary (E); on either side of the sanctuary were side chapels dedicated to a King, who is sometimes Rameses I, sometimes Sethy I, sometimes Rameses II. Unfortunately, the greater part of the buildings round the sanctuary is so utterly ruined that only the foundations can be traced.

Rameses II often represented himself in this temple as one of the gods, and it is usual to suppose that he was the first, or even the only, Pharaoh who did so. But such representations were known in the previous reign, for Sethy I appears as the third in the Triad of Thebes and also in the Triad of Memphis. Even in the XVIIIth dynasty Tehutmes III is shown as one of the gods.

XXII

DÊR EL BAHRI

Queen Hatshepsut's Temple

THE tomb of this great Queen lies in the cliffs on the east side of the Valley of the Tombs of the Kings, in the ridge which divides the plain of the Nile from the Valley of the Tombs. Thus all the worshippers who came to her temple would turn to her tomb, either intentionally or unintentionally.

The temple, with its ramps, its terraces, and its colonnades, was built in imitation of the earlier temple of the XIth dynasty, and follows the usual plan of an Egyptian temple in having an outer court, an inner court, a vestibule, and a shrine, all in the axis of the building. The magnificent situation of the temple, set against the cliffs, makes it one of the most remarkable in the whole of Egypt; and its steady rise from the plain across the foot-hills to the perpendicular wall of rock has no parallel elsewhere, except in the prototype of the XIth dynasty. The whole temple is open to the sky, with the exception of the covered colonnades and the shrines, and even from these the outlook is across the river and the great Theban plain. The darkness and mystery usually associated with Egyptian temples are absent here; sunshine and free air are its main characteristics. A construction of this kind would be impossible in any but an almost rainless country.

The building is undoubtedly all of one period, having been erected in the lifetime of the Queen. Whether she ruled alone as has been supposed, or whether she was the heiress whom the three Tehutmes Kings married one after the other in order to obtain the throne, is not to the point; all that matters in this connection, is that the temple was begun by her, and was finished, all but some minor decorations, before her death. She was associated with her father, Tehutmes I, on the throne, and appears to have begun the temple at that time; she died in the reign of Tehutmes III. This last King is often credited with having murdered her, but the only evidence brought forward in support of this theory is the erasure of her name and figure in the sculptures of this temple, which Tehutmes III is supposed to have cruelly effected to obliterate her memory on earth and even more cruelly to destroy her prospect of eternal life. There is, however, no proof of this statement, for in other places where Hatshepsut built in conjunction with one of the three Tehutmes, her name and figure still remain. It is evident then that another explanation must be found. As her personal name is always preceded in the cartouche by the words Khnemt Amon, Consort of Amon, it would come under the ban of the Heretic King, and would be erased in his great crusade against the Theban god. Later, when the pious Sethy I of the XIXth dynasty restored the temples which Akhenaten had defaced, the names of any one of the three Tehutmes indiscriminately was cut over the erasure by the ignorant stone-masons, who did not realise that so magnificent a building could belong to a queen and not to a king.

The material of the temple is chiefly limestone, with here and there a base course of sandstone; the limestone was probably brought direct from the quarry, but the sandstone was taken from the ruins of the adjacent temple of Mentuhotep III. Throughout the temple the stones are not of any great size. The enclosing wall of the lower court is of small limestone blocks, some of which stand on footings of sandstone, which again are aften set on mud bricks. The wall is built like many of the thick walls in ancient Egypt, by building two thin parallel walls at the desired distance apart, and then filling the intervening space with small stones and rubble, the outer stones not being in any way bonded with the core; the top was finished with a kind of coping.

The entrance was through an avenue of sphinxes across the plain, and the gateway was shaded with persea trees. Through the gateway (A) the worshipper entered a great forecourt (B), now so much ruined that the outline can barely be traced. Here also trees were planted, and there were beds of flowers and pools of growing papyrus reeds; this is perhaps the place to which the queen alludes in her inscriptions when she speaks of the "garden of my father Amon". The roots and stumps of these ancient trees have been found in the pits of good earth in which they had been planted, and the positions of the flower-beds and papyrus-pools have also been traced. Colonnades stretch across the western end of the court, interrupted in the middle by the rising causeway or ramp (C) which leads to the middle court. The colonnades consist of twenty-two pillars (D) on either side of the causeway, arranged in two rows of eleven pillars; these, like the other colonnades of the temple, are of limestone, which has turned in the course of centuries to a beautiful amber colour. The pillars at the back are sixteen-sided, those in the front are square. The wall behind the colonnades has a batter, and is decorated with relief sculpture; the north side is too dilapidated to show more than a scene of bird-catching, but on the south is the extremely interesting representation of the transport of the obelisks from the quarries to Thebes.

The sloping causeway had a parapet on either side, a necessary precaution. The middle or inner court (E) has colonnades at the western end, and also a single row of pillars halfway down each side. The middle court is wider on the north side of the causeway than on the south, and the colonnade has been lengthened by the addition of a chapel dedicated to Anubis (F), which fills the space to the outer wall (pl. XXIX, 1). A chapel dedicated to Hathor is at the south end of the southern colonnade (G), and corresponds more or less with the Anubis chapel, though it is considerably larger and is outside the wall.

The northern colonnade (H) consists of a double row of square columns, eleven in each row, standing on a platform which is approached by a short flight of steps, as it is raised more than three feet above the level of the court. The stone ceiling is painted blue, sprinkled over with five-pointed yellow stars representing the sky at night. The back wall has a pronounced batter to resist the thrust of the court above it; and on the lower half of this wall are scenes and inscriptions recording the immaculate conception and divine birth of the queen. Every Pharaoh claimed to be the offspring of God and a human mother; a claim which is as ancient as the Vth dynasty, when the kings of that period were believed to be the sons of the Sun-god and a priestess. Hatshepsut's record gives the details which the earlier story has omitted; the desire of the god to produce a human child, his visit to the queen whom he had chosen to be the mother of the divine infant, the queen's joyful reception of the deity, the preparations among the gods for the great event, and their rejoicings when the child is born. Though the sculptures have been much damaged the whole story can be traced with the help of the similar scenes and inscriptions in the temple of Luxor, for Amenhotep III copied these records almost verbatim, changing only the names of the mother and child to those of his own mother and himself. Similar scenes and inscriptions are found in those Ptolemaic buildings which are known at the present day as "Birth-houses". In the scene where Queen Aahmes is being led to the birth chamber by the deities of birth, the beautiful head of the expectant mother is worth special notice; it is one of the few pieces of sculpture which survived the iconoclastic fervour of some despoiler of the temple in the XVIIIth dynasty, and the almost equally disastrous attempts at restoration in the following dynasty.

The upper half of the wall shows the coronation ceremonies when Hatshepsut was made Pharaoh. Her age was first recorded by the goddess Seshat in a ceremony which seems to be of the same kind that the Chancellor Nu claims is to be performed for him mystically after death: "There was given to me my name in the Great House, the remembrance of me in the House of Flame, on that night of counting the years and numbering the months." Two gods then baptised the queen with the Water of Life, and set her on the knee of Amon to receive his blessing. She then went on a royal progress with her father, Tehutmes I, to various great religious centres in Upper Egypt, where she received the badges of sovereignty peculiar to those shrines when they had been the capitals of independent states. The actual coronation appears to have taken place on her return to Thebes, and she is shown between two priests representing Horus and Seth, who place the crowns of Upper and Lower Egypt on her head. The wall of the southern colonnade (I) preserves the record of the celebrated expedition to the land of Punt, which Hatshepsut sent out for trading purposes.

Though the colonnades of the two side chapels increase the beauty of the effect, the result on the plan is lop-sided. The small chapel of Anubis is entered by a hypostyle hall, in which there are twelve sixteen-sided pillars; the vistas through these pillars are very beautiful. The shrine is brilliantly painted with scenes of offerings and other ceremonies; among the most famous of these paintings are the hovering falcon and vulture which symbolise respectively the deities of Upper and Lower Egypt, who with outspread wings protect the Pharaoh.

The chapel on the south side is not only much larger than the Anubis chapel but is also entirely different in construction. It could be entered either from the court beside which it stands, or by a flight of steps from outside the temple wall. The entrance was by two roofed colonnades, some of the pillars are sixteen-sided, and some have Hathor-head capitals. The inner part of the chapel is hewn out of the solid rock, and consists of two vestibules and the actual shrine. All the sculptures represent Hatshepsut or Tehutmes III with the goddess Hathor as a cow. It is probable that the narrow shrine was intended to hold a stone image of a cow like the figure found in the adjoining temple of Mentuhotep III.

A causeway (J), similar to the one leading from the lower court, leads to the highest court, which in this temple takes the place of a vestibule. The causeway terminates in a granite doorway, and from here the visitor can see the whole of the Theban plain spread at his feet. The granite doorway is now isolated, but it must once have been the entrance to a hypostyle hall (K), which now lies in ruins. The pillars extended across the whole width of the court, and seen from below gave the effect of two storeys of colonnades, as they stand immediately above the colonnades of the middle court. Beyond the hypostyle hall was an open colonnaded court (L) round which were chapels and small halls for the services for the dead. The western side of the court ends at the cliff itself, in the face of which are several niches painted with scenes of Hatshepsut and Tehutmes III before various gods. Some of these niches probably held statues of the queen. In the centre of the cliff-wall is the entrance to the rock-hewn shrine (M), before which was once a portico of granite. The shrine itself consists of three chambers, now greatly ruined; the innermost was either made or restored

RAMESSEUM: HYPOSTYLE HALL
(1)

RAMESSEUM
OSIRID PILLARS
(2)

Plate XXXII

Ramesseum: Side Aisle

Face page 127]

in Ptolemaic times, and was dedicated at that period to the two deified men, Imhotep and Amenhotep, who appear to have been revered as gods of healing and of oracles.

The temple has had many vicissitudes since Senmut the great architect of Queen Hatshepsut, designed and built it. It has suffered from man and from Nature. Falls from the overhanging cliffs have blocked and destroyed many parts; the forces of wind and sun have disintegrated the stone, and man has been even more destructive. Akhenaten, if indeed it were he, contented himself with effacing figures and inscriptions which he considered offensive, but the building itself he did not touch. Later the chambers of the upper court were used as an undertaker's place of business, with stacks of the chemicals to be used in his gruesome work of embalming; here also he kept specimens of his handicraft in the shape of coffins, so that the relatives of the dead might choose the style in which to bury their friend. The falls from the cliff made a convenient burying ground for those who desired to be within what was still regarded as consecrated ground. When the ancient religion fell and Christianity became the ruling faith, those who desired to retire from the world and devote themselves to a life of prayer found in these courts and colonnades a convenient harbour for themselves. They built a brick monastery on the upper court, with a high tower overlooking the plain, they divided the colonnades with brick walls into cells for the brethren, and as the sculptures of the heathen were always of demons and were undoubtedly inhabited by the devils, whose portraits they were, the monks with zeal as fierce and holy as that of Akhenaten fell upon these accursed figures and destroyed them. Thenceforward there would be nothing to disturb the pious meditations of the recluses, who could fix their thoughts on the world to come, rejoicing that the fate of the worshippers of those heathen images would not be theirs.

It is, however, unfortunate that the early Egyptologists did not realise that every period has its interest, but cleared away Coptic buildings without record, not remembering that the remains of an early Christian monastery, even though it belonged to monks as ignorant as the Copts of the fifth and sixth centuries, might have shed light on the beliefs and conditions of the people of that time. Mariette made a similar clearance at Abydos, also making no record. In archæology a loss or omission can never be retrieved, and our knowledge of the period when Christianity was making its way and fighting for its life is the poorer for these irreparable losses.

XXIII

DÊR EL BAHRI

Temple of the XIth Dynasty

THIS is the most complete temple of the period between the Old Kingdom and the great temples of the XVIIIth dynasty. It is the mortuary temple of two kings, Mentuhetep II who began the building, and Mentuhetep III who completed it. The plan is unique, for it consists of a pyramidal structure in the centre, standing on a platform cut out of the cliff and surrounded by colonnades. The pyramid, of which little remains, was only sixty feet square at the base; it was a purely architectural feature, and was not intended for use, the burial-chamber of the king for whom it was built being entered from the outer court and lying in the cliff behind the pyramid (pl. XXIX, 2).

The temple is built on two terraces; it is orientated east and west, and was approached from the plain by an avenue, where the pits of made earth in which the trees were planted can still be recognised. The avenue led to the great court, which had on the west side a roofed colonnade of two rows of square pillars. The facing wall against the rock base of the upper terrace was covered with sculpture.

From the lower terrace an inclined plane or ramp gave access to the upper terrace; the ramp is not in the exact centre, being slightly more to the south. An unusual feature of the ramp is the use of wooden planks for the roadway; this in unlike any other ramp or causeway known in Egypt where the usual paving material was stone.

On the upper terrace was the pyramid, built with a core of rough stone and rubble and cased with fine white limestone. A colonnade of one hundred and forty octagonal pillars was carried round three sides of the pyramid, and the walls which divided the colonnade from the pyramid were covered with painted relief sculptures representing the King's conquests, the pillars themselves were covered with sculpture in such high relief as to be almost in the round. In the colonnade at the back of the pyramid stood the chapels of the priestesses, who appear to have been sacrificed at the King's death, and who were buried beside him to accompany him to the next world. Such sacrifices occurred but rarely in Egypt, where civilisation reached a high stage of development early in the history of the world. The most notable examples are found in the Ist dynasty round the royal tombs, where by far the largest number of burials were of women, though King Den (Udy-mu) had also dwarfs and dogs for his pleasure in the Hereafter; there were at least a hundred burials round his sepulchre. If such sacrifices were made in later times, which seems doubtful, they were not on so tremendous a scale. The chapels or shrines are fully decorated with scenes from the lives of the ladies, and include such homely representations as the milking of cows and the hair-dressing of one of the priestesses. There is also a fine scene of the King enthroned wearing the crown of Upper Egypt. On the east of the pyramid were the shafts leading to the burial-chambers where these unfortunate victims were buried.

On the west of the pyramid is a court, from which a passage five hundred feet long slopes down to the tomb-chamber of Mentuhetep III who was buried in the alabaster sarcophagus in the granite-lined chamber which are still in existence. The tomb was intact at the inspection ordered by the judges in the XXth dynasty on the occasion when two bands of tomb-robbers were tried at Thebes for breaking open the royal sepulchres and stealing or destroying their contents. But during the three thousand years which have elapsed since the trial the tomb has been ransacked, the mummy removed and utterly destroyed, and of all the riches buried with the Pharaoh only a statuette and a few trifles of no use to the plunderers remain.

A chapel against the cliff and a recess hewn in the solid rock show that the temple was for the worship of a deity other than the King; this deity was probably the goddess Hathor. Though Amon was undoubtedly the god of the eastern bank at Thebes, there is some evidence to show that Hathor ruled the western bank, or at any rate a goddess, who was sometimes worshipped as the Peak of Thebes, and sometimes personified as a cow or a woman. In the XVIIIth dynasty a shrine to Hathor was set up in the corridor on the north-west of the pyramid; it is of stone, richly decorated within with sculptured and painted scenes. Standing in the shrine was the famous figure of a cow, now in the Cairo Museum. The figure is of limestone, life-size, and represents the cow of Hathor pushing her way through a clump of reeds. The shrine and cow are the joint work of Tehutmes III and his son Amenhotep II, who were as closely connected in this work as they were in the building of the temple of Amada. Here it seems that Tehutmes made and decorated the shrine, while Amenhotep was responsible for the figure.

XXIV

RAMESSEUM

The temple, known as the Ramesseum, is the centre of a great mass of buildings, of which it is the chief. It was built by Rameses II for his funerary rites, but like all Theban mortuary temples it was also dedicated to a god; usually, as in this case, to Amon (pl. XXX, 1).

The description given by Diodorus is so accurate that it is obvious he was writing from personal knowledge: "The sepulchre of Simandius contained above half a league about, at the entrance whereof was a gate of porphyry, next to which was a square gallery of stone, in it on the tops of the pillars were architraves all of one stone, and the covering was all of stone, ten foot broad, enriched with azure stars. In front was another gate like the former, but fuller of work and sculpture, where there were three great monolithic statues, the workmanship of Memnon; one of them, representing the King seated, surpassed in size all the statues of Egypt. The work was wonderful, not only for the size, but for the art and also for the excellence of the stone in which, huge though it was, there was neither crack nor blemish. Upon it was inscribed, 'I am Simandius, the King of Kings. If anyone desires to know who I am or where I lie, let him outdo what I have done'." [Diodorus goes on to describe the sculptures on the pylon, the statues on the terrace, and the great hypostyle hall.] " Next after was the sacred library, at the entrance of which was inscribed 'The Medicine of the Mind'." [The sanctuary he calls the Tomb of the King.] "The tomb was surrounded with a golden circle, three hundred and sixty-five cubits in circumference, and a foot and a half thick; in it were described from cubit to cubit the three hundred and sixty-five days of the year, the course of the stars, and what they signified according to Egyptian astrology."

The temple stands on the very edge of the cultivation, so that the entrance through the pylon was from the fields. The pylon (A) though greatly damaged still retains much of the sculpture illustrating the great battle of Kadesh which Rameses II delighted to record in all his temples. Here the "army of Amon", which led the van in this campaign, is shown camping with all the deliberation of fancied security. The unharnessed chariot-horses, the great baggage waggons, the unloaded pack-asses, and the leisurely unconcerned soldiers, make a scene of cheerful animation. The King's council of war is being held, and the enemy's spies, who had lulled the Egyptian generals into a belief that the enemy had withdrawn their troops, are being beaten to make them confess. The confession came too late, for the Hittites are seen bursting into the camp. Another sculpture shows the immediate sequel, Rameses in his chariot is charging the Hittites who fly before him. Both from the illustrations and from the inscriptions it is evident that Rameses, misled by false information from the enemy's spies, had camped in front of the "deceitful city of Kadesh". He had just discovered that the Hittites were holding the town in force when the camp was attacked. The "army of Amon" fled in disorder pursued by part of the Hittite chariotry; the larger part of the enemy forces however executed a circling movement, so that Rameses and his bodyguard found themselves enclosed by the hostile chariots. The desperate position roused all Rameses' fighting spirit, he put himself at the head of his little band and charged towards the river where the Hittite line was weakest. The charge was successful, the Hittites broke and could not recover, panic spread among them, they fled to Kadesh for shelter, and their rout was completed by the arrival of the "army of Ptah"—part of the main body of the Egyptian army—which had hurried up to the rescue of the Pharaoh. The battle, therefore, ended prosperously for Rameses, who was able to continue his campaign, and finally to record on the north end of the pylon a list of cities captured in Syria and Palestine, among which are some with names familiar to us from the Old Testament, such as Merom, Beth Anath, and Salem.

The pylon was the entrance to an outer court (B), now utterly ruined. There appears to have been a colonnade all round; and on one side, through the double row of pillars, is the entrance to the palace of the King (P). A temple-palace such as this was for the use of the Pharaoh as a god; for secular purposes he probably had a less pretentious and more comfortable abode elsewhere. A colossus (C) stood on one side of the entrance to the inner court; it is said to be the largest statue in the world. In the time of Diodorus it was evidently intact, but since then the stone has disintegrated and the upper part of the figure has fallen to the ground and is broken to pieces. Shelley's sonnet on the statue is worth quoting:

I met a traveller from an antique land
Who said: Two vast and trunkless legs of stone
Stand in the desert. Near them, on the sand,
Half sunk, a shattered visage lies, whose frown,
And wrinkled lip, and sneer of cold command,
Tell that the sculptor well those passions read
Which yet survive, stamped on these lifeless things,
The hand that mocked them and the heart that fed;
And on the pedestal these words appear:
"My name is Ozymandius, King of Kings,
"Look on my works, ye mighty, and despair!"
Nothing beside remains. Round the decay

DÊR EL MEDINA

Plate XXXIV

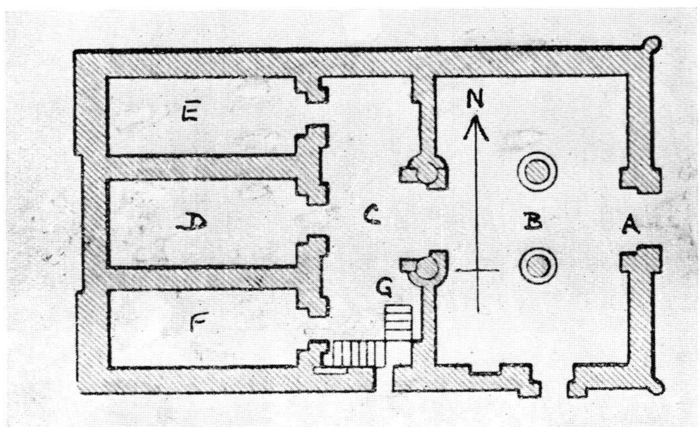

Face page 135]

Of that colossal wreck, boundless and bare
The lone and level sands stretch far away.

The lines show that the statue is even less complete now than when Shelley wrote. The figure is hewn out of a single block of granite, which must have been brought from Aswan. The setting of so large a mass of stone in position is a proof of the complete mastery of the Egyptians in the technique of moving blocks, which were not only of great size and weight but were also of difficult and awkward shapes.

Passing through the doorway, the inner court (D) is reached. On either side was a colonnade formed by a double row of papyrus columns, while at either end was a row of Osirid pillars, the "caryatids" of Diodorus. The few Osirids which are still standing are mournful survivals of past splendour, the figures mutilated, the faces obliterated, the crowns destroyed. On the wall, dividing the outer and inner courts and behind the Osirids, the sculptures repeat the favourite scenes of Rameses II in the Hittite campaign. Here the colour still remains, and the Hittites are seen to be a fair people with light hair and white skins. The prince of Aleppo, who was rescued by his friends from the river in a half drowned state, is represented with red hair. Above are scenes from the festival of the god Min; the King in the presence of the Queen reaps a handful of ears of corn which is taken by the priest of Min and shaken freely so as to scatter the grain. The inscription beside the scene says, "Giving wheat to the earth in the presence of the god." The white Bull of Min takes a majestic though unexplained part in the ceremony. All the columns in the court are decorated with scenes of the King and the gods.

Colossal statues of black granite once stood in the court; now they are broken to fragments. The colossal head now in the British Museum, was brought to England by

Belzoni, who gives an interesting account of the moving of the great block from the court to the boat: "The fellahs of Gournou, who were familiar with *Caphany*, as they named the colossus, were persuaded that it could never be moved from the spot on which it lay; and when they saw it moved, they all set up a shout. Though it was the effect of their own efforts, it was the devil, they said, that did it; and as they saw me taking notes, they concluded it was done by means of a charm." [The means were levers, rollers, and ropes.] "The mode I adopted was very simple; for work of no other description could be executed by these people, as their utmost sagacity reaches to pulling a rope, or sitting on the extremity of a lever as a counterpoise."

At the end of the court facing the entrance is a raised terrace (E), once roofed, approached by three sets of steps, one in the centre, and one on either side. It is on this terrace that the western row of Osirids stand, while behind them is a row of circular pillars with lotus-bud capitals. The wall of the terrace behind the pillars is covered with scenes of the King and gods. Eleven out of the King's innumerable sons appear to be assisting their royal father in some special ceremony, perhaps of victory, for in the registers above them the King is given life by the war-god Mentu, while Thoth records the royal name. The terrace serves as a vestibule to the Great Hypostyle Hall which can be entered by three doors.

The hypostyle hall (F) is the glory of the temple (pls. XXXI, XXXII, I); it consists of a high nave of three aisles with three lower aisles on either side; and, like the hypostyle hall of the Great Temple of Karnak, the lighting was by clerestory windows. The tall columns of the nave are circular in section with capitals like those in the colonnade of Haremheb at Luxor; the shorter columns have the usual lotus-bud capital, now no longer lobed but presenting a perfectly plain surface. The shafts of all the columns in the hall have plain surfaces, offering a good field for decoration, of which the sculptor took full advantage, and every shaft shows coloured reliefs of the King in the presence of the gods. On the walls the Hittite campaign forms the chief decoration; the record is not of the battle of Kadesh, it is the less dramatic but more successful assault on the fortress of Dapur. The citadel was strongly defended, and the Egyptians attacked with vigour; the "storm-troops" are seen coming up sheltered under their shields and commanded by the youthful sons of the King. The final attack was by escalade, and the young princes so distinguished themselves that their names are handed down to posterity in the account; this was unusual on the part of Rameses II who generally preferred to keep all the glory of any military exploit to himself.

Three small pillared halls (G, H, I), one behind the other in the axis of the temple, are entered from the hypostyle hall and lead to the shrine. Each hall had eight pillars. The first hall (G) still preserves the roof on which is a star-map showing, by the Egyptian astronomical method, the position of the stars at the time of some important event in the King's life, perhaps his birth or his accession. The walls are covered with sculpture; conspicuous among the scenes are the sacred boats of the Triad of Thebes. Rameses II plays a large part in all the scenes. An interesting representation is of the King seated under a sacred tree, while the god Atum inscribes the royal name on the leaves, assisted by the two deities of writing, Seshat and Thoth. Sacred trees are always peculiarly interesting, and in Egypt there are many such trees; the nome of Heracleopolis Magna bore one as its totem, a holy sycomore grew at Memphis, and was the habitation of the goddess Hathor; another gave its name to Hierasykaminos (the modern Maharraka) in Nubia, and the most famous is the tree of Heliopolis, which has retained its sanctity to modern times as the tree under which the Holy Family rested during their journey in Egypt. The itinerary of the Holy Family, from the Flight into Egypt till the Return to Palestine, was traditionally preserved, and was recorded by the Arab author Maqrizi. "They halted first at Bosta on Bashans 24 (May 30), there the inhabitants refused to receive them. They camped outside Bosta for some time; then they went to Samannud, crossed the Nile, and thence to Ashmunen. Then they went to Filës, where they stayed a long while, then they moved to Kus-Kam. They were driven out and went to Mirah, and went to Dêr al Moharraq, where after six months and several days Joseph received a dream ordering his return to Syria. From Mirah they travelled to Cairo, then to Heliopolis, and thence to Syria." The account of the route is quite consistent and reasonable; Bosta is probably Tel Bastah (Bubastis) at the mouth of the Wady Tumailat, where the caravan road from Syria enters Egypt. From there the route is uncertain till Middle Egypt is reached in the neighbourhood of Ashmunên. Kus-Kam (Qussiyeh), Mirah (Meir), and Dêr al Moharraq are well-known at the present day. In Cairo the grotto where they rested is now covered by the church of Abu Sargeh (St. Sergius); and the spring at Heliopolis, in which tradition states that the Virgin washed the garments of the Holy Babe, is now used to water the tree which sheltered the Holy Family.

The second of the small halls (H) also had eight pillars, and part of the roof still survives. The walls have been sculptured all over. As is usual in all temples the sculptures become more conventionally religious and less humanly interesting the nearer they are to the sanctuary. This hall is no exception to the rule; here the King is merely making the usual sacrifices to the gods he most favoured, among whom as always are Ptah and Sekhmet of Memphis.

The rest of the temple is ruined to the foundations; all that can be known is that the third small hall (I) had eight pillars, and the shrine four, while the shrine and the three halls were surrounded by a number of small chambers.

The great girdle wall encloses a vast complex of brick buildings of the same date as the temple. Here were the priests' houses, the royal library, quarters for the palace servants, and storehouses of every kind. It was in this part of the temenos that Sir Flinders Petrie found papyri of the XIIth dynasty, among which are the earliest dramas known. The date of the papyri is proof that the royal library of Rameses II contained volumes written in ancient times and valued on account of their antiquity.

The walls of the temple do not run parallel with the girdle wall though built at the same period. The discrepancy is undoubtedly intentional but the reason is not apparent; the obliquity is the more emphasised in that the brick buildings follow the line of the girdle wall.

XXV

DÊR EL MEDINA

THE temple of Dêr el Medina is one of the most beautiful examples of Ptolemaic architecture. It was begun by Ptolemy IV (Philopater) and finished by Ptolemy IX (Euergetes II) half a century later, but the site must have been sacred for at least a thousand years before the Ptolemaic Kings began their building. The dedication is to Amenhotep, son of Hapu, the Hellenised form of the name being Amenothes, son of Paapis. A dedication of a temple to a non-royal human being is rare, for temples belonged only to the gods or to their representative on earth, the Pharaoh. The ordinary man was not considered divine, and Herodotus says that the priests were very positive on this point, "In 11,340 years no god had assumed the form of a man, neither had any such thing happened either before or afterwards in the time of the remaining kings of Egypt." Herodotus was misinformed by the priests who were evidently ignorant of the fact that their ancestors had recognised two deified men, and probably more. Of these two the earlier was Imhotep, who was Vezier, Chief Architect, Chief Magician, and Chief Physician at the court of Zoser; the other was Amenhotep, son of Hapu, who was Vezier, Chief Magician, Chief Physician, and Master-Builder of Amenhotep III. Both men appear to have been the most important persons of their time in the kingdom; and it was probably their reputation as magicians which caused them to be venerated as gods. The cult of Amenhotep, son of Hapu, which began at his death, reached its height under the Ptolemies.

The Nubian temple of Dendur was also erected to the honour of two deified men, but these owed their position to their identification with Osiris, whereas at Dêr el Medina Amenhotep was worshipped as himself; so also was Imhotep, who attained divinity before Amenhotep, and had two shrines dedicated to his cult, one at Memphis and one at Philae. These two deified men, so much alike in their earthly careers, were closely connected in the minds of the Egyptians, and in the temple of Dêr el Medina the figure of Imhotep appears as the equal of Amenhotep.

This little temple is the smallest of all the temples of Egypt, and has, perhaps for that very reason, escaped the hand of the destroyer to a great extent. It stands in a large enclosure of irregular shape surrounded by a high brick wall, which probably dates to the XVIIIth dynasty and is complete over the greater part of its length. The wall rises above the stone gateway, which thus appears to be embedded in the brickwork; it is a good example of the Egyptian manner of enclosing the temples with high encircling walls and so screening the sacred place from the eyes of the multitude. In Christian times a monastery was built within the enclosure, hence the modern name of the building, "The Convent of the Town".

The temple is entered through the stone gateway (A), which opens into a court (B); the roof of which is now destroyed; it was originally supported by four columns, two with the characteristic foliage-capitals of the Ptolemaic period and two with Hathor-head capitals. Pillars with screen-walls divide the hall from the vestibule (C).

As in many other temples several doors open from the vestibule; that in the axis leads to the shrine (D), and on either side of the central doorway is another entrance to a subsidiary shrine (E, F). At the south end of the vestibule is a door leading to a staircase (G); the stairs were lighted by a window, and were intended as a processional way to the roof when the images of Amenhotep were carried forth on certain specified days of the year that he might "breathe the sweet breezes of the north wind" (pl. XXXIII).

The three shrines are now empty, but must once have contained the divine statues. The sculpture on the walls is peculiar and quite unlike the sculpture in any other temple, though closely resembling the decoration of a mortuary chapel. For this reason it has been suggested that this was originally a funerary temple for Amenhotep. If this is really so, the temple is unique in Egypt, for mortuary temples for personages of less than kingly rank are otherwise unknown. It is, however, possible that Amenhotep was regarded as not merely royal but actually divine; as a mortal he would die and be buried, then like the divine kings his worship would continue in his chapel. Although the date is of the middle Ptolemaic period, the decoration would reproduce many of the sculptures of the earlier chapel, and the scene of the Weighing of the Heart at the Judgment of the Dead is one which never occurs in temples of the gods. The gods, being gods, could never be brought to judgment, it was only sinful mortals who underwent the ordeal of the Scales. This sculpture is strong evidence that the temple was originally a mortuary chapel for a human being.

It is evident from the remains near the original chapel that a busy town once existed in that neighbourhood. In all probability the town fell into complete decay before the advent of the Ptolemies, the ruined chapel alone remaining. Ptolemy Philopater rebuilt it as a temple, but with the introduction of Christianity the old religion was abandoned and the temple was deserted. Its lonely position in the midst of ruin made it the obvious place for the abode of those who had withdrawn themselves from the world.

PLATE XXXV

MEDINET HABU: HYPOSTYLE HALLS
(1)

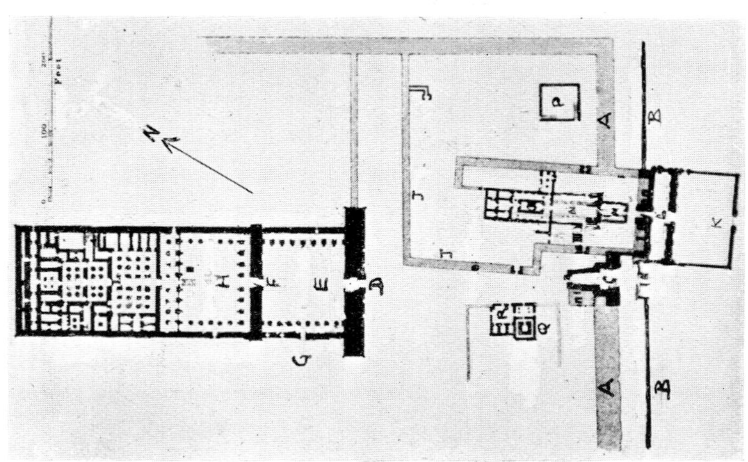

MEDINET HABU (PLAN)
(2)

[*Face page* 142

PLATE XXXVI

MEDINET HABU: SECOND COURT
Showing Pillars of Christian Church
(1)

MEDINET HABU: FIRST COURT AND SECOND PYLON
(2)

Face page 143]

An interesting side-light is thrown on the beliefs attached to the gods of this temple. A large number of votive tablets have been found in the precincts bearing representations of ears, and occasionally of eyes; these are intended as the ears of the god to whom the petitioner makes his prayer, and who is thus forced to listen. The ears are not always in pairs, and the number may vary from one to a hundred according to the urgency of the petition and the piety of the petitioner. These tablets come from two places only, the temple of Ptah in Memphis and the temple of Dêr el Medina at Thebes.

XXVI

MEDINET HABU

Great Temple

THE main temple of Medinet Habu was built by the last of the great Pharaohs, and is itself the latest example of purely Egyptian architecture. It belongs to that group of magnificent temples of the New Kingdom, of which Hatshepsut's temple at Dêr el Bahri was the first. The next great period of building was several centuries later under the Ptolemies, when foreign influence had permeated the whole country.

The girdle-wall (A), nearly sixty feet high and proportionately thick, was intended as the enclosure of this temple alone, but in it is incorporated part of the enclosure wall of the XVIIIth dynasty temple. This is quite in accordance with Rameses III's usual thrifty ways, he invariably used the work or material of his predecessors, often without regard to its suitability. There is also an outer wall (B) standing thirteen feet high, with a crenellated top; and this, in combination with the pavilion, gives the effect of the defences of a fortress. The narrow entrance through the outer wall has a guard-room on either side, and again suggests a likeness to a fortress.

The gateway (C) through the main girdle wall is one of the most remarkable buildings in Egypt; it is known as the Pavilion, and is entirely unlike the architecture of any other period, either earlier or later (pl. XXXIV, 2). The structure consists of two crenellated towers enclosing a courtyard, which is wide at the entrance and narrow at the far end, where it is shut in by a high gateway. On the ground-floor of the towers are guard-rooms; the storeys above contain living-rooms for the King and the ladies of his harem. The walls are sculptured within and without, and the scenes are a curious mixture of warfare and harem-life. On the outside of the walls Rameses III is the formidable conqueror, he slays his enemies in the presence of the gods as Samuel hewed Agag in pieces before the Lord, and he leads files of captives to various gods to be slaves in the temples. In the court are two black granite figures of the lioness goddess Sekhmet, the most savage and warlike of the goddesses; and on the walls on either side are stone brackets held up on the heads of the King's enemies; the brackets probably once supported statues of the Pharaoh who would thus be seen trampling his enemies underfoot. These warlike scenes of victory and death are in marked contrast with the sculptures on the walls of the rooms within the towers. In these apartments are portrayed the beautiful ladies belonging to a monarch who more than any other Pharaoh prided himself on his licentiousness. He is shown as a "King of the harem", and the personal note is intensified by the remembrance that he probably died as the result of a harem conspiracy. One of his queens plotted to kill him, and put her own son on the throne; the conspirators first tried to accomplish their end by means of magical wax figures; these proving ineffectual they resorted to more mundane weapons, and Rameses appears to have received injuries from which he finally died. The conspirators were tried for their lives; those who were found guilty and condemned to death were permitted to commit suicide in the presence of the judges as soon as sentence was passed; the fate of the guilty queen is not recorded.

The gateway (c) admits into the sacred precincts and is in the axis of the great Temple though at a little distance from it. The plan of the temple follows the same arrangement as the Ramesseum; the first, or entrance, pylon (D) gives access to an outer court (E), which is divided from the inner court (H) by a wall with a pylon in the centre. The inner court is on a higher level and is approached by a ramp from the outer court. At the far end of the inner court is a terrace which admits in succession to the great hypostyle hall (I), two small pillared halls and the shrine. Small chambers are built on either side of the three halls and at the sides and back of the shrine.

The first pylon is covered with scenes of the Pharaoh slaying captives before Amon and Harakhti; and there is also a long inscription recording the second campaign against the Western Confederacy, who attacked Egypt in force and were defeated. Much of the inscription is clearly a poem, in which various similes are used to extol the Pharaoh. He is "the great flame of Sekhmet", and "the heart of His Majesty was wroth like Baal in heaven, his strength was mighty like his father Amon. He is like a plundering lion terrifying the goats, like Sutekh when he is enraged. Mentu and Sutekh are with him in every fray, Anath and Astarte are his shield."

Passing through the gateway of the pylon the first court (E) is reached (pl. XXXVI, 2). This has a colonnade on either side; on the north the columns are Osirids of the King, now much damaged; on the south, the columns have circular shafts and papyrus capitals; the asymmetry is not unpleasing. On the south also are three doors which formed the private entrances to the royal palace (G) which adjoined the temple. The most remarkable feature of this wall is a balcony, which the King could enter from the palace to view processions and other religious ceremonies in the court. On either side of the balcony is a bracket supported by the heads of foreign enemies, and the scenes below the balcony show the joyful reception accorded to the royal god when he deigned to make his appearance. The other walls of the court are fully sculptured with scenes and inscriptions recording the Syrian war, which took place partly on the coast of Palestine, against the allied armies of the Libyans and the people of the "land of Amor", presumably the Amorites. The campaign was of course successful, otherwise it would not have been recorded. The enemy were so utterly defeated that they had to beg leave even to breathe: "The miserable chief of Amor and the miserable vanquished chief of Libya say, 'Breath! O great Ruler, strong-armed, great in might! Give us breath that we may bow the knee to thy double serpent-crown, that we may speak of thy might to our sons' sons'." Some of the scenes show the victorious Pharaoh in the presence of Amon, "the King himself presenting the tribute to Amon from the great chiefs of every country, silver, gold, lapis lazuli, turquoise, all precious stones without limit, from the spoil which His Majesty carried off, from that which his valiant sword captured."

The second pylon has a granite gateway and is approached by a ramp (F). The surface of the pylon is covered with inscriptions, chiefly relating to the campaign against the Confederary of the Sea-peoples. The artists of Rameses III had a marvellous facility in depicting the different racial types among both the mercenaries employed by the Pharaoh and the captives taken in the wars; the bearded Amorite, the clean-shaven Philistine with his feathered crown, the Shardana in his horned helmet, are fine examples. The Confederacy appears to have been one of those great movements which, when successful, overthrow old civilisations and force new ideas and new methods on unwilling nations. The Eastern Mediterranean was probably overrun by these people before they ventured to think of Egypt, a country wealthy by reason of its own fertility and by centuries of accumulations of plunder from foreign countries. The riches of Egypt were a temptation not to be withstood, and the Confederacy gathered in force for the attack, only to encounter a military genius and an inspired leader. Whatever may have been Rameses III's faults as a man, there is no doubt that he was an incomparable general. He met the Confederacy by land and sea on the borders of Egypt; though he led the land-forces in person the naval tactics were due to him also. The enemy-fleet was lured into a harbour where the Egyptian fleet was lying in ambush, while on land the army were "a wall of iron". The result was the total defeat of the Confederacy, and Egypt was saved from the horrors of an invasion. It is, however, a moot point whether Egypt would not have gained in the end by the introduction of new blood and new ideas which the conquerors would have brought with them. As it was, this great effort exhausted all the energy and military prowess of Egypt; thereafter rulers and people degenerated steadily, and Egypt sank into a barbarism from which it never wholly emerged, for it fell a prey to Ethiopian, Assyrian, Greek and Persian, before the two first Ptolemaic Kings lifted it again to a semblance of its former glory.

The second court (H) is almost a replica of the second court of the Ramesseum. Rameses III seems to have taken Rameses II as his model, both in the building of his temple and in the records of his campaigns. But whereas the poem of Pentaur on the Battle of Rameses II is often truly poetical and felicitous in expression Rameses III's record of his far more important campaigns is often too much overlaid with metaphor and is apt to become bombastic. "He is like a lion with deep roar upon the hill-tops, who strikes terror from afar; he is a gryphon swift in every stride. This fair god is like Mentu, great of strength, whose heart is glad when he sees the battle; firm on the right, swift on the left, smiting hundreds of thousands, whose lifetime and whose souls are ended, the strong-armed son of Amon is behind them like a young lion."

Roofed colonnades surround the second court on all four sides; on the right and left, i.e. to the north and south the columns have lotus-bud capitals of the later type; on the east the pillars have Osirids of the King; on the west a terrace, approached by a ramp, carries a double colonnade, Osirids in front, columns with bud capitals at the back.

On the walls at the back of the colonnades Rameses made the record of the first Libyan War, which took place in the fifth year of his reign. He had three great campaigns; in his fifth year he fought the Libyans for the first time; in his eighth year the Confederacy threatened Egypt, and he defeated them; and in his eleventh year he fought the Libyans again. The records are arranged more or less in chronological order in the temple; the earliest being in the western parts, and the later towards the entrance. Rameses claimed that in this first Libyan War the enemy lost a thousand men taken prisoner and twelve thousand five hundred and thirty-five killed. The exact number of the slain was always known from the habit of cutting off the right hand of a dead enemy and counting the hands at the end of the battle.

Besides the military records there are also representations of religious ceremonies, some of which are obviously copied from the Ramesseum; for the procession of the god Min with his sacred white bull is found in both temples and nowhere else. But the full ceremony of ploughing and reaping occurs here only; the Pharaoh in his royal insignia ploughs with four oxen, he reaps the ripe corn and presents the sheaf to the Nile-god, behind whom stands the emblem of the inundation, an emblem which also means abundance. This is certainly the record of a fertility rite reminiscent of the ceremonies of Osiris at Abydos, and undoubtedly extremely ancient.

Many of the hieroglyphs in the second court are startling by their size and the depth to which they are cut. The colour in the hollows is often well preserved; Miss Edwards remarks on the beauty of some of the effects: "Struck by an unusual splendour in some of the blues, and by a peculiar look of scintillation which they assumed in certain lights, I examined them particularly, and found that the effect had been produced by very subtle shades of gradation in what appeared at first sight to be simple flat tints. In some of the reeds, for instance, the ground colour begins at the top of the leaf in pure cobalt, and passes imperceptibly down to a tint that is almost emerald green at the bottom." She adds in a note: "The grand blue of the ceiling of the colonnade of the great hypæthral court is also very remarkable for brilliancy and purity of tone; while to those interested in decoration the capital and abacus of the second column on the right on entering the courtyard, offers an interesting specimen of polychrome ornamentation on a gold-coloured ground."

The reliefs, being sheltered by the roofs of the colonnades, also retain their colour, and it is interesting to see how much of the detail was painted. On the field of battle the dead are shown lying on the ground which is sprinkled over with a profusion of wild-flowers, these being rendered in colour, not in sculpture. Details of the horses' harness and the men's armour are also represented in paint, and the scenes are consequently much more vivid and lifelike than when only sculpture remains. If the earlier temples were decorated with the same delicate particularity, the amount that is lost to us by want of the painted detail is incalculable.

Beyond the second court the temple has been destroyed almost to ground level (pl. XXXV, 1). The foundations of walls and the bases of columns show that the hypostyle hall (1) had twenty four pillars and probably a high nave with clerestory windows like the Ramesseum. The two vestibules

Medinet Habu: Temple and Sacred Lake of Tehutmes III
(1)

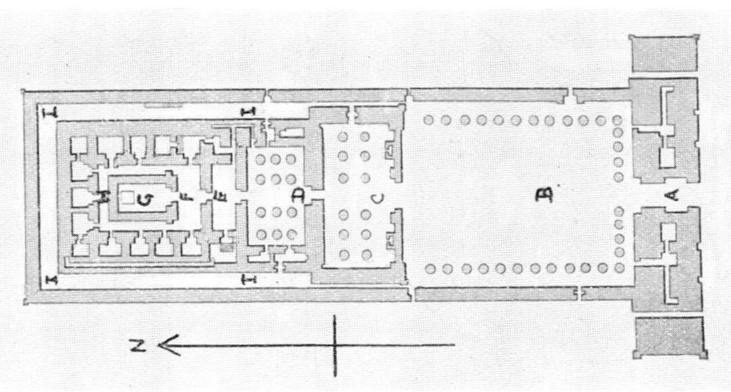

Edfu (Plan)
(2)

PLATE XXXVIII

EDFU PILLARS

[*Photograph by Mr. Percival Hart*

ESNA PILLARS

Face page 151]

had pillars, so also had the shrine. One of the chambers to the south of the shrine still retains its roof, which is decorated with maps of constellations, perhaps representing a horoscope.

Leading out of the south side of the hypostyle hall are several rooms which were the treasuries of the temple. The inscriptions and scenes show the immense wealth of the priesthood, wealth showered upon them by the victorious and pious Pharaoh: "Speaks Rameses to his father, Amon-Ra, King of the gods, 'Take thou gold and silver like sand of the shore, I produce them for thee by the measure. I bring to thee lapis lazuli, turquoise and every precious stone in chests, and fine gold'." Another inscription says: "I bring to thee silver, gold, copper, royal linen, perfumes of Punt; I fill thy treasury with every splendid precious stone with which to brighten thy beauty to all eternity."

The outside of the temple is covered with reliefs and inscriptions. On that part of the first pylon which stretches beyond the temple wall are the spirited scenes of the King in his chariot hunting wild asses, mountain goats and wild bulls. Along the south wall of the temple is a list of the feasts celebrated annually within the building; the record of five months only is preserved, and this shows that the average number of feasts was one every three days. The principal festival was the anniversary of the coronation; at first it was quite a small affair, but later Rameses caused it to be observed with festivity for twenty days.

On the west wall the scenes give the details of a campaign in the Sudan, with long rows of captured negroes. There are also scenes of the first Libyan War; these continue to the north wall, where they conclude with the Pharaoh watching the counting of the hands severed from the dead bodies of the enemy. As the Negro campaign occupied only a part of the wall, the rest of the space is filled with scenes of the Syrian war, which include the famous naval battle. These are given with great spirit and with much detail; the Egyptian ships are distinguishable from those of the enemy by the lion's head at the prow. Further scenes from the Syrian and Libyan campaigns continue along the wall and the pylons.

The second court was used in Christian times as a church (pl. XXXVI, 1). The court was too large to be roofed, therefore small pillars were erected within it and the roof was carried across the narrower space. An altar was set up at the east end, and the figures and inscriptions of the older religion were defaced or covered with plaster. The smaller chambers to the west became sacristies and priests' houses, and it was in one of these that Wilkinson found "one of the large gilt crosses which ornamented the dresses of the priests." All this Christian building has been recently swept away, and the court is now in the same condition as when the Christians took possession. The early Christians had much to answer for in the demolition of ancient records and works of art, but at least they were actuated by a fiery zeal for their religion, and thought they were serving God by their acts of destruction. What, however, is to be said for the later Christian, who, pledged to preserve the vestiges of the past, recklessly destroys the remains which do not interest him? The modern pseudo-archæologist has cleared many an ancient temple of its so-called encumbrances, utterly destroying them, so that they disappear in the Sea of Time *spurlos versenkt*.

XXVII

MEDINET HABU

Temple of Tehutmes III

At Medinet Habu, as at Karnak, the girdle-wall encloses a group of independent temples of various periods. The earliest on this site was built in the XVIIIth dynasty, the Great Temple belongs to the XXth dynasty, and the shrines of the Queens are of the XXV and XXVIth dynasties.

The temple of the XVIIIth dynasty was begun by Amenhotep I. It was orientated rather to the north of west, and was enclosed by a girdle-wall, part of which was incorporated by Rameses III in the great brick wall round the temenos of his temple. The original wall remains only on the north and west (J). It is a processional temple, but as Amenhotep was very definitely a god the building may have been his funerary temple as well. Five monarchs of the XVIIIth dynasty were concerned in the building of this holy place, Amenhotep I, Hatshepsut, and the three Tehutmes. It was in use and kept in repair till the XXth dynasty; then it fell into decay and was restored and partly rebuilt by Shabaka and Taharqa; the Ptolemies and the Romans also added to it and restored parts of it.

The forecourt (K) is large in comparison with the rest of the building; the entrance door in the axis of the temple bears the name of Antoninus Pius, and at the north end of the court is a colonnade (L), originally Ptolemaic, but altered and inscribed by the same emperor. Behind the colonnade stands the Ptolemaic pylon, which is peculiar in being for outward show only; it is merely a shell, for the walls facing towards the temple have never been built.

Passing through the pylon a small court (M) is reached; this is often called the Court of Nectanebo, but it dates to the XXVth dynasty. Nectanebo followed the example of many Egyptian Pharaohs in erasing a previous King's name and substituting his own. The court is small, being little more than an enlarged colonnade with screen-walls between the columns. Taharqa decorated the walls with building-inscriptions, and Nectanebo claimed the court as his by scenes and inscriptions referring to the building of the court and its dedication when completed.

At the far end of the court is a pylon with the names of Shabaka and Taharqa; this leads into another court (N) which had a row of nine columns on either side. It was probably the hypostyle hall of the original temple, in which case it would belong to the XVIIIth dynasty, though restored or rebuilt later. The granite doorway on the right is of the XXVIth dynasty, and the inscription on it gives the high-sounding name of the temple, "The Splendid Throne of Amon-Ra". Hakar, a king of the XXIXth dynasty, seems to have rebuilt the hall. He was one of the native rulers who rebelled against the Persian rule and so paved the way for the establishment of the last of the native dynasties.

A doorway in the axis of the hall leads into a pillared gallery surrounding the actual sanctuary. The pillars are square in section, and are connected by screen-walls, the first instance of the use of such walls. As this gallery is of the time of Tehutmes III, it is possible that the screen-walls are due to the influence of a foreign architecture from a country where sunlight was more welcome than in Egypt. The reason for the screen-walls is probably due to the abandonment of the outer wall of the temple, its place being taken by pillars, but as the religion of Egypt was a mystery religion the inner court had to be hidden from the public eye; the low screen-wall, of rather more than man-height, did this effectually while at the same time admitting light and air and without interfering with the artistic effect (pl. XXXVII, 1).

The sanctuary (o) is of the processional type, and the inscriptions show that Amon was the god of the temple. Ptolemy IX (Euergetes II) restored the sanctuary in the usual Ptolemaic manner. The outer walls of the sanctuary are also fully decorated.

Behind the sanctuary are several chapels sculptured with religious scenes. These have the names of Tehutmes I and Tehutmes II superposed indiscriminately over the name of Hatshepsut.

To the east of the temple is the Sacred Lake, of the same date as the temple itself; round about it were the gardens which were always a feature of the XVIIIth dynasty temples.

In Christian times the temple was used as a church and dedicated to St. Menas, a legendary saint, but so highly popular as to suggest that he was a pagan deity under another name. His chief shrine was near Alexandria but churches dedicated to him are found in all parts of Egypt, even as far south as Elephantine.

XXVIII

MEDINET HABU

Shrines of the Queens

THE miniature temple of Queen Amenardys (Q) is one of the few buildings of the XXVth dynasty still remaining. It is aligned with the Pavilion and Temple of Rameses III, and consists of an entrance pylon, a colonnaded court, and a sanctuary surrounded by an ambulatory. The texts in the court are entirely funerary and are for the benefit of Queen Amenardys, who is styled the daughter of King Kashta. The temple was erected by Queen Shepenupt II, the adopted daughter and immediate successor of Amenardys; she is shown measuring the foundation of the temple by the help of the goddess Seshat.

The pylon is sculptured with figures of some of the nomes of Egypt carrying offerings, while above are representations of Amenardys performing religious rites in the presence of Amon and Mut. The text above the doorway states that the chapel was for the benefit of childless women and expectant mothers as well as for the cure of diseases. Many pilgrims seem to have resorted to the shrine, and deposited votive offerings in the form of figures of gods. The colonnade is now destroyed, evidently by a fire which occurred in Christian times when the chapel was used as a storehouse. The stones of the court still bear the marks of the fire, which destroyed many of the scenes both there and in the sanctuary. The scenes are funerary in character, and show Shepenupt making offerings to the dead Amenardys and to the gods of the dead.

The sanctuary is important architecturally as having a true vault in stone; probably the earliest example in Egypt of a stone roof so built. Both in the sanctuary and the ambulatory the scenes and texts are funerary, with Amenardys as the chief recipient of the offerings or as being in the presence of the gods of the dead.

The outer faces of the temple walls are covered with inscriptions in honour of Amenardys, and she is represented with a King who may be her father Kashta or her husband Piankhy II. Kashta's name has been erased, more or less successfully, throughout the temple; another instance of unexplained hatred of which Egypt furnishes so many examples. There is also a scene of Shepenupt II making offerings to her adopted mother, Amenardys, and to Amenardys's adopted mother, Shepenupt I.

At the west side another building adjoins the temple of Amenardys, built for three Queens, Shepenupt II, Nitocris, and Meht-en-wesekht. The entrance pylon was evidently intended at first to admit to one shrine only; when the second shrine was built a second door was opened to the left of the central gateway; but as there was not room for a third door the enclosing wall is narrowed suddenly on the west by a right-angled turn to fit into the façade.

The shrine of Shepenupt II was the first of the three to be built; it stood alone, and the pylon formed the entrance to the court (R) from which it opened. Later, the shrine of Nitocris was erected on the east side; it was aligned with Shepenupt's chapel and filled the space between it and the wall enclosing the shrine of Amenardys. The second door of the façade is in the axis of the shrine of Nitocris. Later still Meht-en-wesekht's shrine was built on the west and the court was enlarged to admit it.

The sculptures in the court give the titles and genealogies of the three queens; there are also scenes of the royal ladies making offerings to the Triad of Thebes, as well as to their adopted ancestresses, Amenardys and Shepenupt I.

The interior of the shrines of Shepenupt II and Nitocris are copied from the shrine of Amenardys, the roofs are vaulted in the same way, and the sculptures are reproduced, word for word and scene for scene, from the same source. Meht-en-wesekht's shrine has a flat roof, and the style is reminiscent of a tomb-chamber of the Old Kingdom.

Under each of the four shrines is an underground chamber of unknown use. The walls of Meht-en-wesekht's crypt are covered with funerary texts, now greatly damaged by the infiltration of the annual inundation. The other crypts are plain.

Meht-en-wesekht re-appears unexpectedly as the wife of Setme Khamwas in the demotic story. She is represented as a childless woman who, by means of a magical charm made from a melon-vine, is enabled to bear a child.

These shrines are important from the religious point of view, for the position of Queens in Egypt has been very little studied so far. It is known vaguely that the throne went in the female line, but it is still uncertain whether a Pharaoh had a right to the throne by birth, or whether he succeeded by right of marriage with the heiress. The divinity of the Queen is hardly recognised by modern writers, yet the Queen was actually Isis, "She of the throne"; and as the position of Isis was higher in the eyes of the people than that of her husband Osiris it follows that to her subjects the Queen was as important, if not more so, than the King. From the scanty records which remain it is clear that certain Queens had a special cult. Aahmes-Nefertari, Nefertiti, and Nefertari-mery-Mut were divinities, but the details of their worship have not yet been recognised. At Medinet Habu alone in these small chapels there are preserved texts which show some of the beliefs in the divine power of Queens.

PLATE XXXIX

EDFU: PYLON

[*Face page* 158

Kom Ombo: Hypostyle Hall
(1)

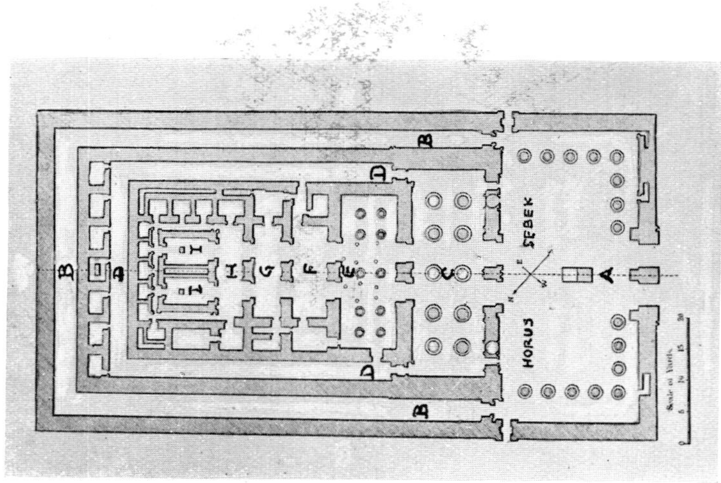

Kom Ombo (Plan)
(2)

XXIX

ESNA

THE name of Esna is one of the many place-names which have descended from the ancient Egyptian, and have not changed through the course of the centuries. To the Greeks the town was known as Latopolis, for the *latus*-fish (*perca Nilotica*) was the deity of the city; but the Egyptians never adopted the Greek name, and from the earliest times to the present day the town has been called Esna.

The temple is almost entirely unexcavated, as the greater part still lies under the houses of the modern town; and to buy up the land and remove a large number of the inhabitants of a thickly-populated district is too expensive a matter for the archæologist. All that can be seen, therefore, of the building is the first hall with its pillars; and this is accessible only because it was used for many years as a warehouse for wool. The level of the ground has risen so high above the temple that the roof of the hall is on a level with the foundations of many of the houses; and the modern entrance is down a steep flight of stairs, making the hall still darker than was originally intended.

The hypostyle hall is built in the majestic style of the Ptolemaic period; twenty-four pillars in six rows support the roof, which is still intact (pl. XXXIX, 1). The pillars are not so large as at Dendera, being thirty-seven feet in height, and about eighteen feet in circumference. The front row of columns which faced the outer court are divided as at Kom Ombos by screen-walls, and have the beautiful foliage-capitals so characteristic of Ptolemaic work. In the axis of the entrance is a doorway in the back wall, leading to the main temple, now buried and consequently inaccessible.

It is more than likely that the buried part of the temple was considerably earlier than the hypostyle hall, but until excavations can be made nothing is certain. Weigall suggests that the hall was added in Ptolemaic times, forming a portico (on the model of the portico of Dendera) in front of a temple of the Pharaonic period, possibly of the XVIIIth dynasty, for fragments of a granite building with cartouches of Tehutmes II were found at Esna by Champollion. The hall was completed by the Ptolemaic builders, but was not decorated; the Roman emperors took advantage of the bare walls, and inscribed their names there in Egyptian hieroglyphs. The emperors even followed a custom common to Egypt (a custom which is both the help and the despair of the historian), of erasing the name of a ruler and inserting the name of his successor. In the temple of Dêr el Bahri these usurpations are extremely frequent, Hatshepsut's name being obliterated and that of one of the Tehutmes being superposed. Rameses II was one of the chief sinners in this respect; he acquired any fine piece of sculpture or architecture belonging to one of his predecessors by the simple means of cutting out the name of the original owner and substituting his own. On the walls of the temple of Esna this system is found unexpectedly among the records of the Roman emperors. The emperor Caracalla, who murdered his brother the emperor Geta, has had Geta's name erased from all the inscriptions where it occurred and has replaced it by his own in the approved Egyptian style.

The dedication of the temple was to Khnum, the sheep-god of the Cataract. The sheep of Khnum differs from the ram of Amon by having horizontal pointed horns, entirely unlike the curved horns of the Theban god. Khnum is one of the creator-gods, and in the New Kingdom is represented as forming the body of the unborn child on the potter's wheel. His cult is found in so many parts of Egypt that it has been suggested that Khnum has superseded early and more primitive gods who had fallen into disrepute. He appears to be indigenous at the Cataract only, for in other places where he is the deity, the worship is often of a more savage character than could be reasonably expected of a sheep-god. At Herakleopolis Magna, for instance, the sheep deity, to whom human sacrifices were offered, has the punning name of *Her-shefi*, which may mean either "Sheep-faced" or "Face of Terror". The real deity of Esna was the fish, a very primitive totem; and it is not at all improbable that the original cult included certain bodily mutilations and sacrifices which were suggested by the legend of the dismembered body of Osiris and the fish. Plutarch points out that the legend of Osiris gives the explanation of the tabu which the Egyptian priests practised regarding the eating of fish, though undoubtedly the real reason was the sanctity of the creature as a totem, the legend connecting it with Osiris being much later.

XXX

EDFU

At one time Edfu was an independent princedom, possibly with its borders extending as far as the Cataract; it was thus the neighbouring principality to Thebes, and though the Pharaohs at Memphis might exercise a nominal suzerainty the rulers of Edfu were probably independent for all practical purposes.

Nothing, however, of an early period has been found in the neighbourhood of the temple; and the building being in good condition little or no excavation has been made there since it was cleared by Mariette in 1860; but there is a record that Imhotep, the great architect of the IIIrd dynasty, built a temple on the site on a plan "which fell from heaven." There are many indications to show that a temple existed at Edfu throughout the historical period, and it must still have been of very great importance when the Ptolemies took over the government of Egypt and built this magnificent sanctuary for the worship of the local god. The earliest remains are of the XIXth dynasty, but these are hardly more than foundations. In the temple itself there is a granite shrine, which stood in the Holy of Holies and was presented by Nectanebo I of the XXXth dynasty; but the temple as it stands at the present day is entirely Ptolemaic. The exact date of the building is known; the foundations were laid on the 23rd of August, 237 B.C., in the reign of Ptolemy III, and the last stone was laid on the 17th of August, 212 B.C., twenty-five years later. This was only the shell of the building; then troubles (riots and consequent bloodshed) broke out in Upper Egypt, and continued for several years; and until peace was restored nothing could be done towards the completion of the temple. Then Ptolemy VII put in all the doors and fittings; the paintings and sculptures were carried out; the temple vessels were prepared, and the furnishings for the worship of the deity were completed; finally on December 10th, 42 B.C. the opening ceremony took place with exceeding great pomp and splendour. The time from the laying of the foundations to the completion of the whole temple was one hundred and eighty years, including the long interruption. Weigall remarks that the temple "was built at the time when Julius Cæsar was setting out to conquer Britain, and when the Roman Imperial age was about to begin, and it had not been in use more than a score of years when the deaths of Antony and Cleopatra brought Egypt under the rule of Rome."

The dedication from the earliest times was to a local deity who was called the Horus of Edfu. It is a noticeable fact that, though this Horus is sometimes identified with the sun-god, and though he is often represented as the Winged Disk, the temple is not orientated by the sun; but, in accordance with the inscriptions in the temple itself, the orientation lay from Orion in the south to the Great Bear in the north. The legend of Horus of Edfu shows clearly that he and the sun-god were two distinct deities.

The legend is found on the walls of the temple, and must therefore have been the authoritative account of the events, which are said to have happened in the one hundred and sixty-third year of the reign of Ra-Harakhti; which points to the fact that the legend records actual battles. The account shows, in more or less poetical language, that Horus of Edfu, presumably a pre-dynastic king, fought the god Seth and his allies (the native inhabitants), defeated them, and took possession of Egypt. The battles traditionally took place on the water; one at Dendera, one in the Fayum, and one on the borders of Nubia. The triumph-song to commemorate these victories is said to have been chanted by the priests of Edfu, the King's daughters, and the women of Busiris and Pe. Though the date is Ptolemaic the hymn preserves the savagery of the primitive time in which it was first composed and sung. "Eat ye the flesh of the vanquished, drink ye his blood, burn ye his bones in the flame of fire," are not the sentiments of the Ptolemaic era, but reflect the fierceness of the uncivilised hordes who established themselves in the Nile Valley, and were perhaps the founders of dynastic Egypt.

The great pylon (A), which gives access to the temple, is divided almost into two parts by the lofty entrance door. The effect of firmness and stability, in which the Egyptian architect so delighted, is very marked; it is chiefly given by the contrast between the slope of the pylon walls and the vertical lines of the doorway. The batter of the walls is still further emphasised by the vertical grooves to hold the flagstaffs, whose fluttering pennons announced to the world that the god was in residence. The pylon is decorated in the usual Ptolemaic manner with gigantic figures of the King slaying his enemies; as this king was Ptolemy XIII, who probably had never seen war in any form, the sculpture is merely an interesting survival of a conventional subject of decoration. The flagstaffs as well as the sculpture on the pylon seem to have been painted, and the flags waving from the top of the masts would also have been brilliantly coloured, so that the first effect of the whole structure would be of vivid colour (pl. XXXVIII).

The long paved forecourt (B), which lies between the pylon and the temple itself, has a covered colonnade on three sides; the walls behind the colonnades were decorated with painted reliefs, which continued the blaze of colour once seen on the pylon outside.

The proportions of the hypostyle hall (C) are deceptive on account of the size of the columns; for though there are only twelve of these, they are so large as to dwarf the rest of the hall (pl. XXXIX, 2). The chambers which lead out of either side of the second hypostyle hall (D) are of special interest, partly because of their names, and partly because of the sculptures which indicate the uses to which the rooms were put. One chamber was the library for the sacred books, and the careful librarian has had the list of books engraved on the walls, and so obviated any possibility of losing or mislaying the catalogue. In the other chamber were kept all the vessels for the ceremony of purification, which every worshipper, from the king down to the poorest fisherman, was expected to undergo; possibly the ceremony was as perfunctory as the ceremonial ablution of the Moslem.

As the temple was built all at one period there has been no alteration in the plan, and the axis runs without deviation from the entrance, through the pylon, to the sanctuary, passing through the forecourt, the great hypostyle hall, the small hypostyle hall, and two vestibules, before reaching the shrine. The small hypostyle hall is almost complete and is a good example of the method of lighting an Egyptian temple; the small apertures in the roof give a purity of illumination which is not obtainable by side-lighting.

In the first vestibule (E), which was called the "Hall of the Altar of Offerings," the daily sacrifice and liturgy were celebrated, and the sculptures represent the King making offerings to Horus. The second vestibule (F) has the curious name of "Hall of the Repose of the Gods;" it is uncertain what was meant by this name, for to the modern mind the sanctuary would be the place where the god would rest. It is possible that the portable shrine, in which the god was carried round the temple on festival days, remained here after the procession, while the priests went away and took some refreshment and repose before putting the image back in the safety of the sanctuary. The stand on which the shrine rested when not being taken in procession is in the sanctuary (G); and at the far end of the holy chamber is a shrine of polished granite for the image of the god.

So far the plan of the temple is simple; but there is a large complex of passages and chambers round the sanctuary. A passage (H) opening from the second vestibule on each side of the sanctuary leads all round the holy chamber, and from it open a number of small rooms. Each room is named, and many of the names have a poetical touch, "The Chamber of the Thrones of the Gods," "The Chamber of the Spread Wings," and the small altar standing in another chamber is called "The Great Throne of the Dispenser of the Sun's Rays." Whoever had the naming of these rooms had a pretty turn of words.

An ambulatory (I) is taken completely round the northern part of the temple; it is entered from the forecourt, or from either of the two hypostyle halls. On the walls of the ambulatory are the records of the Battles of Horus against Seth, illustrated with scenes from the ritual which commemorated the victory. The King, or in his absence the High-priest, represented Horus, and appears to have despatched a certain number of human victims, who were called the allies of Seth and the enemies of Horus.

Stairways led from the first vestibule and the small hypostyle hall to the flat roof of the temple. On New Year's Day the statues of the gods were carried round the temple, partly to be seen of all men, and partly, as Weigall suggests, that the gods might view their lands and possessions. In the processions the lesser folk went first, then came the nobles and priests in order of their importance, the greatest last; and at the end of the procession came the gods. The King or his representative the High-priest walked either at the head or at the end of the procession; there was apparently no rule as to his position in this

Kom Ombo: Hypostyle Hall

[*Face page* 166

PLATE XLII

[*Reproduced by Courtesy of the Oxford University Press*

PHILAE: TEMPLE OF IMHOTEP
(From " IMHOTEP " by J. B. HURRY)
(1)

PHILAE: COLONNADE, SHOWING METHOD OF ROOFING
(2)

Face page 167]

ceremony, and he could choose his own place, either near or at a distance from the divine images.

A number of priests' doors lead from the forecourt to the outer precincts, so that the priests were not obliged to enter by the great main entrance; and by the system of doors and passages within the temple they could pass from any part of the building to any other part without crossing immediately in front of the sanctuary.

There is a Birth-house at the west of the pylon, built in the same period as the temple. The sculptures are chiefly concerned with scenes of rejoicing at the birth of the child-god; the god Bes and various goddesses play on musical instruments, and Khnum, the creator god, forms the body of the child on the potter's wheel.

It was in the temple of Edfu that there occurred the extraordinary phenomenon described by Maspero. In 1901 two of the roofing slabs gave way and others showed signs of collapsing; they were therefore repaired by piercing each slab "by a om. o5c. boring machine, iron stirrups were passed through, bolted below by a nut and plate, and fixed above to iron girders of the necessary strength, which were laid on the upper surface and along the full length of the long axis of the slabs." Maspero then describes the result: "Aussitôt le travail achevé, la pierre, qui était demeurée muette jusqu'alors, prit soudain la parole, à l'étonnement des visiteurs et à l'effroi des indigènes: chaque matin, au moment où le soleil, montant sur l'horizon, se trouvait assez haut pour que ses rayons vinssent effleurer la face supérieure des blocs, des détonations faisaient entendre d'intensité diverse, sèches, courtes, strépitantes, tantôt isolées, tantôt se succédant par series de trois ou quatre." His own experience was that "dès que la lumière toucha la pierre un éclat se produisit, semblable à l'explosion d'un revolver de fort calibre, puis, après un silence de quatre ou cinq minutes, une décharge de bruits moindres, qui rappelait à s'y méprendre le crépitement d'une fusillade

M

lointaine. Deux gros coups résonnèrent ensuite à trois ou quatre secondes d'intervalle, un long silence et, enfin, une sorte de soupir, clair et vibrant." The phenomena ceased abruptly in 1905 when the iron bars above the roofing slabs were removed and replaced by iron girders below, while the spaces of the fallen blocks were filled with wood and concrete.

XXXI

KOM OMBOS

THE name of Ombo or Ombos is taken from the Greek form of the Egyptian Nbi or Nubi through the Coptic Embo. At one time this village was identified as the site of the Ombos of Juvenal's *Satires*, where the poet describes a battle between the inhabitants of Ombos and the inhabitants of Tentyra (Dendera). "A long-standing and ancient grudge, an undying hatred, and a wound that can never be healed, still rages between the neighbours, Ombos and Tentyra. On both sides there is the utmost fury on the part of the vulgar, from this cause, that each locality hates its neighbour's deities, since it thinks those alone should be accounted gods whom it worships itself." [Here follows a long description of the fight with sticks and stones.] "Those who inhabit Tentyra press on (their opponents), all showing their backs in rapid flight. One who through excessive fear was precipitating his pace falls and is captured; whereupon the victorious crowd, after he had been cut into a number of morsels and small portions, that one dead man might suffice for many, eats up the whole of him and gnaws his very bones. . . . The very last of them who came up after the entire body had been consumed, drew his fingers along the ground and tasted some of the blood" (*Satire* XV 11. 33–92). Internecine struggles between villages, although not ferocious as in Roman times, are still a feature of life in the country parts of Egypt. Strabo also notes the hatred of the people of Dendera towards the sacred animal of Kom Ombo: "Tentyra, where the crocodile is held in peculiar abhorrence, and is regarded as the most odious of all animals. Other Egyptians, though acquainted with its mischievous disposition and hostility towards mankind, yet worship it and abstain from harming it. But the people of Tentyra track and destroy it in every way. . . . The people of Tentyra have a dislike to crocodiles, yet suffer no injury from them, but dive and cross the river when no other person ventures to do so."

The worship of the crocodile presents many peculiarities. It was probably an indigenous cult throughout Egypt, except perhaps in the Fayum where the worship may have been introduced from the Delta, for Sobk, the crocodile god of the Fayum, was called the son of the Delta-goddess Neith; in historical times Sobk was the supreme god of the Fayum to the exclusion of all other gods in that district. In Upper Egypt the crocodile was identified with the primitive god Seth, and when the cult of Seth roused the enmity of the Osiris-worshippers the crocodile fell into disrepute as a god in many parts of Egypt. The nature of this savage animal is sufficiently alarming to account for the respectful fear in which it was held. Its cunning habit of lying on the banks of the river looking like a stranded log, its extreme quickness of movement, its immense strength and its invulnerable hide make it an insidious and formidable enemy. It is equally at home on land or in water, travelling long distances in either element, and its ferocity is unequalled among animals; any creature caught in its locked jaws cannot escape. No wonder that it was feared and propitiated by the early inhabitants of the Nile Valley, who may have believed, as so many primitive people believe, that their totem animal would not attack them. Until the introduction of steamers on the Nile the river was infested with crocodiles who levied a heavy toll on the lives of human beings and animals. The river between Silsilis and Kom Ombo was a special resort of the creatures, and Fairholt remarks on "the abundance of crocodiles that infest the stream here, and may be seen basking in great family groups, of all ages and sizes, on the sunny islands of sand in the centre of the river." The tradition of a chain between the rocks on the two sides of the river at Silsilis still continues, and it is said that the chain was used to prevent the crocodiles from passing the narrow strait.

In the myth of Horus of Edfu the Allies of Seth changed themselves into crocodiles in order to escape from the attacks of the Winged Disk; this is a legend founded on early tribal wars and conquests, when the aboriginal crocodile-worshippers (Seth) were conquered by the falcon-tribes (Horus) of Edfu. The modern Kom Ombo, though a centre of crocodile worship in Roman times, was not the Ombos of Juvenal; that city lay at the modern Naqada, which is the next village on the north of Dendera, and was a centre of Seth worship from the earliest times.

The temple of Kom Ombo is peculiar as being in duplicate; the eastern half is dedicated to Sobk, the western to Horus, and each side is merely a reflection of the other, although there is no division by a wall. The greater part of the temple is in ruins, but enough remains to show the beauty of the Ptolemaic architecture. The building occupies a low hill overlooking the river, where the Nile turns from south to west. The encroaching sand on one side and the undermining water on the other have left little of a temple once as large as Dendera but now only a "magnificent torso". Fairholt notes that "the stream is very rapid here, and strikes with great violence on this eastern bank." The temple, therefore, now stands at the edge of the water though originally built at some distance from it; the Nile has evidently changed its course somewhat and has flooded over the flat ground which lay below the building.

The encircling wall of brick is still extant in many places on the landward side; it was pierced with stone gateways, of which the eastern gate bore the cartouches of Hatshepsut and Tehutmes III, showing that a great temple stood on the site in the XVIIIth dynasty.

As the entrance pylon has almost entirely disappeared, having been undermined and washed away by the river, the present entrance is directly into the outer court (A). This is greatly ruined; the roofed colonnade on the three sides has vanished, leaving only the remains of the columns. An altar once stood in the middle of the court, indicated now by a square base with granite troughs for carrying off the blood of the victims. From this court starts the outer ambulatory (B) which surrounds the whole of the more sacred parts of the temple.

A hypostyle court (C) of ten columns is entered by four doorways from the outer court (pls. XL, 1, XLI). The four columns on the east belong to Sobk, the four on the west to Horus, and the two in the middle to both gods equally. The capitals are fine specimens of the foliage capitals of the Ptolemaic era; and there is an added interest in the unfinished carving, which shows that the artists of this late period carried on the method of their earliest predecessors by setting the rough stone in position and carving it when *in situ*. This method is known as early as the pyramid-temple of Zoser, where unfinished capitals were found; and it is seen also at Tel el Amarna in the tombs in the cliffs, and again at Philae. The ceiling of this hall is decorated with flying vultures, whose spread of wing represented protection to the royal founder; and the architraves are covered with astronomical designs. The scenes on the walls are entirely religious, and show Euergetes II and his queen Cleopatra making offerings to various gods. From this hall starts the inner ambulatory (D), which surrounds the second hypostyle hall (E), the three ante-chambers (F, G, H), and the two shrines (I). The inner hypostyle hall is lower than the outer; it also has ten columns with foliage capitals, and its walls are covered with reliefs.

Throughout the temple the sculptures and inscriptions have been painted in brilliant colours, showing that the Ptolemaic artist like his Pharaonic ancestor regarded colour as one of his principal decorative effects. The inner hypostyle hall is much ruined, the roof has gone and the outer walls have been broken down. Of the three ante-chambers and the two sanctuaries, little more than the foundations remain to tell of their glories.

The outer ambulatory is decorated with scenes of offerings of the usual type, the only interesting feature is the representation of a set of surgical instruments, which suggests that the temple was once a centre of healing. The inner ambulatory is of more importance; at the north end there are six chambers, possibly small shrines, these were intended to be decorated with painted sculpture, but the scheme of decoration was never finished, and the sculpture remains in various stages of completion. The centre chamber, which lies in the axis of the temple, is peculiarly interesting, for in the floor is a movable stone, which when raised gives admittance to an underground passage beneath the wall dividing the two sanctuaries. The passage was connected by an opening in its roof with another passage in the thickness of the same wall; and an opening in the roof of the second passage led to a third passage on a higher level; in other words, there are in the one wall three levels of passages, one above the other, entirely hidden from those in front of the sanctuaries, and of which the secret entrance could have been known only to the priests. These facts suggest that the passages were used as a means of impressing the ignorant peasants who worshipped in the temple, and making them believe in miraculous voices and miraculous visions. The priest could enter the room at the back of the sanctuary, and could then appear unexpectedly above the third ante-chamber, having apparently passed through solid roofs and walls; he could also speak in either sanctuary without being seen and so give the oracle of the god to an anxious enquirer. This simple explanation of the mystery which must have surrounded the gods of Kom Ombo is probably true of so-called miraculous performances in the sacred places of every religion in the world.

On the terrace, which once formed the entrance to the temple, is a small birth-house, standing at the south-west angle of the main building. It is so greatly ruined that hardly any of the walls and their decoration survive; only enough remains to show that Euergetes II was the founder. As there were two co-equal gods in the great temple, and their consorts were co-equal also, the deities of the birth-house may have been either Hathor and Khons-Horus, who were associated with Sobk, or they may have been "The Good Sister" and "The Lord of both Lands", who were consort and child of Horus. It is unfortunate that the dedication is unknown, as it might have thrown light on the connection of the two gods of the temple and the reason for the double worship.

Plate XLIII

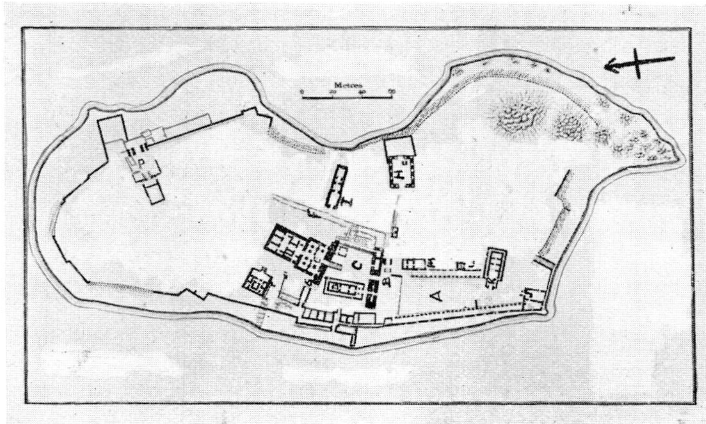

Island of Philae
(1)

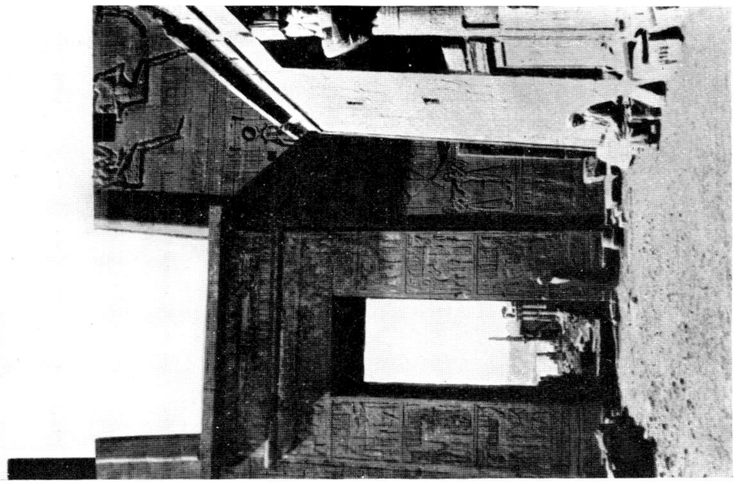

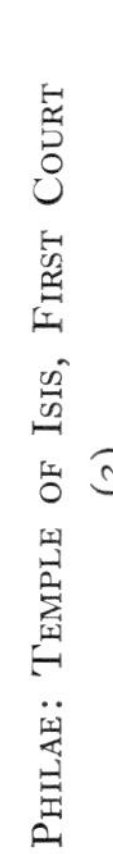

Philae: Temple of Isis, First Court
(2)

PHILAE: BIRTH-HOUSE AND SECOND PYLON
(1)

PHILAE : TEMPLE OF ISIS
(2)

Face page 175]

XXXII

PHILAE

PHILAE is traditionally considered the most beautiful temple in the Nile Valley, but this is due more to its situation than to the architecture; and since the palm-groves, which constituted more than half its charm, have been cut down the temples now have value only as examples of Ptolemaic and Roman architecture. The temples, however, can only be seen when the water is low (pl. XLIV, 2); from December to May the river is held up by the *barrage* and the temples are so completely flooded that only the architraves and cornices are visible.

In ancient times the sanctity of the island was so great that in that small area—500 yards by 160—there are not less than six temples besides other buildings. There is no apparent reason for the extreme holiness of Philae. It is one of the large group of islands strewn along the river for several miles; it is neither the largest nor the smallest of the islands, it is not at either end of the series, it is neither nearer to nor further from the shore than many others, and as the whole district is granitic it cannot have been the rocky character of Philae which distinguished it above all others. It lies where the river suddenly widens before narrowing to the cataract, where the current is consequently slacker, and the accessibility of the island may be the reason for erecting the original shrine, but why the shrine should become so excessively holy is as yet unexplained.

The chief deity of the island was a goddess, who was known in Ptolemaic and Roman times as Isis, but the wild Nubian tribes who worshipped her were the avowed enemies of Egypt, and would hardly have adored an Egyptian goddess or called their own deity by an Egyptian name. Whatever her name may have been, it is certain that she was the great divinity of Lower Nubia, and even "the Ethiopians of the south came down the river yearly to pay their devotion at Philae and to carry away the image of the goddess to their own country in order to bring fertility to their land and their people. The image was duly returned when the ceremonies were ended." The priesthood of the goddess rose to great power in consequence of the importance of their deity, and in the reign of Ptolemy VI (Philometor) they actually administered and ruled the whole of Lower Nubia. It is possible that the beginning of their political power took place under King Ergamenes, a contemporary of Ptolemy II. His capital was at Meroë where the priesthood claimed the right to inform the King when the time had come for him to be slain. When they sent this information to Ergamenes they found they had met their match; he refused to obey their mandate, collected his soldiers, marched on the temple, and slew all the priests. This act, however, appears to have made him unpopular, and he retired to the northern part of his kingdom and made Philae the chief religious site.

But the priests of Philae, though not quite so fierce as their brethren of Meroë, were also capable of trying to strike terror into the hearts of their co-religionists. There are still extant three oracular warnings conveyed by a priest apparently to some great personages of the district; the date is in the mid-Ptolemaic period. "Saith to me the Boy born in Elephantine Espmêti, son of Petarhensnufi, I being at the gates of Khnum-Re, Sopti, Isis and Anuki, and waiting for that which they should desire; for he in whom they shall find guilt, him they put into my hand, saying, 'Make his punishment.' I am the Osiris Espmêti si-Khnum. Say unto Ptra, son of Pshenpwer, I have not allowed thy name to be pronounced, the name which thy mother gave thee, but since I learned thy heart thy name is pronounced Ptra, son of Petarhensnufi. Loathsomeness to the god is that which thou hast done. Thou knowest what thou hast done. Thou hast drunk wine in the garden and the grove which are for the pleasure of User-Wennofri, thou hast done the abominations of Isis; thou hast drunk wine by night when the goddesses were in mourning robes. While the Mourners went with bare breasts, thou didst call to thy wife saying, 'As to Tefni, there is no goddess to compare with her'. Thou hast caused the singers to sing and hast spent a gay hour, awakening User-Bai from his sleep; thou hast cast away the wrapping with the mixed-wine of the Beginning of the Year, drinking with the Blemmyes." Clearly the gentlemen in question had been revelling when they should have been fasting, and the priests were displeased. The second and third oracles show that the god or goddess was slow to punish without giving due warning. "I have said to Patow, son of Harpaesi, saying: 'Write it as a document, let it be taken unto them; there is no causing accusation to be found against thee.' But if thou do not read this before them, crime will be found in thee." And in the third oracle comes the statement, "I do not punish him who doeth ill, until I have opened his eyes."

The Ptolemaic temple shows that, though Isis was the supreme deity, other gods were also worshipped on the island, particularly those most closely connected with her, her husband Osiris and her sister Nephthys. Khnum and Satet as the deities of the Cataract have shrines; Hathor, regarded at this time merely as another manifestation of Isis, has a small temple.

Temple of Isis

The whole island was once surrounded by a stone-built quay-wall with landing steps at many points. At the south end of the island the Porch of Nectanebo (J), standing actually on the quay-wall, is the earliest portion of the temple; it now forms the entrance of the Ptolemaic temple, but was built as the entrance of a magnificent temple which Nectanebo designed to erect. Little of the original structure remains, for the continual wash of water in the annual inundations damaged it so greatly that it had to be restored under Ptolemy II.

The line of the temple follows the curve of the island; Nectanebo's Porch is orientated slightly north-west, the pylons and outer court run due north, and the temple proper points north-north-east (pl. XLIII, 1).

The colonnades (A) which lead up to the first pylon are a good example of Ptolemaic architecture, and are interesting as showing the usual Egyptian method of roofing with blocks of stone which stretch from the wall to the outer columns (pl. XLII, 2). Another interesting point is that out of the seventeen columns of the eastern colonnade only six capitals are finished (pl. XLV, 1, 2); as was the common habit of Egyptian builders, the plain capital was set in place and carved afterwards. Though the processional way between the colonnades is not in the exact axis of the pylon it forms a fine approach to the temple. On the east side in front of the pylon stands the elaborately decorated doorway (B) built by Ptolemy II. Weigall suggests that it was the entrance to a sacred way leading eastwards; if this were indeed the case the sacred way would have led to the so-called kiosk (H), which was another temple of Isis. This doorway is the best-known part of the temple as being the most photographed.

The first pylon, the towers of which stand sixty feet high, was part of Nectanebo's plan, for in the main gateway are scenes of that king in the presence of various gods. The sculptures on the outer walls, however, are in the usual grandiose style of the Ptolemies, whose artists had little sense of proportion in their decorative sculpture,

Philae: Detail of Colonnade
(1)

Philae: Eastern Colonnade
(2)

[*Face page* 178

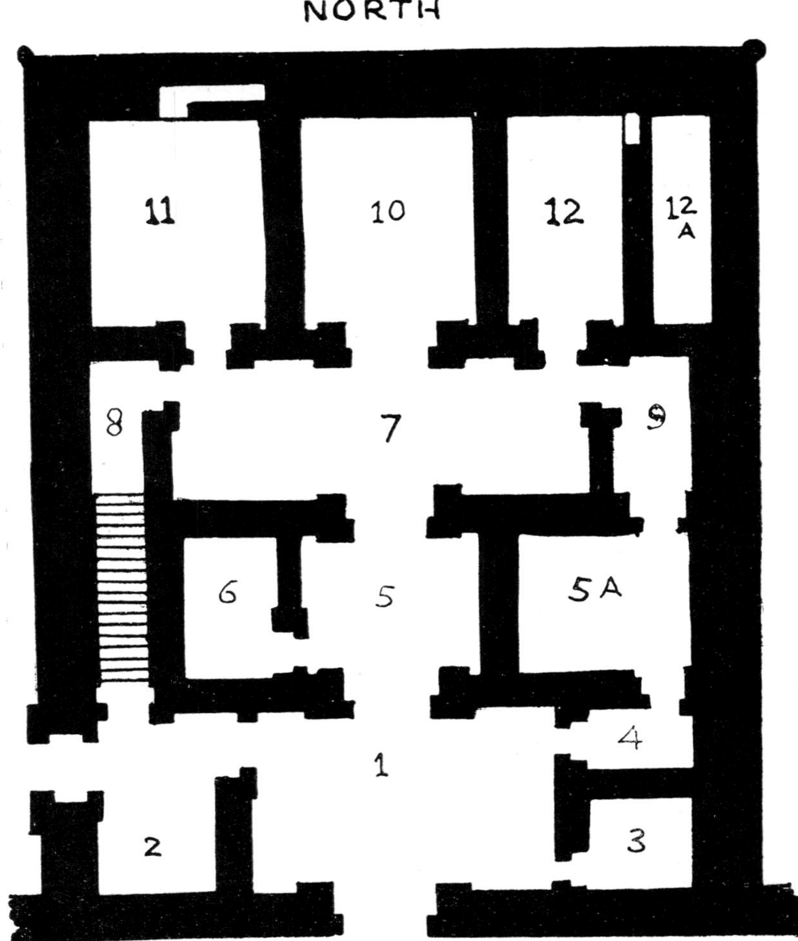

PHILAE: TEMPLE OF ISIS
From Hypostyle Hall to Shrine

and made their figures either so large as to dwarf the building on which they were placed, or so small as to produce a confused effect. The scenes on the pylon are conventional and show a gigantic Pharaoh (the degenerate Ptolemy XIII) slaying a group of enemies at a single stroke before various deities.

In front of the pylon stood two obelisks set up by Ptolemy IX (Euergetes II), both of red granite. They are covered with Greek and demotic inscriptions, of which the most important is engraved on the base of one of the obelisks; it consists of a petition of the priests of Philae to Ptolemy IX and shows that they were suffering from a very real trouble. "To King Ptolemy, and Queen Cleopatra his sister, and Queen Cleopatra his wife, gods Euergetes, welfare. We the priests of Isis, the very great goddess in Abatōn and Philae,—seeing that those who visit Philae, generals, chiefs, governors of districts in the Thebaid, royal scribes, chiefs of police, and all other functionaries, as well as their soldiers and other attendants, oblige us to provide for them during their stay; the consequence of which is that the temple is impoverished, and we run the risk of not having enough for the customary sacrifices and libations for you and your children—do therefore pray you, O great gods, if it seem right to you, to order Numenius, your cousin and secretary, to write to Lochus, your cousin and governor of the Thebaid, not to disturb us in this manner, and not to allow any other person to do so, and to give us authority to this effect; that we may put up a stele with an inscription commemorating your beneficence towards us on this occasion, so that your gracious favour may be recorded for ever; which being done, we and the temple of Isis shall be indebted to you for this, among other favours. Hail!" Painted higher up on the same pedestal was the answer, "To the priests of Isis in Abatōn and Philae, Numenius, cousin and secretary, and priest of the god

Alexander, and of the gods Soteres, and the gods Adelphoi, of the gods Euergetes, of the gods Philopatores, of the gods Epiphanes, of the god Eupator, of the god Philometor, and of the gods Euergetes, greeting. Of the letter written to Lochus, the cousin and general, we place the copy here below; and we give you the permission you ask of erecting a stele. Fare ye well." Then follows the copy of the letter, "King Ptolemy and Queen Cleopatra the sister and Queen Cleopatra the wife to Lochus our brother, greeting. Of the petition addressed to us by the priests of Isis in Abatōn and Philae we place a copy here below; and you will do well to order that on no account they be molested in the matters which they have detailed to us. Hail!"

The forecourt (C) (pl. XLIII, 2) is irregular in plan owing to the angle at which the second pylon is set. On the west side is the birth-house; this shows that the forecourt was not part of the temple proper, as in Ptolemaic times the birth-house is usually distinct from the temple near which it stood. It is, as the name implies, entirely dedicated to the cult of the divine Mother and Child, and in places where there was a Triad of gods the birth-house is for the special worship of the second and third members of the Triad. An entrance has been made in the western part of the pylon to form a processional way into the birth-house (D), which consists of a court, two vestibules and a shrine, the vestibules and shrine being enclosed by colonnades; the pillars of the colonnade on the west of the forecourt have every capital different, giving symmetry of appearance though not of detail (pl. XLIV, 1). The whole of the inside of the building, walls, pillars and screen-walls, are covered with relief sculptures and inscriptions, all of the Ptolemaic and Roman periods. In the shrine the chief scenes are of a falcon standing under a clump of papyrus-reeds, and below this is a seated figure of the divine Mother with her newly-born child in her arms. On the east side of the forecourt is a colonnade which gives access to a series of rooms, probably once intended for the use of the priests, or perhaps for the troublesome guests of whom they complained to the King. It is likely that one at least of these chambers was used for making up the temple-incense, for on the doorway is an inscription giving the proper method for its preparation.

On the north of the forecourt is the second pylon which is reached by a stairway as the temple is on a slightly higher level than the forecourt. The pylon is decorated in the usual ungainly style of the later Ptolemies; more interesting than these sculptures are the faded Christian paintings within the doorway. In front of the pylon and to the east a mass of the natural rock protrudes, which has been worked down and inscribed with a record of lands granted to the temple.

The inner court (E) of the temple proper is unusually narrow; this is clearly done by intention in order that the open space between the roofed colonnades at the sides could be covered with an awning; the rope-holes for securing the awning are still visible in the stone cornice; in the fierce heat of a Nubian summer this protection was very necessary. At the east side the natural rock has not been cut away and the pavement has been laid round it; Weigall notes this fact and suggests that the rock was too sacred to be removed. A similar example of the sanctity of the rock on which a temple is built is seen in the mosque of Omar at Jerusalem, which stands on the site of the temple of Jehovah; the rock comes through the pavement and according to Muhammedan tradition is too holy to be levelled as it was on this rock that Abraham was about to sacrifice Isaac (the Muhammedans say Ishmael), and that when Muhammed took his flight to heaven, he was caught up from this spot. The reliefs on the walls of the inner court are of religious subjects, showing the Ptolemaic Pharaohs performing ritualistic acts before various divinities. There is here a mixture of religions, for the early

Christians used the court as a church, and crosses of the usual Coptic form are cut in the walls in every direction. A Greek inscription commemorates the conversion of the heathen temple into a Christian church, "This good work was done by the well-beloved of God, the Abbot-Bishop Theodore. The cross has conquered and will ever conquer." Modern Christians have followed the example of their predecessors in disfiguring the temple by placing in 1841, a large inscription of Pope Gregory XVI over one of the doors.

A vestibule (5) and an antechamber (7) lead from the inner court to the sanctuary (10). On either side of the ante-chamber and the sanctuary are rooms which receive light only through the dimly lighted chambers from which they open. They are practically completely dark, yet the walls are as much and as carefully decorated with sculptured reliefs as the well-lighted parts of the temple. On the east side doors are so arranged that a priest could pass to the holy place without going through the antechamber. From this side also is the entrance to the stairway leading to the roof of the sanctuary (pl. XLVI).

The sanctuary, unlike the generality of shrines, has two windows which admit the light freely. The sculptures show very definitely the supremacy of Isis in the temple, for on the principal wall of the shrine—the one facing the doorway—she, and she alone, is represented. No statues of her remain, as they were probably destroyed by the iconoclastic zeal of the Christians.

The roof has a sunk chapel at each corner, the walls of which are covered with religious sculpture. The most important of the four chapels is at the south-west corner, where on one wall the death and resurrection of Osiris are depicted. Specially interesting is the strange scene of the reconstruction of the dismembered body of Osiris. According to the legend Osiris' body was torn in pieces by his murderer Seth and scattered broadcast over Egypt; Isis searched for and recovered all the fragments, and so

DEBOD: SECOND PYLON
(1)

PHILAE: HYPOSTYLE HALL
(2)

[*Face page* 182

PLATE XLVIII

DEBOD: CHAPEL OF AZREKH-AMON
(1)

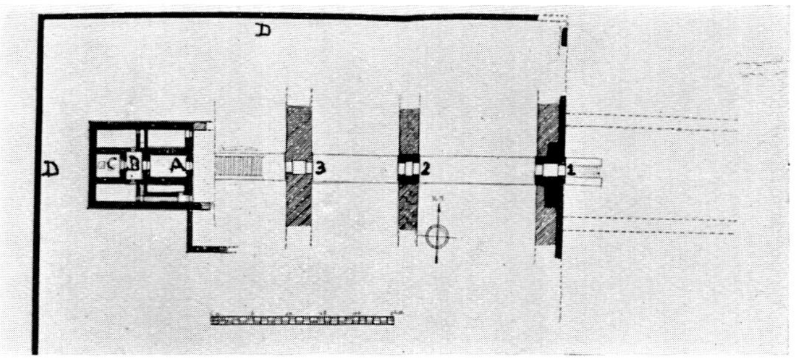

DEBOD (PLAN)
(2)

DEBOD: SHOWING THE THREE GATEWAYS
(3)

was able to reconstruct the body and put life into it again. In this scene two goddesses are engaged in the work, and have been so far successful as to reconstruct the legs and lower part of the body. Another scene shows the god in the form of a mummified falcon lying on a bier; and in a third scene Osiris lies dead on his bier while a priest pours water over him and causes flowers and plants to spring up from his body. This is an illustration of the hymn to Osiris, which says that all things come from him, "the tree and its foliage, reeds, barley, wheat, and fruit trees."

The outside of the walls of the temple are covered with sculptured scenes, showing the emperor Tiberius offering human and other sacrifices, and standing in the presence of the chief gods of Philae and a host of minor deities. As is the case throughout the entire temple, the gods represented are Egyptian, no Nubian deities occur here; Mandulis of Talmis had a small chapel leading off the east colonnade, but was not worshipped in the temple itself.

The remains of the girdle-wall (F) are found along the east side of the temple. It has vanished on the west; the only vestige of it on that side is the gateway of Hadrian (G), a stone portal which admitted into the precincts through a vestibule. As the door looks out on the island of Bigga, the sculptures refer almost entirely to Osiris. The chief scene is the king carrying a box on his shoulder and with Thoth and Isis approaching a building with two doors; beyond these is the Nile with a crocodile bearing Osiris on its back and swimming towards a pile of rocks, probably intended for the island of Bigga, which contained the peculiarly holy shrine known as "Abatōn" dedicated to Osiris. Another sculpture shows the figure of the Nile-god within a cave surrounded by a snake, representing the "hidden cavern" from which the river was supposed to rise. The priests of Philae and Bigga clearly claimed that their islands were the source of the great river, a claim which would enhance the sanctity of the site.

XXXIII

PHILAE—THE SMALLER TEMPLES

THOUGH a considerable number of small temples and shrines existed on the island, there are only four which are worth noting; these are the Kiosk, the temple of Hathor, the temple of Nectanebo, and the temple of Arsnuphis (Yri-hes-nefer).

The Kiosk (H), also known as "Pharaoh's Bed", is a small hypæthral shrine, which was never finished. Fourteen pillars connected by screen-walls enclose a rectangular space, which has neither roof nor floor. Above the foliage capital of each pillar the abacus rises to such a height that the capital appears as a kind of excrescence on the column; a plain architrave with a cavetto cornice above increases the peculiar effect and makes the temple look as though the roof had been unskilfully raised half a storey higher.

There are three entrances; a wide door on the east and west sides, and a small door on the west; the plan is therefore like the kiosk of Qertassi, which also is rectangular, and has fourteen pillars and three doorways. Like Qertassi also there is little decoration; only two reliefs were finished; these show the emperor Trajan making offerings to Isis and Osiris in one scene, and to Isis and Horus in the other; the dedication is inferred from the fact that Isis is represented in both sculptures.

The Kiosk is considered one of the most beautiful buildings in Nubia. The group of pillars with their richly sculptured capitals and the plain entablature give a wonderful effect of lightness, which is increased by its being open to the sky.

Kiosks appear to have been introduced by Romanised architects, and are found chiefly in Nubia; the explanation of these roofless buildings is obscure, unless it is for the same reason that colonnades are built in Italian gardens, as a place in which to sit in the cool of the evening. As the gods had the same feelings and desires as their human creatures, the Kiosks may have been built in order to give them the same kind of pleasure.

Philae: Temple of Hathor

Due east of the Great Temple, and just outside the temenos wall, stands the miniature temple of Hathor (1). Though small it is more than a chapel, for it consists of a hall, a vestibule, and several other chambers which though now entirely ruined must have included a shrine and side-chapels. It was built by Ptolemy VI (Philometor) and Ptolemy IX (Euergetes II), and was added to and partially rebuilt by the emperor Augustus. The dedication was to Hathor; a Greek inscription on the wall announces to the world that "Hiertia directed a prayer to Aphrodite"; though the fact in itself is not so interesting to posterity as it was to Hiertia it shows clearly that the Greeks regarded Hathor merely as another name for their own goddess Aphrodite.

The style of the architecture is of no special interest; the columns and screen-walls being in all respects like those in other temples of the period. Where this temple differs from any other is in the reliefs, for they are more in accordance with the Hellenistic conception of Aphrodite than with the stately Egyptian Hathor. The god Bes is shown playing on a musical instrument and dancing, musicians play on harps and flutes and reed-pipes, and an ape performs on a guitar. The King's offerings are very unusual: he gives sistra to Sekhmet, a coronet to Hathor, wine to Isis and Hathor, and an ape-amulet to Tefnut. Seven goddesses are represented as receiving gifts or worship; Mut of Thebes, Sekhmet of Memphis, Satet of the Cataract, Isis, Nephthys, Tefnut and Hathor. The subjects of the reliefs and the number of the goddesses suggest that this temple commemorates the birth of a god, the seven Hathors being in attendance, Bes dancing the birth-dance, and all the world rejoicing. It is singularly unfortunate that the sanctuary is so utterly destroyed, for there if anywhere would have been the image of him whose birth caused so much joy. As all the deities of the island bear Egyptian names the Divine Child was probably called Horus, although it was at the birth of Osiris that the oracle spoke, "at his entrance into the world a voice was heard, saying, 'The lord of all the earth is born'."

Philae: Temple of Nectanebo

The temple or Porch of Nectanebo I (s) stands on the brink of the river at the south end of the colonnades which lead to the Great Temple. The entrance was from the north, i.e. in the reverse direction from the entrance of the Great Temple. The "porch" consists of a kiosk-like structure with a hypæthral court on the west side. The kiosk has pillars on both sides, those on the east are greatly ruined, though the foundations are preserved. The pillars on the west, however, are in almost perfect condition; the capitals are peculiarly interesting as showing the transition between the Pharaonic and Ptolemaic form of foliage capital. The architectural fault so common everywhere in Philae is seen here in the tall abacus, which owes its height to the desire of the architects for ornamentation and to the desire of the priests for religious emblems; the head of Hathor surmounted by a headdress formed of a shrine and a sistrum is the decoration almost invariably used. The result of the high abacus is to weaken the effect of the capitals, which do not support the architrave and appear in the wrong place. Between the pillars are screen-walls, on which are scenes of Nectanebo in the presence of various gods; it is noticeable that the deities are almost entirely Egyptian, not Nubian. The repetition of the goddess Isis suggests that she was the deity of the temple. As in other Nubian kiosks there are three doors; here they are placed on the north, east and west sides. The door on the west leads into the hypæthral court, a plain structure without colonnades.

Philae: Temples of the Eastern Colonnade

Leading from the southern end of the eastern colonnade is the ruined temple of Arsnuphis (K). This name is the Hellenised form of the Egyptian Yri-hes-nefer, "The Good Guardian". He is one of the many obscure deities who may be little known only because no excavations have yet been made in the centres of their worship. Arsnuphis belongs to northern Egypt, possibly even the Delta, as he is called the son of Ra and Bast; but his cult is best known at Aphroditopolis, the tenth nome of Upper Egypt. The chief deity of that district is indicated by the name, and his connection with the goddess in her own city may perhaps account for his shrine at Philae.

The temple is entered from the east at the south end of the colonnade, of which it appears to be entirely independent; it is enclosed by a high wall, and consists of four chambers, the last of which was the sanctuary where a granite altar once stood. All the walls were covered with reliefs, inside and out, but these are of little interest, consisting only of religious scenes.

The temple was erected by Ptolemy IV (Philopator) and the Nubian King Ergamenes, and was enlarged by Ptolemy V who seems to have erased the cartouches of

Ergamenes. Ptolemy VII (Philometor) and the emperor Tiberius are represented in the presence of various gods, among whom Arsnuphis is conspicuous. Unfortunately the inscriptions are too greatly destroyed and too conventional to give any real information about the deity of the temple, who is addressed in one place as "Great god, lord of Philae. Thou art as a negro, O lord of Punt. For thee is set up a great flagstaff."

The temple of Mandulis. Of the seven doors which open out of the eastern colonnade five lead into the court to which the shrine of Mandulis belongs. This chapel is now so ruined that it is impossible to be certain if it were ever of any importance. It consisted of two axial chambers with the sanctuary to the north. The real interest of this little shrine lies in the dedication, as it is the only temple on Philae dedicated to a Nubian god. Mandulis was one of the great gods of Nubia, but the Egyptians preferred their own deities.

The temple of Imhotep. The temple lies at the north end of the colonnade, from which it is entered by one of the seven doors, though there is also an entrance from the south in the axis of the temple; the door from the colonnade and the axial door both lead into the forecourt. The temple itself consists of two small chambers, neither of which is decorated. It is possible that the chapel was never finished, for the only inscriptions are on the entrance doorway, as though the sculptors had begun the decoration where it would be first seen, meaning to continue in the less visible parts later. The inscriptions are in the name of Ptolemy V (Epiphanes), who is also shown in the presence of Imhotep and other gods (XLII, 1).

XXXIV

DEBOD

The ancient name of this temple was *Ta-het*, "The Abode", or "The Dwelling-place". The dedication offers some difficulty, for Isis of Philae and Amon of Thebes and of Napata were equally worshipped; and the two shrines within the sanctuary show a double cult as at Kom Ombo (pl. XLVIII, 2).

The temple is orientated east and west with the sanctuary to the west. The approach is from a stone quay on the river-bank, then by a paved road of a few yards in length. At high Nile the water rises over the remains of the quay and the road, and nearly reaches the first gateway. The road, now almost entirely destroyed, was continued to the entrance of the temple; the axis of the temple is not quite straight with the quay, as the building follows the line of the rocky knoll on which it was erected.

The stone girdle-wall (D) has been largely destroyed within the last hundred years; in 1821 it was in sufficiently good condition to be measured. It was approximately rectangular, the difference in length between the north and south sides was eight feet, between the east and west sides ten feet. The temple was not in the exact centre of the temenos, but stood nearer to the north. There was only one entrance to the precincts, this was through the first gateway.

Three stone gateways (1, 2, 3) stand between the river and the temple (pl. XLVIII, 3); all are built like pylons, with battered walls, vertical doorways, cavetto cornices, and torus rolls. The north and south sides show that each gateway was the entrance through a thick wall, which presumably stretched across the whole width of the temenos (pl. XLVII, 1). Such an arrangement of gates suggests the outer and inner courts of an Egyptian temple, but the extreme thickness of the walls and the fact that they were of brick militates against this suggestion.

The three gateways are on the same level, but the temple itself is slightly raised, and was reached by an inclined way or steps. The columns and screen-walls which formed the façade have collapsed, the remaining fragments show that the capitals were unfinished when erected, they were merely rough hewn and the foliage detail was never completed.

The so-called "Chapel" (A) probably comprised the whole of the original temple (pl. XLVIII, 1). It was built by the Nubian King, Az-kher-Amon, who reigned in the second century B.C., and was contemporary with Ptolemy V (Epiphanes). It is a plain rectangular chamber without niches; the walls are covered with sculpture which, although it is of the kind demanded by the Egyptianised taste of the Nubian King, is effective and appropriate. The scenes are entirely religious; the King, wearing one of the surprising head-dresses dictated by the ecclesiastical fashions of the period, worships various deities, with a special devotion to Isis and Amon.

Round this chapel the rest of the temple was built in late Ptolemaic and Roman times, the walls of the newer part are not bonded with the walls of the chapel, but are quite distinct. The vestibule (B), which is undecorated, lies between the chapel and the sanctuary; the roof still remains, and the chamber would be entirely dark but for a large window in the wall above the level of the chapel roof.

The sanctuary (C) leads out of the vestibule. It is a dark chamber in which two rose-granite shrines once

Qertassi
(1)

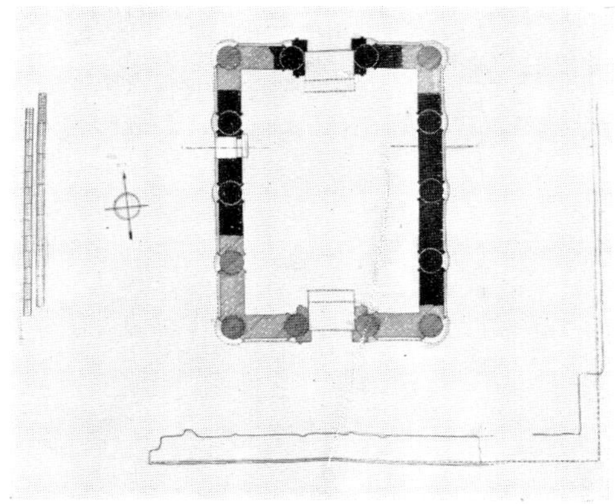

Qertassi (Plan)
(2)

Plate L

Kalabsha
(1)

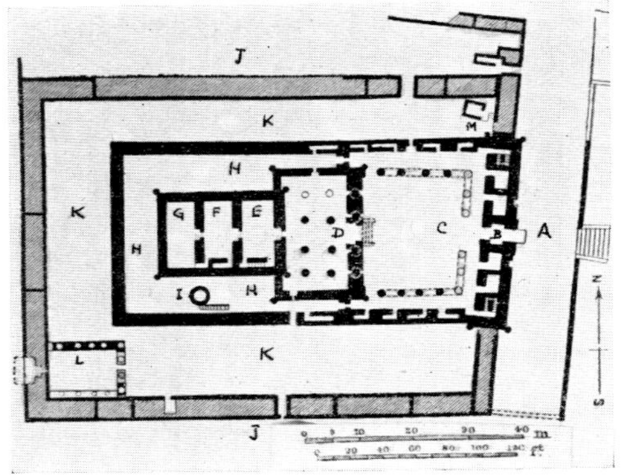

Kalabsha
(2)

Tâfa
(3)

Face page 191]

stood; the larger, dedicated by Ptolemy IX, stood in the centre of the sanctuary; the smaller, dedicated by Ptolemy XIII, was at the north side. Both shrines were *in situ* at the beginning of the last century and were in sufficiently good condition to be deciphered. Since then both have been broken by the local inhabitants of the village; the larger shrine was removed altogether, the pieces of the smaller were left lying on the floor of the sanctuary, they have been put together, and the shrine now stands in the centre of the chamber.

At the north side of the sanctuary is a plain chamber entered from the vestibule; it is undecorated, and the roof is still intact, but a window just under the ceiling admits a small amount of light. On the east side there is an opening, only large enough to admit a human body, leading to a small chamber in the thickness of the wall, obviously the treasury of the temple. The room to the south of the vestibule leads to the stairs which ascend to the roof with an opening to an upper chamber above the room to the south of the sanctuary. The other chambers of the temple are undecorated and of no interest.

XXXV

QERTASSI

QERTASSI (also spelt Kertassi, Gertassi, and Jertassi) lies on the west bank of the Nile. The village evidently took its rise when the sandstone quarries in the cliffs began to be worked, this was probably in the early Ptolemaic period, as the stone for building the Great Temple at Philae was brought from here.

The little temple stands on a rocky platform, and it could never have been any larger, as it just fits the rock on which it is built. In form it is a kiosk like "Pharaoh's Bed" at Philae, though considerably smaller. The dedication is uncertain, as the temple is uninscribed. Inscriptions in the neighbouring quarries refer to Isis of Philae, but mention is also made of a Nubian god and goddess, whose names are given in the Greek as Pursepmunis and Sruptikhis. The harshness of sound and complication of form suggest that the names are composite and contain more than one element. This is one of the most northerly places in which the names of Nubian deities are encountered; the deities of Qertassi are probably entirely local, as they are not found elsewhere.

The temple is of one period, the second or third century A.D., but the dating cannot be fixed precisely. The whole building is only twenty-five feet square, and consists of a single hall or court orientated north and south, and originally surrounded by fourteen columns connected by screen-walls. These walls are decorated with the torus roll and have a cresting of snakes. Of the fourteen pillars six remain, and on one side the whole entablature is still in place. At each end of the court is a doorway, so that the building is the same at each end and has no shrine. The south part is destroyed, but at the north the doorway is still intact; it is flanked on either side by a Hathor-headed pillar. As is usual with capitals of this type they are square though the pillars are round; and the head of Hathor, with cow's ears and surmounted by a pylon, is placed on all four sides of the capital. The stonework shows that the doors were folding, probably two-leaved like Egyptian doors, and opening inwards; the holes in the stone for bolts and other metal fixtures are still to be seen.

The pillars of the hall on the east and west sides are of the ordinary Ptolemaic type, the foliage capitals being particularly rich. The capitals were arranged in pairs, the northern pair are alike and differ from the others, which again seem to have been each like its opposite. Stone architraves were laid from pillar to pillar, and above these the long stones with cavetto moulding completed the entablature (pl. XLIX, 1, 2).

The cutting of the stone shows that wooden fixtures were placed above the screen-walls, probably some kind of wooden screen. A great deal of wood seems to have been used throughout the temple: the screens, the high doors on the north and south, and the small square-headed door cut through one of the screen-walls on the west were of wood which has disappeared long since; for in timberless countries like Nubia and Egypt, wood is the first building-material to be removed from a disused structure, whether dwelling-place or temple.

XXXVI

TÂFA

Two temples stood in this once populated spot, and until as late as 1870 both were above ground. Now the northern building has disappeared, pulled down for material to erect the houses of the neighbouring village; but travellers of the nineteenth century saw, sketched and planned it. Weigall also records an interesting local belief that "travellers returning to Tâfeh from the north see the temple standing as it used to do, but as they approach nearer it vanishes."

The southern temple stands on a platform of masonry which must have raised it well above the village surrounding it, and makes it now a conspicuous object. Only what may be termed the "kernel" of the original building is still in existence, and consists of one chamber with six pillars, all of which, as well as the roof, are intact. Roeder conjectures that originally the building was much larger and had at least a façade, but he acknowledges that his investigations have yielded no trace of any further structures (pl. LI, 1).

The axis of the temple runs due north; the entrance was by two doors in the south wall, a large one in the centre and a smaller one to the east of it. The main doorway is flanked on either side by a pillar with foliage capital and plain abacus, so built into the wall as to appear like a pilaster; above is a cavetto moulding ornamented with two winged disks and with a cresting of disk-crowned snakes. The eastern doorway is lower and narrower than

TÂFA: PTOLEMAIC CAPITAL

(2)

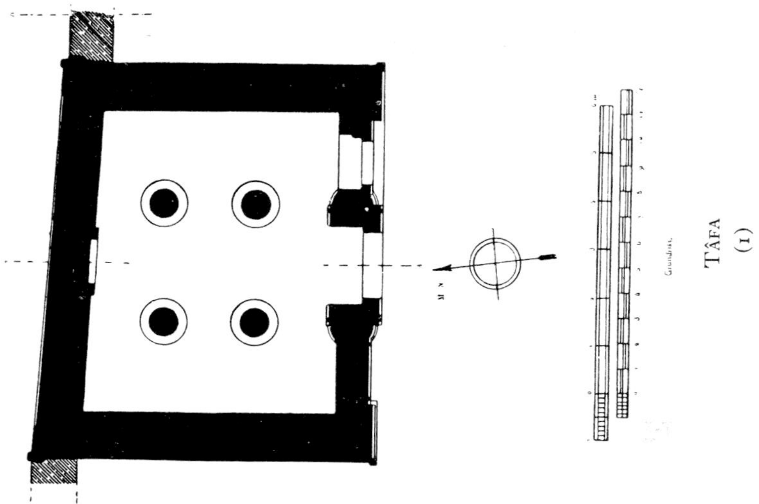

TÂFA

(1)

PLATE LII

BÊTEL WALL: FLUTED COLUMNS

Face page 195]

the central; it also has pilasters, cavetto moulding, winged disks and snake-cresting. On the west side of the main doorway, where another door might have been expected to correspond with the one on the east side, the space is filled by a plain slab of stone with torus roll and cavetto moulding. The front is thus divided into three parts, and above each part between the top of the doorway and the architrave is an open space which admits air and light to the interior of the building. The whole front is outlined with a torus-moulding, above which the entablature consists of a cavetto cornice with the winged disk as the central ornament. Roeder points out that the whole front has been considerably altered from its original appearance; the two pillars now built into the wall having been free-standing and enclosed later (pl. L, 2).

The hall to which the doors give access is of an irregular shape, as the north wall is not parallel with the south wall, nor at right angles with the east and west walls. Four pillars with foliage capitals support the stone roof (pl. LI, 2). The pillars beside the main entrance are of the same type as those within the hall, and bear the same architraves as the pillars on the corresponding sides of the hall.

The date of the temple is probably within the Christian era, it is one of the last pagan buildings to be erected in Nubia. It was seized by the Christians and turned into a church, and a Greek inscription found in the precincts records the fact: "In the name of God the Father, the Son, and the Holy Spirit. Written on the 18th of the month Khoiakh, indiction 9, year of Diocletian 427. In the year 13 of the Christ-loving King, Mercurius, was accomplished this good work of sanctifying this place in the year 5 of the God-guarded priest Johannes, the 18th of the month Khoiakh. Amen." The actual date according to our calendar is December 14th, 710. The inscription is historically important as fixing the exact date of King Mercurius, "who was called, on account of his good works, the New Constantine."

Tâfa is also the scene of a surprising story about Moses, related by Abu Salih. "It is said that the prophet Moses before he went out from the face of Pharaoh was sent by the latter upon an expedition into the land of the Soudan. Now in this land, into which Pharaoh commanded Moses to make his expedition, there were many adders and noisome beasts. But the prophet Moses was wise and was assisted by God in all his actions; so he marched into the Soudan with his army, accompanied by birds such as cocks and owls, and entered into the uninhabited deserts where the ancient and noisome beasts and reptiles dwelt; and when they heard the voice of the cocks and of the owls sounding by night and by day, they fled away and remained no longer in their habitation, but vanished from the path of Moses; and so he marched onwards and saw none of them. Then Moses came to the city of Tâfeh, and halted before the city; and the king's daughter saw him and the birds with him, and she loved him; and so she sent messengers to him offering to open the city to him, and pointing out to him the road he should take in order to conquer the city, and thus she made the capture of the city easy to him. So Moses captured the city by offering general quarter, and he granted immunity to the inhabitants, and they brought him money."

XXXVII

KALABSHA

THE modern town of Kalabsha, which is situated almost on the line of the Tropic of Cancer, stands on the site of a city known to the ancient Egyptians as Thelmes and to the Romans as Talmis. It was of great importance at one time as the principal town of the Dodekaschoinos, the country ruled over by the priests of Philae.

The original temple was built in the XVIIIth dynasty either by Tehutmes III or by his son Amenhotep II, was added to by various later Kings, fell into ruin, and was entirely rebuilt under the Ptolemies and decorated by the Roman emperors. It was dedicated to the Nubian god Marul or Malul, whose name was Hellenised as Mandulis. He was entirely local but had a widespread reputation and is often mentioned in other temples, though always as Malul of Talmis. Little is known of Mandulis; he is usually equated with Osiris, showing that he was a god of fertility; and Weigall suggests that he was a deified man, arguing from the fact that the hieroglyphic determinative after the name of Malul is of a man and not of a god. As Osiris was certainly a god incarnate in human form this suggestion is probably the true explanation.

There is an interesting Greek hymn to Mandulis in the temple, of which the following is a translation: "When I had gone to contemplate this blessed place of peace, to breathe in the air the sweet breath of life, new ideas, strange to my former life, whirled round my spirit on all sides. Since my conscience had no vice with which to reproach me, my nature then called on me to cultivate the mystic works. Then, becoming a scholar, I composed a varied song, thanks to the noble eloquent spirit which the gods bestowed on me. When the Muse made me clearly pleasing to the gods, I shook the Bacchic crown adorned with flowering grass, and then a grotto of sleep invited me to descend thither, although I feared a little to give myself up to the visions of a dream. And sleep stealing me straightway, transported me quickly into a country which is dear to me. For it seemed to me that I was bathing my body in the streams of a river, and that the sweet abundant waters of the Nile laved me pleasantly. I thought that I was singing a beautiful song in noble words inspired by the Muses, in harmony with all the nymphs. Thinking it a dainty left by Greece I have written on the stone this inspiration of my wise heart. After having moved my limbs as one moves in tune, obeying the baton, I called in, to join with the song, the help of this inscription, without knowing whether I was leaving a cause for blame to unsympathetic souls; but the Master called me to speak this learned poetry. Then the great Mandulis descended from Olympus. He softened the barbaric style of Ethiopia, and exhorted me to sing in sweet Hellenic verse that, thanks to thee, man's life can vaunt that it is foreseen, that Day and Night adore thee, and all the Hours; they call thee Breith Mandulis of the same parents, divine stars rising to heaven together in one constellation. Thyself, thou badest me to come and inscribe this in thine honour, and to expose these learned writings to the harsh judgment of all men." Mandulis is also described as "with shining cheeks, going on Isis' right, and, as if proud of the grandeur of the Romans, giving oracles like the Olympian god that he is." This mention of Isis suggests that the

PLATE LIII

DENDUR: ENTRANCE PYLON
(2)

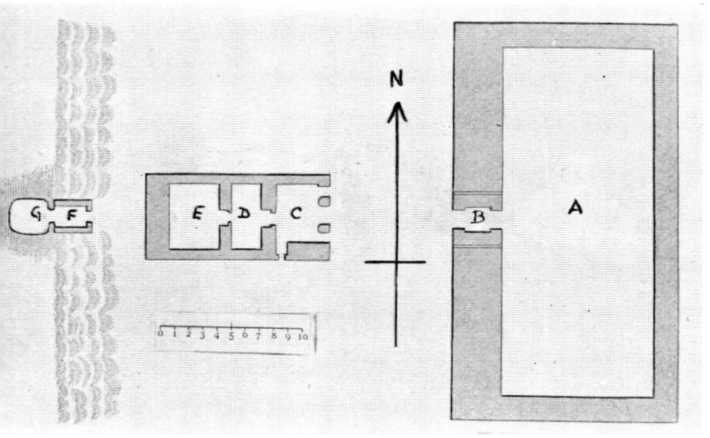

DENDUR (PLAN)
(1)

[*Face page* 198

PLATE LIV

[Photograph by Mr. Percival Hart

DENDUR: COLUMNS

Face page 199]

companion deity, Breith, is the Nubian equivalent of the great Egyptian goddess, and is again a proof that Mandulis was the Nubian Osiris.

Viewed from without the temple presents a magnificent sight. Brockedon's description is worth quoting: "Its noble elevation, the two magnificent terraces by which the entrance is approached, the grand range of mountains by which the scene is backed, the rich groves of palms and acacias in front, and even the mud houses of the population, add to the striking grandeur of the temple and the picturesque character of the whole scene."

The temple stands on the west bank of the Nile, and is orientated east and west. The approach was by a causeway of masonry leading from the river and ending in a flight of steps, which rise to a long terrace (A). The terrace continues the whole length of the façade, with which it is parallel; but both the façade and the pylon (B) are skew to the rest of the building. The reason of this is unknown; the angle is original, and there seems to be no defect in the ground, as at Abydos, to account for the eccentricity of the ground-plan. Thus the entrance is directed to the north-west while the temple is orientated due west (pl. L, 1).

The two towers of the pylon still stand and were entered by doors from the court. Stairways lead to the top, and it is not unlikely that the priests of ancient days, like the modern tourist, climbed the stairs in order to enjoy the view of the temple and the surrounding country.

The outer court (C) had a row of columns on three sides, north, east and south. The greater number of these columns are still standing, they have the usual Ptolemaic foliage-capitals. On account of the angle of the east side the pillars of the north and south sides are not equally spaced. The screen-walls are sculptured, and one bears an historical inscription written in red paint, the language being Greek of a sort. "I, Silko, King of the

Nubadae and all the Ethiopians have come to Talmis and Taphis once. Twice I fought with the Blemmyes, and God gave me the victory with the three. Once I conquered again and took their cities; I sat down with my people at first. Once I conquered them and they did me honour, and I made peace with them, and they swore to me by their idols, and I believed their oath that they were good men. I went away to the upper regions where I became ruler. I was not at all behind the other kings but even before them; for as to those who contend with me, I do not cease to occupy (lit.: sit down in) their country until they have honoured me and besought me, for I am a lion to the lower districts and a citadel to the upper. I fought with the Blemmyes from Primis to Lêlis once, and the other of the Nubadae; I laid waste their country since they would contend with me. The lords of other nations who contend with me, I do not suffer them to sit down in the shade, only in the sun, and I have not permitted water [to be taken] into their houses, for my servants carry off their women and children." Though the style is like the Triumph-songs of the Pharaohs, Silko appears to have been a Christian; the humiliation of the conquered chiefs by making them sit in the sun is an interesting touch.

This temple was apparently a favourite place for learning to be exhibited, for there is also a poem in Latin in which the first letters of each line spell out the name of the author, Julius Faustinus. It is a eulogy of Hadrian, but the corruptness of the Latin and the floweriness of the verses make it impossible to translate; only here and there can a few words be understood, "The Muses, Pallas and Apollo have fled from the wickedness of the world to the pious time (*pia saecula*) of Hadrian."

Small chapels or crypts were constructed in the thickness of the walls on the north and south sides of the outer court, and a door in the north wall gives access to the outer passage or ambulatory round the temple precincts, and also to a crypt.

The hypostyle hall (D) was never completed as regards the decoration, though this cannot be considered as a defect, for the sculptures are coarse and the colouring crude throughout the temple. Miss Edwards says that the taste displayed "was of the vilest"; she adds in a note: "I observed mauve here for the first and only time; and very brilliant ultramarine. There are also traces of gilding on many of the figures." Champollion also criticises the decoration in no measured terms: "Les sculptures barbares du temple de Kalabschi, qu'on a fait riches parce qu'on ne savait plus les faire belles." The roof of the hall was intact when Burckhardt visited the temple, he describes it as "formed of single blocks of stone reaching the whole breadth, and upwards of three feet in thickness". This, like so many other temples in Nubia, suffered at the hands of the local inhabitants in the nineteenth century.

Three chambers lie in the axis of the hypostyle hall; an outer vestibule (E), an inner vestibule (F), and a shrine (G). Both vestibules are a bewildering mass of stairs, chapels and crypts in the thickness of the walls. In the wall of the inner vestibule is a chapel with a crypt; it has been suggested that these were for the cult of Osiris, who as a chthonic god was often worshipped underground or in darkness.

The inner ambulatory (H) opens from the outer court and forms a passage round the vestibules and shrine. Within it and to the south of the shrine is a Nilometer (I), still in a good state of preservation; Nilometers are generally late in date, and this is no exception to the rule.

A girdle wall (J), twelve feet thick and built of masonry, enclosed the precincts, leaving an open space—the outer ambulatory (K)—between it and the temple wall; in accordance with the general irregularity of the plan, the space on the south is considerably wider than the corresponding space on the north. In the south-west corner of the ambulatory there is a chapel (L) with an open court and a rock-hewn shrine; this was probably the birth-house, so commonly found as an adjunct to Ptolemaic temples. At the north-east corner is another small chapel (M) also of the Ptolemaic period.

Like almost all the temples of Nubia, Kalabsha was used as a church by the Christians. The terrible dilapidation of the building is generally attributed to an earthquake, but it must be remembered that the fierceness of the early Christians, when at last they gained power, was often wreaked on the heathen places of worship, and that to burn and destroy the heathen and all their works was accounted as pleasing in the sight of the Lord. How much ruin can be wrought by human hands can be seen in the destruction of the solid stone roof of the Hypostyle Hall of this temple (pl. L, 3).

XXXVIII

BÊT EL WALI

WILKINSON says that the temple of Bêt el Wali is, next to Abu Simbel, the most interesting monument in Nubia.

The hill on which it is situated is within a mile of the temple of Kalabsha, and though the two temples are near together in date of foundation and in distance they were dedicated to different gods. Kalabsha worshipped Malul and Wazt, at Bêt el Wali the deities were Amon-Ra, Khnum and Anuket.

Compared with the great fortress-like temple of Kalabsha the temple of Bêt el Wali is very small, consisting only of a rock-cut shrine, a pillared hall also cut in the rock, and an outer court. It was founded by Rameses II, whose interest in Nubia is shown by the number of temples for which he was responsible.

The outer court is greatly ruined, for only the two side walls remain. On these Rameses is represented as charging furiously against the Nubians in his chariot; other scenes show the dismay of the enemy and their flight, and finally the presentation of the "tribute" of Nubia to the Pharaoh by the Viceroy of Nubia and other Egyptian officers. Nubia was a rich country, and the tribute included large quantities of gold, leopard-skins, elephant-tusks, decorated chairs, plants and ostrich eggs, as well as live animals such as cattle, antelopes, and giraffes. Other scenes represent campaigns against the Libyans and Syrians; and here, as is usual with the sculptures of Rameses II, the detail and the human interest are very great; in many cases also the spirited figure of the King as he fights in single combat is worth noting.

Three doorways lead into the rock-cut hall. The pillars in this hall are fluted, and are of the type known as proto-Doric, a type not found in the other temples of Nubia; they are inscribed with vertical lines of hieroglyphs (pl. LII). All the walls of the hall are sculptured with religious scenes and ceremonies, such as the sacred dance before the god, the burning of incense, and the presentation of offerings; the king is also shown on familiar terms with the various gods and goddesses, who treat him as one of themselves. There are two scenes; in one the King is shown smiting a negro, in the other his victim is a Libyan. It is possible that these scenes actually represent human sacrifice of the type recorded by Amenhotep II at Amada, but Rameses II, though always rejoicing in being depicted as a great warrior, does not appear to have been unnecessarily bloodthirsty.

The sanctuary is decorated with reliefs, on which the colour is still visible and is of the same beautiful quality as in the temples of Egypt, quite unlike the coarse style of the Roman period. At the end of the sanctuary are three statues of gods, probably Amon-Ra and Harakhti with Rameses himself between, but they have been so violently defaced that they are unrecognisable.

The Christians took possession of this temple, and used the two rock-cut chambers as chapels, while in the court they built a brick church. Few traces remain of these sacred places, but the domes in the court and the destruction of the "idolatrous" sculptures and statues still bear witness to the fervour of the newly-converted.

XXXIX

DENDUR

THE little temple of Dendur—one of the smallest in Nubia—lies on the west bank of the Nile, and is orientated east and west. The entrance is from the river, and the magnificent terrace (A) which overlooks the water is extremely fine. A short causeway leads up to the pylon, of which only the richly decorated stone gateway remains (B), the sculptor has left no blank spaces on the stone work, the whole surface of the door—inside, outside and on the reveals—is covered with decoration. Under the cavetto cornice on the river-face is the winged disk, and below that is the torus-roll; the architrave had scenes of offerings, now greatly damaged; down either side of the door are again scenes of offerings with appropriate inscriptions. The landward face of the door has similar ornamentation (pl. LIII, 1, 2; LV).

The court, to which the doorway gives access, is on a higher level than the terrace. The brick wall which once enclosed the court on the north and south has almost disappeared, only enough remains to ascertain that the walls were of the same materials as the now vanished pylon which bounded the east side of the court. There were originally entrances on the north and south sides, for inclined ways lead up from the lower precincts.

At the west end of the court is the tiny façade of the temple itself, formed of two columns with foliage capitals, (pl. LIV) and with screen-walls between them and the walls of the inner court. The screen-walls are almost entirely destroyed, but there is still enough to show the original serpent-cresting. Across the façade the cavetto cornice has disappeared but it remains at the sides of the building. The pillars as well as the whole of the façade are ornamented with relief-sculptures of scenes of the worship of various deities. Throughout the temple the officiant in the religious scenes is the Pharaoh of the period, i.e. the emperor Augustus.

The roof of the inner hall (C) is intact, and is decorated with flying vultures and with yellow stars on a blue ground. The walls are also covered with sculpture of the coarse Roman type, chiefly representing religious scenes. The most interesting sculpture is of a large figure of a couchant lion, with its face turned to the spectator; it is painted yellow, and has a green (originally black) mane, beside it is a tall stand on which is a small bowl, both stand and bowl painted yellow to represent gold; the bowl is an incense-burner for in it are two balls of incense from which rises a green flame. The doors which pierce the west and south walls are part of the original plan, but the door in the north wall is a later alteration for it has been ruthlessly cut through a sculptured scene; this was probably done when the temple became a Christian church. The west door, leading to the ante-chamber and the sanctuary, is fully decorated with the winged disk above and scenes at the sides. Here again a lion is reproduced as a separate and important entity; he sits on his haunches holding the flowering head of a reed between the front paws and another between the hind paws; behind him is a sheaf of lotus-blossom; he faces inwards towards the door, and the figure is duplicated on the other side of the doorway.

The ante-chamber (D), is roofed, but is entirely undecorated, and the sanctuary is also plain with the exception of a stele on the west wall. This stele, which takes the place of the divine image in other temples,

DENDUR: SHOWING PYLONS AND TEMPLE
(1)

DAKKA
(2)

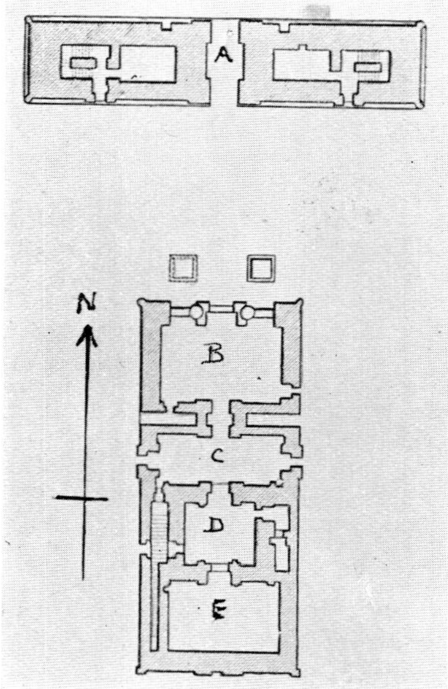

DAKKA
(1)

GERF HUSÊN [Photograph by Mr. Percival Hart
(2)

has a cresting of serpents above the cavetto moulding below is the winged disk, and the main part of the stele is divided into two panels, in the upper panel the deified Pa-Hor worships Isis, in the lower the deified Petisi adores Osiris. The sanctuary (E) is partly built and partly cut out of the rock which here begins to rise very sharply.

The chief interest of the temple lies in the dedication, which is to two brothers, Pa-Hor and Petisi, the sons of Kuper; these men were deified, though for what reason is as yet uncertain. Both of them met their death by drowning, and it is noteworthy that in many parts of the world certain forms of death by drowning appear to confer deification on the victims; in medieval Christian Europe this deification was modified to canonisation. In the ancient world the reason seems to be that the drowned person was either the King himself or his substitute, who was put to death as a means of ensuring a rainfall (in Egypt the inundation) sufficient for the proper watering of the crops and the consequent abundance of the harvest. In the temple of Dendur the two men are called *Hsy*, "The Drowned", or *P-shai*, "The Protective Deity" (the Greek equivalent of this word being Agathodaimon). When they are called "The Drowned" they wear the insignia of royalty; when they are called "Agathodaimon" they wear the insignia of the god Osiris. They are then, like Antinous, the substitutes for the King, drowned in his stead for the fertility of the country. As substitutes they represented the King and wore the royal crown, and because the King was Osiris, the giver of fertility, they wore the head-dress of the god. This would account for the fact that the Emperor himself was not ashamed to be represented kneeling in worship before the divine men who were sacrificed for him and who by giving their lives brought prosperity to his country.

Behind the temple is a small rock-hewn chapel (G), which may have been the tomb of the two deified brothers and possibly the original shrine for their cult. The entrance is by a plain square-headed door cut in the rock; in front of the shrine was a small open court (F), of which only traces remain. Probably the shrine was abandoned when the temple was built, though it may have retained some of its original sanctity. The temple does not seem to have been built altogether in connection with this shrine, as its axis does not lie directly in the axis of the shrine but rather to the south. The axis of the shrine is in a direct line with a peculiar cavity made in the back wall of the temple-sanctuary, and Blackman suggests that the cavity may have been used for oracles of the deified brothers.

The temple was used later as a Christian church, which was consecrated in A.D. 577. The date can be recovered from the Coptic inscription, which runs thus; "By the will of God, and the command of the King Eirpanomë and Joseph the exarch of Talmis zealous in the word of God, and by our receiving the cross from the hand of Theodorus the bishop of Philae [Pilak], that I Abraham, the humblest priest, should place the cross on the day of the foundation of this church, which is the 27th day of Tobë, Indiction 7, there being present Shaï the Eunuch, and Papnoutë the Stepharis, and Epiphanios the Keeper of the Seal, and Sirma the Courier. May every-one who shall read these writings offer of his charity a prayer for me."

XL

GERF HUSÊN

THE temple of Gerf Husên is on the west bank of the Nile, and is partly rock-hewn, partly built. It is one of the many temples with which Rameses II enriched Nubia, and is often said to be a poor and inferior copy of the great rock temple of Abu Simbel. Unfortunately the exact year in which Rameses founded either temple is unknown, so that it is impossible to be certain from the date alone whether Gerf Husên is a copy, a prototype, or even an independent creation. But a comparison of the plans of the two temples shows that the outer parts of the temple of Gerf Husên have no parallel at Abu Simbel, and the inner chambers of the two are alike only in having Osirid columns of the Pharaoh who was responsible for both temples (pl. LVI, 2).

The pylon, which once stood at the entrance of the temple of Gerf Husên, was seen and noted by various travellers of the early 19th century; it has now disappeared entirely, probably undermined and then carried away by the inundation. With it went also an avenue of sphinxes and the four statues which stood outside the pylons, and which appear on Gau's plan.

The forecourt (A) is entered by a flight of steps and is partly excavated in the rock, which forms the wall for about half its length on each side, the rest of the wall being built of blocks of stone. The court originally had a colonnade round all four sides, which was roofed with stone; the pillars of the eastern side were of the papyrus-type, those on the west had Osirid figures of Rameses standing against the square piers (pl. LVI, 1).

At the west end of the forecourt is a narrow doorway (B) into the cliff, the whole front of the rock being carved in the form of a pylon. The narrow door leads into a rock-hewn hall (C) decorated with six colossal statues of Rameses as Osiris, three on either side, marking the axis to the shrine. The hall is forty feet square, and the pillars are twenty-eight feet high. On each side of the hall are four recesses, so arranged as to be seen in the spaces between the pillars; in each recess there are three figures sculptured out of the solid rock representing the King between two deities as being himself a god. The arrangement of the recesses and the pillars indicates that in every direction to which the worshipper might turn he would there behold the divine King, the royal god. The divinity of the king is still further expressed in the scene sculptured in relief on the east side of the hall, where Rameses is shown as King making offerings to himself as god.

Through another narrow door opposite the entrance access is obtained to a smaller hall (D) with two square pillars; this is the vestibule from which the shrine opens. The walls of the vestibule are covered with relief-sculptures showing Rameses making offerings to the various gods of Nubia and Egypt, he himself being included among the number. North and south from the vestibule are long narrow chambers for storage of the sacred vessels used in the services of the gods or for the reception of offerings.

On the west side of the vestibule are three doors leading to shrines, the centre shrine (E) is the main sanctuary of the temple; and there the sculptures show that the figures of the gods were carried in sacred boats as at Abydos. A stand for supporting the divine boat stands in the centre of the main sanctuary, hewn out of the rock.

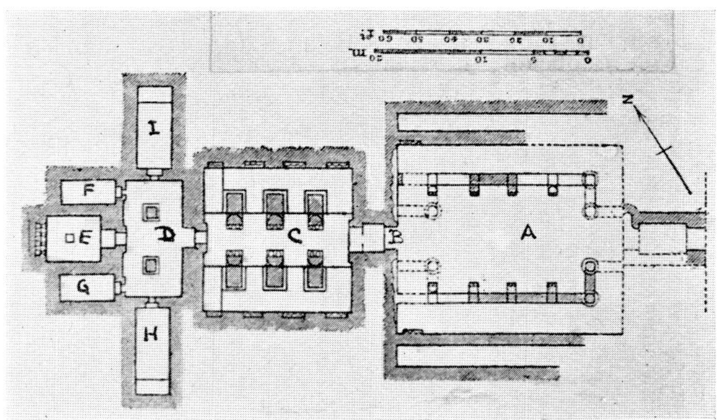

GERF HUSÊN (PLAN)
(1)

GERF HUSÊN: TEMPLE OF RAMESES II
(2)

EL MAHARRAKA
(3)

Plate LVIII

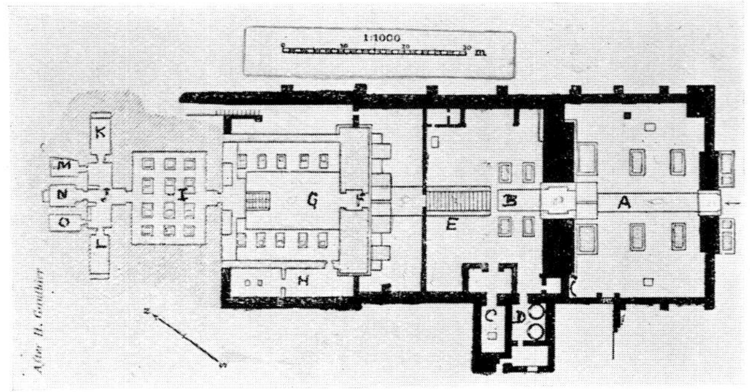

Es Sebua

(1)

[*Photograph by Mr. Percival Hart*

Es Sebua

(2)

Behind it is a recess where, seated in row in the solemn darkness, are the four chief deities of the temple, Hathor, Ptah-Tatanen, Rameses himself, and Ptah. The two smaller shrines are undecorated.

With the exception of the four plain chambers (F, G, H, I) leading out of the vestibule the whole temple was originally covered with painted relief-sculptures. The Osirid-pillars also were undoubtedly painted, so that the whole temple glowed with colour. But the effect could never be so fine as in an Egyptian temple, for the Nubian sculptor was not on the same artistic level as the Egyptian. The gigantic figures standing against the columns in the halls are impressive owing to their size, but they are not of the same fineness and beauty of execution as the figures of the same king in his own mortuary temple, the Ramesseum at Thebes. The Nubian sculptor tended to make all the human figures short and fat and heavy, whereas the Egyptian figures are inclined to be thinner than nature, but with a dignity and beauty all their own.

It is not certain why the gods of Egypt should have been carried so far south when there were so many local gods in Nubia, although the Egyptians, like the Greeks, were apt to give the names of their own gods to foreign deities. Yet it is surprising to meet Ptah of Memphis at Gerf Husên and in other parts of Nubia in company with Mandulis or the local forms of the falcon god.

There is nothing to show whether Rameses II ever inspected this temple personally; the Viceroy of Ethiopia was responsible for the making and decoration, and it seems hardly likely that he would have been at the expense without some prospect of showing the result to his royal master.

XLI

DAKKA

THE oldest part of the present temple of Dakka was built by that King Ergamenes who had the courage to defy the whole priesthood of Meroë when commanded by them to submit to be sacrificed. But the history of the site reaches back to the Middle Kingdom as shown by the size of the cemeteries of that period which exist in the desert to the west. Wherever the Egyptians went they built temples; and though one generation might pull down and destroy the work of its predecessors, it was only to build again in the fashion of the newer period. It was not for nothing that the Egyptians had achieved so great a reputation for piety in the time of Herodotus, who says that "they were the first to assign altars, images and temples to the gods." It is therefore extremely probable that a temple of the Middle Kingdom once existed on this site. The Greek name of the place was Pselkis, closely following the original Egyptian form *Per-Selk*, "The House of the Scorpion". The temple is not, however, dedicated to the Scorpion-goddess, as might have been expected, but to Thoth of Pnubs, the word *Pnubs* refering to that tree which here was accounted holy.

Ergamenes was contemporary with Ptolemy II, Ptolemy III and Ptolemy IV, the last of whom is responsible for some of the sculptures; Ptolemy IX (Euergetes II) built the hall, and finally the sanctuary was rebuilt and the pylon added under Roman rule.

The temple, which lies north and south, is built on the west bank of the Nile, in a desolate open spot not far from the river. It was approached by a road outlined by stone walls and ending in a terrace; though these are now almost completely destroyed there is evidence that they date to the XVIIIth dynasty (pl. LVII, 1).

The Roman pylon (A) is almost complete, and though of late date it preserves all the features of the earlier Egyptian work; the slope of the walls, the two towers, the central gateway, the cavetto cornice and the grooves for flagstaffs, show that the old tradition was still in full vigour. The stone used in building appears hardly affected by the passage of time, it still presents a smoothness of surface almost as fresh as when first erected. The internal arrangements of the pylon, with guardrooms and stairways, are worth noting. Greek and Roman visitors to the temple made their way up the pylon steps, not to admire the view, but to make their orisons to Thoth of Pnubs, and they cut in the stone the outline of their feet to show where they had stood and as an everlasting memorial of their piety; but like tourists of both ancient and modern times they could not resist the temptation of cheap notoriety by cutting their names as well.

That the pylon ever gave access to an outer court cannot be stated with certainty as nothing now remains but an open space without any trace of building between the gateway and the temple proper (pl. LV, 2).

The temple consists of four chambers: a hall (B), a transverse chamber (C), an antechamber (D), and the shrine (E). The façade of the hall is formed by two pillars with foliage capitals, the pillars being connected with the side walls by screen-walls in the usual way. This part of the temple was used later as a Christian church, and Christian paintings once covered the sculptures; now the paintings have peeled off or powdered away and the gods of the old religion have become visible again.

The doorway in the rear wall of the hall leads into the transverse chamber, which was originally the outer court of the temple of Ergamenes. In Roman times a staircase was built leading from this chamber to the roof, where a hidden chamber was contrived in the thickness of the wall. Such hidden chambers are not uncommon in Ptolemaic and Roman temples; they may sometimes have served as strong-rooms for the temple treasures, but in many cases they were certainly for magical and oracular purposes.

The ante-chamber is all that remains of the work of Ergamenes. Part of the roof is still intact, and the walls were once completely covered with reliefs; these are all of religious subjects, the most interesting being a scene of Ergamenes making an offering to the goddess Anuket and the "Pharaoh of Senemt". This last epithet rouses some curiosity as to which god was intended. Senemt is the ancient name of the island of Bigga, where stood the *Abatōn* or Tomb of Osiris, but the figure of the "Pharaoh of Senemt" is not that of Osiris. It is possible that it is an epithet of the god Seth, who was always the chief god of the south, for at this time his name had so fallen into disrepute that it might have been more politic to use a respectful designation rather than the name. Isis was important in the eyes of Ergamenes, for he records that she gave him all Ta-kens (Lower Nubia) from Aswan to Takhompso, the district which is mentioned in the Greek *ex votos* as lying between Egypt and Ethiopia.

The sanctuary has little of importance. The reliefs are truly Egypto-Roman in style; Miss Edwards describes them as "atrocious; such mis-shapen hieroglyphs; such dumpy smirking goddesses; such clownish kings in such preposterous head-dresses." The only scene which is of any interest shows the sacred tree, under which sits the baboon of Thoth while the Nile-god pours water over its leaves. The doorway of the sanctuary is axial but the chamber is asymmetrical, as a wall was built on the west side to enclose a staircase.

Round about the whole temple, enclosing all the

Amada [Photograph by Mr. Percival Hart
(1)

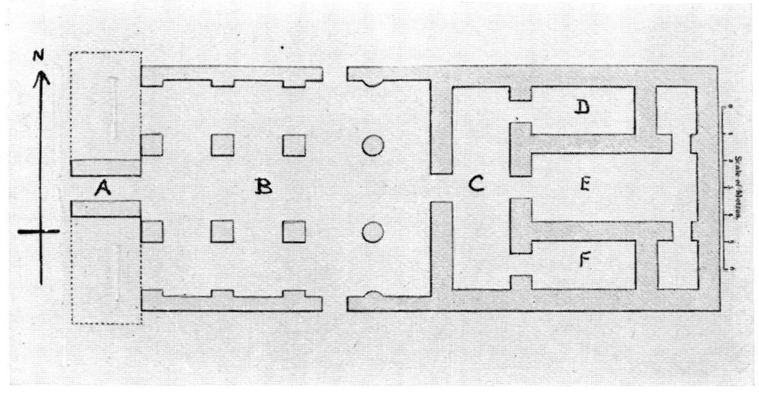

Amada
(2)

[*Photograph by Mr. Percival Hart*

AMADA: HYPOSTYLE HALL
South Row of Osirids

precincts, was a brick girdle-wall, the scanty remains of which can still be traced.

The temple had a great vogue among Greek and Roman visitors to Nubia, many of whom recorded their vows and prayers to the god. The usual form of acknowledgment of the divine grace and favour is as follows: "I Sarapion, son of Euphron, strategos, came and adored the very great god Hermes". Rather more elaborate and pompous is Apollonius's inscription: "Apollonius, strategos, came to give justice to mortals. As to thee, O King of Pselkis, who guardest the country between Egypt and the distant land of Ethiopia, he addressed to thee this day his prayers, and has sacrificed to thee". An ardent worshipper records the fulfilment of a vow: "To the very great god Hermes Paytnubidis, who presides over the frontier regions of Egypt and Ethiopia, Saturninus Vetranus Aquila, zealous for religion, executed the gilding of the temple in accomplishment of a vow for the safety of his children and his wife."

XLII

EL MAHARRAKA

THE cult of a sacred tree was so important at this place that the town was known in Greek times as Hierasykaminos, the Holy Sycomore. It marked the boundary between the Ptolemaic Kingdom and Ethiopia proper and formed part of a small buffer state.

There was probably a temple on the site at an early period, but of this nothing remains; the present building dates to the time of the Roman occupation and was never completed. On one of the pillars is an inscription giving the dedication, which is unique in Nubia. The god of the temple is Sarapis, whose temples were usually in the north of Egypt, where the cult was introduced by the Ptolemies. Sarapis was popular where European ideas prevailed, as at Alexandria, and had a considerable vogue in the Roman Empire, even in Rome herself. His popularity at Rome may have been due to the mystery which surrounded Egypt in the eyes of the fashionable Romans, for as Egypt was the personal property of the Roman Emperor and did not belong to the State it became invested with an air of secrecy and strangeness. A Roman official, even a Senator, could no more enter the country without a permit from the Emperor than he could enter private grounds without permission from the owner. Egypt was, therefore, an object of much curiosity to the Romans; marvellous stories as to its prodigies were current, and its gods were credited with great magical powers. Under the Ptolemies Sarapis was the chief god, completely ousting Ra and Amon; he continued as chief god till the introduction of Christianity when his magnificent temple at Alexandria was attacked by the fanatical followers of the new religion, the image destroyed and the building burnt down.

Miss Edwards speaks of the temple of El Maharraka as "picturesquely desolate". There is reason to suppose that it was overthrown by an earthquake while still incomplete, for Burckhardt's description shows that some convulsion of nature caused its utter ruin. "The southern wall has fallen down, apparently from some sudden and violent concussion, as the stones are lying on the ground in layers, as when placed in the wall; a proof that they must have fallen all at once" (pl. LVII, 2, 3).

The temple consists of only one small hall, round which was a row of pillars joined by screen-walls. The entire building is unfinished, the pillars still in the rough, the capitals unworked, the screen-walls uninscribed. The whole appearance of the temple suggests that the catastrophe, which overtook it while in course of erection, so discouraged the builders that they abandoned the work. That it was intended to be different in detail from other temples is shown by various architectural features, particularly the spiral staircase which led to the roof of the colonnade.

The temple stands a little way inland, and between it and the river was a shrine, which may have been entirely independent of the temple or may have been attached to it in its cult; the connection between the two is uncertain. The shrine is of the late Roman period, and was presumably dedicated to Isis, for on one of the walls is a rudely carved relief of Isis dressed like a Roman lady and seated under the sacred sycomore, while her son Horus, most inappropriately garbed in a Roman toga, offers her a cup of wine; on one side stands Thoth, on the other is Isis again, both represented in the Egypto-Nubian manner.

There are a few Greek inscriptions from the temple, of which the one found by Miss Edwards is the longest, "The vow of Verecundus the soldier, and his most pious parents, and Gaius his little brother, and the rest of his brethren."

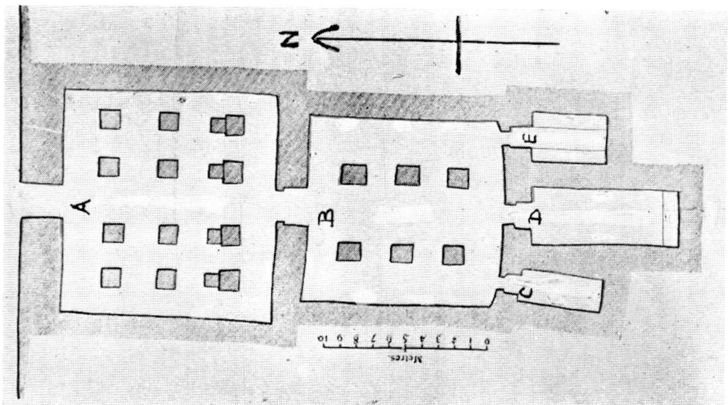

DERR
(2)

DERR: HYPOSTYLE HALL
(1)

[*Face page* 218

Abu Simbel: Showing Sand-river and both Temples
(1)

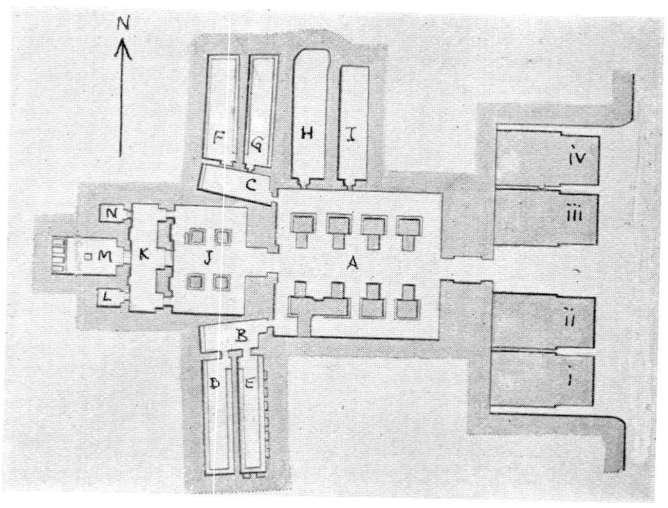

Abu Simbel: Great Temple
(2)

XLIII

ES SEBUA

The elaborate temple of "The Lions" was probably erected on an earlier site, as pottery of the Middle Kingdom has been found in its near neighbourhood. If, however, there was a Middle Kingdom temple here it has vanished long since; but it is quite possible that the present sanctuary was begun in the XVIIIth dynasty, for Amenhotep III made a rock-cut shrine near by. The existing temple was dedicated to the gods Amon and Ra-Harakhti, which also suggests the XVIIIth dynasty as the period when the temple was begun, though the decoration is of the XIXth dynasty.

The plan of the rock-cut halls and chambers, as well as of the hall immediately outside the cliff, is the same as at Gerf Husên, Derr, and other cliff-temples of Nubia.

A girdle-wall of brick originally enclosed the whole outer structure, and a gateway of stone set in the wall gave admission to the first of the forecourts. Outside the gateway on each side stood a statue of Rameses II and a sphinx. Within the court (A) the axis of the temple is marked out by a double line of sphinxes; as these are in the form of lions they have given the modern name of Es Sebua (The Lions) to the temple and to the village. On either side of the court, between the sphinxes and the wall, stands a stone basin for ceremonial purification.

At the further end of the court another pylon gave access to a second forecourt (B), and here the axis is marked by two hawk-headed sphinxes on either side; these represent Ra-Harakhti, one of the protecting deities of the temple. A double forecourt, such as is seen here and also at Luxor, shows that an addition has been made after the completion of the original temple; the addition at Luxor was probably due to Rameses II, and it appears to be the same at Es Sebua. On the west side of the court is a small temple (C) containing an altar dedicated to Amon-Ra and Ra-Harakhti; in the store-room (D) of this shrine there are two circular corn-bins, evidently for keeping the corn for the offerings.

Continuing up the axis of the temple a long stairway (E) starts about half way along the court, and leads through a pylon (F) to the terrace on which the temple itself is built; this pylon is perhaps the original entrance to the sacred precincts. Though the pylon is decorated with scenes of Rameses slaying enemies, and though the colossi fronting it are also of Rameses, it is quite possible that the actual structure is of the XVIIIth dynasty. The central doorway of the pylon leads into what was probably the original forecourt (G) of the temple, with colonnades of square pillars supporting Osirids of the King. These colonnades were roofed, leaving only the centre of the court open to the sky. The sculptures on the walls and the pylon are of little interest, except for the two long processions of Rameses' daughters. On the west is the Sacrificial Chamber or Slaughter House (H), where the animals were killed and dismembered before being offered to the gods. All ancient temples must have been similarly equipped, but it is seldom that the actual place survives as it does here.

A staircase at the north end of the court ascends to a small terrace on which stands the great hypostyle hall (I), partly hewn in the rock, partly constructed of masonry. In the axis of the hall are six square pillars with colossal Osirids of the king; and behind them are six more plain square pillars, making twelve pillars in all which support the roof.

From the hypostyle hall opens the usual transverse vestibule (J), with two lateral chambers (K, L) and a triple sanctuary (M, N, O), as at Gerf Husên. The main shrine (N), in the axis of the temple, contains a niche with three statues of the deities worshipped in the temple, Amon, Rameses, and Ra-Harakhti.

Like so many Egyptian temples Es Sebua was turned into a Christian church, after the conversion of the country. By the exigencies of the situation the church had to be orientated west and east, as the remains of the apse and the altar show. Fanatic zeal was not so strong here as at Derr, and the sculptured scenes were merely painted over with figures of saints instead of being ruthlessly destroyed. The result of this partial obliteration has often a strange effect, to which Weigall calls attention as "the rather curious spectacle of Rameses IInd offering flowers to St. Peter, who is shown with a large key in his hand."

XLIV

AMADA

Miss Edwards describes this temple as "a shed without and a cameo within". It stands on the left bank of the Nile, which here flows round a bend almost due south through barren uninhabited desert. The reason for building a temple in such a place is not apparent, but it seems to have been a sacred spot from the XIIth dynasty. It is possible that Senusert III erected the first shrine, for his name occurs in the temple, and the names of persons of the Middle Kingdom are found inscribed on the rocks in the neighbourhood, Senusert's shrine, if there ever was one, has disappeared long since, and the present building dates to the middle of the XVIIIth dynasty, having been erected by Tehutmes III and his son Amenhotep II; the figures and cartouches of the two Kings alternate throughout the temple. Tehutmes IV made some additions and alterations, and the Pharaohs of the XIXth dynasty continued the decoration, after which the Egyptian Kings appear to have lost interest in the temple and it was left to decay.

The dedication is to Amon-Ra and Ra-Harakhti, showing that these gods were regarded as the protectors of Nubia as early as the time of Tehutmes III. The figures of Amon did not escape the iconoclastic zeal of Akhenaten, whose hatred of Amon induced him to erase the figures and name of that god wherever they occurred, although when he came to the throne he seems to have been an ardent worshipper of Amon. Sethy I restored the erased figures and name at Amada as he did in so many temples in Egypt; he appears to have devoted much of his time and wealth to this pious duty.

Abu Simbel (Interior)
(1)

Abu Simbel: Temple of Rameses II
(2)

[*Face page* 222

Plate LXIV

Abahuda
(2)

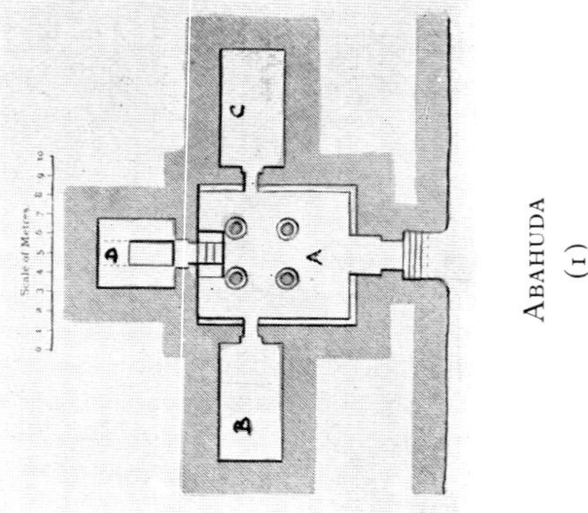

Abahuda
(1)

Of the brick entrance-pylon which faced the river nothing now remains but the stone doorway (A), which led into an outer court (B) built by Tehutmes III and Amenhotep II. The court was open and was surrounded by a brick wall, and had a small colonnade of four sixteen-sided pillars at the far end. Tehutmes IV altered this court and made of it a hypostyle hall by covering it in and erecting twelve square columns to uphold the roof (pls. LIX, 1, 2; LX). The decoration of the walls by Tehutmes IV is of peculiar interest as showing some unusual ceremonies which may belong to the ritual of the coronation. The recording of the Pharaoh's age and the baptism with the Waters of Life occur in the coronation scenes of Hatshepsut; the baptism scene is not uncommon in Ptolemaic sculptures, but is rare in the earlier periods. In Egypt there were certain temples where the newly-appointed Pharaoh had to perform and undergo special ceremonies of consecration on his accession, and it is not unlikely that this was the case in Nubia also, and that Amada may have been one of the temples set apart for the purpose. Another interesting scene shows the King kneeling before a sacred tree, a survival of a primitive cult of tree-worship. It is noticeable that the King in these ceremonies is connected with the gods of Egypt and the goddesses of Nubia—Satet of the Cataract and Hathor of Abu Simbel—but the gods of Nubia are conspicuous by their absence. The records of the XIXth dynasty are also interesting; the Viceroy of the time of Rameses II is shown worshipping the Pharaoh's name; and there is a portrait of Tausert, daughter of Rameses II and queen of Siptah, on the south wall of the court; Siptah himself is not portrayed though his name occurs.

Through a doorway in the axis of the court a vestibule or transverse chamber (C) is entered; from this three doors lead into as many chambers (D, E, F), of which the central one is the shrine (E). In the reveal of the door between the court and the vestibule is a representation of Amenhotep II's baptism, he stands between Horus and Thoth who pour over him the Waters of Life.

On the rear wall of the shrine is an inscription set up in "the Station of the King", which is where the King stood during the religious ceremonies. The inscription is of Amenhotep II and is a record of human sacrifice, reminiscent to us of the description of Samuel hewing Agag in pieces before the Lord: "when His Majesty returned joyously to his father Amon, he himself slew with his mace the seven princes who had been in the district of Tikhsi, and had been placed head downwards at the prow of His Majesty's boat. Six of these fallen ones were hanged before the wall of Thebes. Then the other fallen one was taken up-river to Nubia and hanged on the wall of Napata in order to make manifest the eternal victories of His Majesty in all lands and countries of the Negroes." A door to the north and a door to the south of the shrine lead into small chambers in which probably the temple vessels were kept.

In the south chamber (F), leading from the vestibule are sculptures representing the ceremonies at the foundation of a temple. These are historically important for they show the part the two royal founders played in the founding of the temple. Tehutmes III performs the ceremonies for the actual foundation, but Amenhotep II makes the sacrifice when the temple was completed.

On the walls of the temple there are a few inscriptions of various periods; the most surprising are two of the seventeenth century, one of which states that "Herodotus beheld and admired"; under this, also in Greek but in a later style of writing, are the words, "No, he did not."

The Christians dealt gently with the temple when it was converted into a church; they merely covered the walls with plaster and whitewash, and so preserved the sculptures from the Moslems who followed them as well as from the destroying hand of Time.

XLV

DERR

THE rock-temple of Derr lies in the cliffs on the east bank of the Nile, and was founded, or at least decorated, by Rameses II, who appears to have made a speciality of Nubian temples. He claimed to be the actual author of this temple by calling it the temple of "Rameses in the House of Ra."

The rock, in which the temple is hewn, was so unsuitable for the purpose that the sides of the chambers and halls are only approximately straight, the walls curving in a way unknown elsewhere. In this respect the temple of Derr compares unfavourably with the other rock-cut temples of Nubia (pl. LXI, 2).

A pylon, now completely destroyed, led to a forecourt (A), which was partly cut out of the rock, as at Gerf Husên. This court was originally roofed, the roof being supported by twelve square pillars (pl. LXI, 1); the four pillars at the southern end (i.e. the most distant from the entrance) are Osirid columns, a type greatly favoured by Rameses II in all his temples. The figures appear to have been destroyed by Christian or Moslem iconoclasts, who also destroyed, whether intentionally or unintentionally, the remarkable historical sculptures on the walls. This is the more unfortunate as the sculptures represent incidents in the Nubian wars of Rameses II, of which very little is known. The scenes give a great deal of detail, and show fugitives carrying away their wounded from the field of battle, goats and cattle of the Nubians wandering unattended, and many other incidents of unexpectedly human interest, besides the conventional scenes of the Pharaoh in battle with his lion at his side. Among the inscriptions and scenes are representations of some of Rameses' children; he is known to have had one hundred and eleven sons and sixty-seven daughters, and there may have been even more; the whole number are never represented together, and their names can only be recovered from the representations in various temples. Nine daughters and eight sons are mentioned here; and of these, the names of only seven of the daughters and five of the sons are legible.

The hypostyle hall (B) is entered by a doorway carved in the cliff, and is itself entirely rock-hewn; the pillars are merely portions of the rock left standing. The sculptures in this hall are of a religious nature, and have not the historic interest and importance of the scenes in the forecourt.

The sanctuary and its two side chambers (C, D, E) lead directly out of the hypostyle hall without a vestibule. At the far end of the sanctuary are enthroned figures of the four gods of the temple cut out of the solid rock; these gods are Ptah, Amon-Ra, the King himself, and Ra-Harakhti. The presence of the King, enthroned as an equal with the heavenly divinities, shows his absolute belief in his own godship. According to the usual scheme of a Nubian rock-temple the sanctuary and its two side-chambers are decorated with scenes of worship of the divine boats; the boat-shaped shrines, which may have been actual boats, were probably kept in these sacred caverns. On the walls of the side-chambers the King is shown standing or dancing sacred dances before various deities, including himself.

The temple has suffered considerably from falls of rock from the roof which, in spite of cross-walls and pillars, was not sufficiently strong to support the weight above; the rock was of too poor a quality for excavation on so extensive a scale. Besides this natural disadvantage the temple also suffered in Christian times by being made a habitation of monks, iconoclasts of the fiercest type who joyfully destroyed the works of the heathen. Still later the temple was used as a dwelling place by the local inhabitants who, by slower but equally sure methods, continued the destruction. After the temple was abandoned by human beings, bats took up their abode in the once holy places, and completed the wreckage.

XLVI

ABU SIMBEL

The Great Temple

THE great rock temple of Abu Simbel (Ibsambul) is the finest of all the rock temples in the Nile Valley, whether in Egypt or Nubia. If it ever had pylons they have now disappeared, and the outer court is so small as to be insignificant, so that the great façade with its giant figures bursts upon the spectator without any preliminary buildings. Belzoni had the glory of being the first to excavate this enormous cavern, which he compared for size with the tomb of Sethy I in the Valley of the Tombs of the Kings.

The site appears to have been sacred for many centuries before Rameses II chose it for his Nubian *chef d'œuvre*, for in the inscriptions both at Abu Simbel and Abahuda the hill is already known as "The Hill of Libations". The hill is of sandstone and ends in a bold headland on the river. The entrance is to the side and on the east of the headland (pl. LXII, 1), and the temple is hewn out of the rock in a manner suggestive of a natural cavern rather than of human work.

Like so many temples in Nubia the dedication is to the deities of the three chief cities of Egypt, Amon-Ra of Thebes, Ra-Harakhti of Heliopolis, and Ptah of Memphis; co-equal with them in divinity and worship was Rameses himself.

The axis of the temple is almost due east and west, the entrance being to the east in order that the rays of the sun as it rises may pour through the whole interior and shine on the divine statues in the innermost shrine. To quote Weigall: "The whole temple is designed for the one hour of sunrise. Those who visit it at dawn and pass into the vestibule will be amazed at the irresistible solemnity of that moment when the sun passes above the hills, and the dim halls are suddenly transformed into a brilliantly lighted temple; and, though one has sickened of the eulogies of the literary traveller in Egypt, one may in this case adopt his language, and describe the hour of sunrise here as one of profound and stirring grandeur." Here indeed the worshipper could behold with his bodily eyes the Glory of the Lord. Though the sunrise is the chief hour of the day, the sunset has its special charm also. The temple is then in darkness, the towering figures in the hall are seen vaguely in the gloom, but through the doorway the hills glow softly with tints of rose and amber, the waters of the river reflect the colour of the sky, the whole scene is glorified by the darkness from which it is viewed. This magnificent conception of a shrine for the glory of the Living God was designed with all the splendour which even Rameses could devise, and it remains as the most colossal monument that the proudest of the Pharaohs has left to perpetuate his memory.

A brick wall enclosed the outer court on three sides; the original entrance was possibly through a pylon, which has now vanished, though there is still an entrance by a stone gateway to the north-east from which a path appears to have led to the Small Temple dedicated to Hathor and the queen. At the west the court is bounded by the hill itself, which is cut to make the fourth side of the court.

A short ramp with a stairway on each side leads from the court to a terrace which extends across the whole width of the façade. At the south-west corner of the court is the entrance to a small chapel, partly rock-hewn,

of the King who, in this hall as well as in the colossi of the façade, has given expression to his love of the immense. The walls of the hall are covered with sculpture on which the colours are still vivid; the scenes are chiefly battle-pieces, for the temple was founded in commemoration of the campaigns of Rameses II, and especially to record the war against the Hittites when the King distinguished himself at the battle of Kadesh by a desperate charge against overwhelming numbers, thereby turning defeat into victory. Pentaur's poem gives the facts with some poetic license: "Then like Mentu rose the King, seized his arrows and his bow; like to Baal in his hour with his panoply of war. When he turned to look behind chariots closed the outward way; Kheta, Kadesh, and Arvád in their thousands ringed him round. [The King speaks:] There was never chief with me, not a soldier, horse or foot, they had fled to save themselves and abandoned me, their King; there remained not one to fight, while about me came the foe, they in thousands, I alone. [The King prays to Amon:] At the cry of my despair swiftly came the god to me, took my hand and gave me strength till my might was as the might of a hundred thousand men. With the rapid onward sweep of a fierce consuming flame I destroyed their serried ranks; like a hawk among the birds, striking down on either side, slew and wearied not to slay. In their terror did they flee, to the water's edge they fled, deep, like crocodiles, they plunged. Rotted were their hearts with fear as they tasted of my hand; and amazed they shrieked aloud, 'Lo, no mortal man is he; this is Sutekh in his might, this is Baal in the flesh.'"

Among the scenes are two rows of the King's children, daughters on one side, sons on the other. Below the reliefs is a small inscription: "Made by the sculptor of the King, Piaay, son of Kha-nefer." So few sculptors of ancient Egypt signed their work that this inscription is of great value. The ceilings of the nave and side-aisles are painted in colour, the nave has a design of flying vultures, while the side-aisles are decorated with stars on a blue ground.

Two narrow chambers (B, C) lead out from the west side of the hall, one at each corner. Both are excavated at an angle in order to give room to the inner court, and each in its turn gives access to two lateral chambers (D, E, F, G). These were probably store-rooms for the temple vessels, which may have been kept on the stone shelves which run round three sides of each chamber. Non-perishable offerings could also have been stored here. The scenes on the walls are entirely religious and show Rameses in the presence of many gods, including himself. On the north side of the hall are two more chambers (H, I) (pl. LXII, 2).

In the axis of the temple a door leads into a hypostyle hall (J), which has four square pillars decorated, like the walls, with painted sculpture. Three doorways lead from this hall into the vestibule (K), from which open three shrines (L, M, N), as at Gerf Husên. The central shrine is the main sanctuary of the temple and contains the four gods whom Rameses most delighted to honour, Ptah, Amon-Ra, himself and Ra-Harakhti. The sanctuary is completely dark, except at sunrise when the rays of the sun pass through the whole length of the temple and strike full on the enthroned deities.

XLVII

ABU SIMBEL

The Small Temple

ON one side of a valley, now filled with a river of sand is the Great Temple of Abu Simbel; on the other side is the Small Temple, dedicated to the goddess Hathor and to the deified queen Nefertari-mery-Mut. It owes its existence to the piety of Rameses II; and were it not in close proximity with the Great Temple, its colossi would be regarded as among the most impressive in the world.

The present entrance is at the façade, for any pylons or outer court which may have once existed have long ago been washed away by the river. The façade fronts the Nile, and is cut, like that of the Great Temple, in imitation of a pylon with a cavetto cornice. The composition of the façade is of importance as showing that sculpture was essentially an architectural decoration in Egypt. Flanking the entrance are six colossal standing statues; two on either side represent Rameses II, with the figure of the queen between the two statues of her husband. The figures are set in niches cut vertically in the rock and divided from one another by a vertical band of inscription. The whole façade shows the regular contour of an Egyptian building, with vertical and horizontal lines, and the figures have been made to conform to those lines as nearly as possible. On either side of each colossus is one of the royal children, the princes beside the king, the princesses beside the queen. Though these gigantic figures are not so well proportioned as those of the Great Temple, and though the standing position is not so impressive and magnificent as the seated, yet the façade when seen from a distance is very fine.

The hypostyle hall is entered by a doorway between the colossi. The hall is square, and has six square pillars; the front of each pillar is decorated with the head of the goddess Hathor surmounted by her emblem, the sistrum; and the first pillar on each side bears also a figure of the queen, so that she is placed in the most prominent position possible. The other sculptures in the hall bring the queen again into prominent notice; when the king is represented in adoration of the gods, the queen adores them too. The king slays a negro in the presence of Amon-Ra, and the queen looks on; he smites a Libyan before Ra-Harakhti and the queen is there to help and encourage her husband. The scenes where the king takes part are on those walls which are not seen at once on entering the hall; on the walls facing the entrance the queen is represented alone before Hathor and before Mut.

The vestibule is entered by three doors cut in the rock, and here again are reliefs sculptured on the walls. The goddess holds the place of honour, standing in the form of a cow in a boat in the reeds of a papyrus marsh. The sanctuary shows most clearly the dedication to Hathor, for in the recess at the end is the figure of a cow in high relief; under its head is a human figure, probably the king, whom she protects. The emblem of Hathor is represented on each side of the cow, with the king in the attitude of adoration. On the side walls is a scene of the queen burning incense to Mut and Hathor; and on the opposite wall the king makes offerings to his own image and that of the queen. This scene is a proof of the deification of the queen, and shows that Rameses acknowledged her to be as divine as himself.

XLVIII

ABAHUDA

THE rock-cut temple of Abahuda (Gebel Adda) was founded by Haremheb and dedicated to Amon-Ra and to Thoth of Eshmun. Haremheb names the site *Amon-heri-yb* "Amon whose heart is content", the god being presumably happy because the temple was made there.

The temple is excavated in a rocky headland which rises direct out of the water; it consists of a hall (A) of four pillars with lotus-bud capitals (pl. LXIV, 1, 2); from the hall lateral chambers (B, C) open out to the north and south; and in the axis of the entrance a short flight of steps leads to the sanctuary (D). In the floor of the sanctuary there is a shaft opening down into a crypt, of which the use is not apparent.

The reliefs throughout are of Haremheb and the gods, and are interesting only as being a record of this King, who was not of the blood-royal but came to the throne on account of his military genius. The best preserved reliefs are above the doorways into the side chambers, they consist of the winged disk, below which are the Pharaoh's titles and names. On the north wall the King offers to four falcon-headed deities, called respectively Horus of Maam, Horus of Buhen, Horus of Bak, and Horus of Maha; these being the Egyptianised names of local gods. In another scene Haremheb stands between Horus and Seth; this is one of the few instances in Nubia where the place of Seth has not been usurped by Thoth. Seth is here called "He of Nubt, great god, Lord of the South Land"; these are his correct designations, for he was essentially of the south in contradistinction to Horus who was as essentially of the north. The scene therefore symbolises the north and the south uniting to honour the Pharaoh. In Egypt the name and figure of Seth are rarely found, for they were as rigorously erased by the anti-Sethites as the name and figure of Amon were obliterated by the Aten-worshippers; in Nubia Seth's figure is not erased but Thoth is put in his place, though why Thoth rather than one of the other gods is unknown.

In the sanctuary the Pharaoh is represented standing before the sacred barque, which according to the accompanying inscriptions contained the images of Amon-Ra and Thoth.

The most interesting point about the temple is that it was used in Christian times as a church, and the ancient sculptures were painted over with figures of saints. Fortunately these paintings are very little injured for, as Weigall says, "the archæologists who destroyed the less ancient remains in their search for the work of the earlier periods have become more rare now that archæology has been placed on a scientific basis." The paintings are still fresh as regards colour; one represents the figure of Christ clothed in a dark-red robe, his hand raised in blessing, and it should be noted that only the two fingers are raised, the thumb is kept bent down over the third and little fingers. There are also angels, one with long yellow wings; but the most dramatic are the pictures of riders. It is possible that these riders are intended for Mari Girgis (our St. George) who in Egyptian Christian art has taken the place of the pagan god Horus. One of these riders wears long draperies and a jewelled crown, and he thrusts with a long spear at a dragon; this may be either St. George or the archangel Michael. The two saints were often commemorated in neighbouring churches, perhaps because they were and still are extremely popular, the dragon-slayer always having a great appeal to everyone. The body of St. George, though without the head, was still to be seen in the Oasis of Bahriya in the time of Abu Salih, who tells us that "on the festival of his martyrdom, the body is brought out from the shrine, and a new veil put over it; and it is carried in procession all round the town, with candles and crosses and chanting; and then it is carried back to the church. It is said that the limbs of this body were not separated from it, but that it was found entire, without any change." It is evident from this account that the festival of St. George was kept in more seemly wise than that of St. Michael when sheep were slaughtered by hundreds for the feast.

LIST OF AUTHORS QUOTED BY NAME IN THE TEXT

BELZONI, G., Narrative of Operations and Recent Discoveries in Egypt and Nubia.

BROCKEDON, W. (and D. ROBERTS), Egypt and Nubia.

BURCKHARDT, J. L., Travels in Nubia.

CHAMPOLLION, J. F., Lettres d'Égypte.

EDWARDS, AMELIA B., A Thousand Miles up the Nile.

FAIRHOLT, F. W., Up the Nile.

GAU, F. C., Antiquités de la Nubie.

LEGRAIN, G., Louqsor sans les Pharaons.

MASPERO, G., Annales du Service. 1910, p. 14.

PETRIE, W. M. F., Temple of the Kings; Religious life in Ancient Egypt.

WEIGALL, A., Guide to the Antiquities of Upper Egypt; Lower Nubia.

WILKINSON, G., Modern Egypt and Thebes.

Department of Antiquities, Temples immergées de la Nubia, Blackman, A. M., Roeder, G., etc. etc.

INDEX

C

D

Q

R